*f*P

Do Not Ask What Good We Do

✧

INSIDE THE U.S. HOUSE
OF REPRESENTATIVES

ROBERT DRAPER

FREE PRESS

New York London Toronto Sydney New Delhi

FREE PRESS
A Division of Simon & Schuster, Inc.
1230 Avenue of the Americas
New York, NY 10020

First Free Press hardcover edition April 2012

FREE PRESS and colophon are trademarks of Simon & Schuster, Inc.

For information about special discounts for bulk purchases, please contact Simon & Schuster
Special Sales at 1-866-506-1949 or business@simonandschuster.com.

The Simon & Schuster Speakers Bureau can bring authors to your live event.
For more information or to book an event contact the Simon & Schuster Speakers Bureau
at 1-866-248-3049 or visit our website at www.simonspeakers.com.

DESIGNED BY ERICH HOBBING

Manufactured in the United States of America

1   3   5   7   9   10   8   6   4   2

Library of Congress Cataloging-in-Publication Data is available.

ISBN 978-1-4516-4208-7
ISBN 978-1-4516-4210-0 (ebook)

ALSO BY ROBERT DRAPER

Hadrian's Walls

Rolling Stone Magazine:
The Uncensored History

Dead Certain:
The Presidency of George W. Bush

TO MY BROTHER JOHN
AND IN MEMORY OF
OUR BROTHER ELI

Do not ask what good we do: that is not a fair question, in these days of faction.

> —U.S. Representative Fisher Ames, member of the First Federal Congress, after concluding that he would not seek a fifth term in the House, May 30, 1796

CONTENTS

CAST OF CHARACTERS

(in order of appearance)

KEVIN McCARTHY: Three-term Republican, California, 22nd District, House Majority Whip

PAUL RYAN: Seven-term Republican, Wisconsin, 1st District, chairman of the House Budget Committee, leading GOP voice on economic policy

JEFF DUNCAN: Freshman Republican, South Carolina, 3rd District, former state legislator and real estate auctioneer, rated most conservative House member in 2011 by Heritage Action for America

JOHN DINGELL: Twenty-nine-term Democrat, Michigan, 15th District, dean of the House, former chairman of the House Energy and Commerce Committee

ALLEN WEST: Freshman Republican, Florida, 22nd District, retired lieutenant colonel, U.S. Army, only Republican member of the Congressional Black Caucus

BLAKE FARENTHOLD: Freshman Republican, Texas, 27th District, former radio talk show cohost

GABRIELLE GIFFORDS: Three-term Democrat, Arizona, 8th District, member of the moderate Blue Dog Coalition

JOHN BOEHNER: Eleven-term Republican, Ohio, 8th District, Speaker of the House

ANTHONY WEINER: Seven-term Democrat, New York, 9th District, New York City mayoral aspirant

NANCY PELOSI: Thirteen-term Democrat, California, 8th District, House Minority Leader, former Speaker

JO ANN EMERSON: Nine-term Republican, Missouri, 8th District, member of the moderate Tuesday Group coalition and "Cardinal" of the House Appropriations Committee

WALTER JONES: Nine-term Republican, North Carolina, 3rd District, opponent of the war in Afghanistan

SHEILA JACKSON LEE: Nine-term Democrat, Texas, 18th District, liberal member of the Congressional Black Caucus

CHRIS VAN HOLLEN: Five-term Democrat, Maryland, 8th District, ranking member of the House Budget Committee, member of the Democrat leadership team

RENEE ELLMERS: Freshman Republican, North Carolina, 2nd District, former intensive care nurse

RAUL LABRADOR: Freshman Republican, Idaho, 1st District, former state legislator and immigration lawyer

Evening, January 20, 2009

You could fit the number of Republicans who were out on the town the night of Barack Obama's inauguration around a single dining room table.

There were about fifteen of them, all white males, plus a few spouses. The venue was the Caucus Room, an expense-account steakhouse halfway between the White House and the Capitol. A seething winter chill was the least of their discomforts that evening. Nearly a half-million people had begun to congregate on the National Mall on Sunday, January 18, 2009—two days *before* the inauguration. By the time Obama was sworn in on Tuesday, the number had reached 1.8 million. The nation's capital had never hosted a crowd that large, not for any reason. Definitely not for the previous president, George W. Bush, who had been jeered that afternoon as a helicopter whisked him off to Texas. Now the occupant of the White House was a Democrat. The House and Senate were controlled by Democrats. Barricades still lined the streets outside, as if at any moment the ruling party might engulf the Caucus Room and finish off what was left of the Republicans.

On such a night, it was a comfort to suffer among friends. Most of them—Eric Cantor, Kevin McCarthy, Paul Ryan, Pete Sessions, Jeb Hensarling, Pete Hoekstra, and Dan Lungren—were members of the U.S. House of Representatives. Five served in the Senate: Jim DeMint, Jon Kyl, Tom Coburn, John Ensign, and Bob Corker. The other three invitees were conservative journalist Fred Barnes of the *Weekly Standard,* former House Speaker (and future presidential candidate) Newt Gingrich, and communications specialist Frank Luntz. Most of them had attended the inauguration. That astounding vista of humanity on the Mall would haunt them more than last November's electoral margins. McCarthy, a California congressman who had thus far served only a single term in the House, had made a game effort of viewing the event for the historic moment it was. He'd procured Obama's autograph and even that of Obama's sister. As the unworldly progeny of the Bakersfield working class, Kevin McCarthy had been dazzled to be included in such a tableau. As a Republican, he and the others in the room were devastated.

Luntz had organized the dinner—telling the invitees, "You'll have nothing to do that night, and right now we don't matter anyway, so let's all be irrelevant together." He had selected these men because they were among the Republican Party's most energetic thinkers—and because they all got along with Luntz, who could be difficult. Three times during the 2008 election cycle, Sean Hannity had thrown him off the set at Fox Studios. The top Republican in the House, Minority Leader John Boehner, had nurtured a dislike of Luntz for more than a decade. No one had to ask why Boehner wasn't at the Caucus Room that evening.

The dinner tables were set up in a square, at Luntz's request, so that everyone could see each other and talk freely. He asked that Gingrich speak first. It was Newt, after all, who had pulled the Republicans out of a far deeper hole fourteen years ago, leading the GOP to a takeover of the House for the first time since 1955.

Gingrich was happy to oblige. Obama's inaugural speech was impressive, the former Speaker said. The evocations of constitutional principles, pragmatism, and risk-taking—"those could have been our words." Someone ought to laminate Obama's speech and disseminate it, the better to hold the president accountable to his pledges.

Being competitors, however, they did not dwell on Obama's seeming invincibility. They'd been thrashed, it was roundly agreed, because they had it coming. They ended up chucking their own principles and standing for nothing. They'd spent the last eight years defending policies they never should have signed on to in the first place. They'd lost their way.

"We got obsessed with governing," Ensign said—adding with distaste, "making sure the trains run on time. Well, what if the train is heading towards the cliff?"

They picked at their salads and drank their wine and tried not to think about the thousands now dancing at the ten inaugural balls that the new president and his wife would be attending before the night was through.

Luntz was secretly overjoyed. When had Republicans in a group setting *ever* acknowledged how badly they had blown it? When had they *ever* recognized that they had become part of the problem rather than the solution? *Maybe they don't see how big this is,* he thought.

"So we're in the depths," said Pete Hoekstra, who as a freshman in January 1993 had attended Bill Clinton's swearing-in and had seen the GOP survive that particular downer. "The discussion we're having tonight about President Obama, and where our party is, is no different than the discussion I came into as a freshman—except that it was even worse."

Laughing, Hoekstra reminded them, "We'd been a minority party for forty years! And two short years later"—Hoekstra gestured to Gingrich, the field general of the 1994 revolution—"it's a whole new world."

How to regain that whole new world—that was now the question.

The men in the room were, behaviorally speaking, Washingtonians. Unlike ordinary Americans, they lived by a biennial calendar, the rhythms of their lives propelled by the electoral cycle as insistently as the migratory and mating habits of winged creatures. What their party had done from 1994 to 2000, and what the Democrats had then done from 2006 to 2008, the Republicans would once again do. They would take back the House in November 2010. They would use the House as the Republicans' spear point to mortally wound President Obama in 2011. Then they would retake the White House and the Senate in 2012.

They would do all this, but only if the American voter blessed them to do so.

It made no sense, they all agreed, to attack Obama personally. The man was too popular.

"It's got to be about ideas," said Eric Cantor, the House minority whip, in his honeyed Virginia drawl. The Democrats now controlled everything and were already, with a monstrously priced economic stimulus package, showing their true colors. Give them time—they would screw things up, just as the GOP had.

"But everyone's got to stick together," said Paul Ryan, a thirty-eight-year-old Wisconsin congressman and numbers fetishist whose shiny earnestness recalled an *Ozzie and Harriet* America. Ryan hated squabbling amongst conservatives—the paleos versus the neos, the socials against the moderates, on and on for as long as he'd been on the Hill, which was all of his adult life. Ryan had long sought to be the GOP's glue, pleading for adherence to the principles and the data. At times he looked like the underfed, hollow-eyed child of alcoholic parents.

"The only way we'll succeed is if we're united," Ryan told the others. "If we tear ourselves apart, we're finished." But, he added, he liked what he was hearing now. Everyone at the table sounded like a genuine conservative. It was a place to start.

"If you act like you're the minority, you're going to stay in the minority," said Kevin McCarthy. "We've gotta challenge them on every single bill and challenge them on every single campaign."

Luntz viewed McCarthy as one of the Republican Party's emerging stars: an easygoing, unthreatening guy who understood that language and appearance mattered at least as much as substance. Nonetheless, the pollster and media guru interjected a cautionary note. "One of the worst political performances I've ever seen," he said, "was when the Democrats took over the House in 2007 and Nancy Pelosi shut out the Republicans. And everybody whined about it. If any of you behave that way, I'll go on TV and hold you accountable! If you're whiners, you're losers!"

Luntz tended to get carried away, but everyone knew he had a point.

Senator Jon Kyl began to focus on immediate tactics. He pointed out that Tim Geithner, Obama's nominee to be secretary of the Treasury, had failed to pay his Social Security and Medicare taxes during his three-year employment at the International Monetary Fund. Kyl sat on the Senate Finance Committee, which would be conducting Geithner's confirmation hearings the next morning. The Arizona senator intended to go after the nominee. "I'd like to hear your thoughts on the approach I should take," he said to the others.

There was a pattern here, Gingrich pointed out. Charlie Rangel, the new House Ways and Means chairman, hadn't paid taxes on his rental property income in more than two decades. Rangel and Geithner would be wielding more power over how taxpayer dollars would be spent than anyone else in America—and yet these guys couldn't even be trusted to pay their own taxes?

"And there's a web," chimed in McCarthy. "There are freshmen who accepted campaign money from Rangel. They're caught in the web." McCarthy suggested that they waste no time smacking the new Democrats with attack ads.

The dinner lasted nearly four hours. They parted company almost giddily. The Republicans had agreed on a way forward:

Go after Geithner. (And indeed Kyl did, the next day: "Would you answer my question rather than dancing around it—please?")

Show united and unyielding opposition to the president's economic policies. (Eight days later, Minority Whip Cantor would hold the House Republicans to a unanimous No against Obama's economic stimulus plan.)

Begin attacking vulnerable Democrats on the airwaves. (The first National Republican Congressional Committee attack ads would run in less than two months.)

Win the spear point of the House in 2010. Jab Obama relentlessly in 2011. Win the White House and the Senate in 2012.

"You will remember this day," Newt Gingrich proclaimed to the others as they said goodbye. "You'll remember this as the day the seeds of 2012 were sown."

✦ ✦ ✦

Forgotten, or at least not discussed that night in the Caucus Room, was what had been sown in America by January 20, 2009.

On that evening, while the ruling party celebrated in tuxedos and the minority party retrenched over steaks and red wine, the U.S. unemployment rate climbed to 7.6 percent, the highest such indicator of national misery in eighteen years. Things would get much worse. Joblessness in America would exceed 8 percent the following month. By May 2009, the number would climb to 9.4 percent, and by October to 10.2 percent. The avalanche of the financial markets during the summer of 2008, and the global recession it triggered, had dealt America a battering that the Bureau of Labor Statistics would be at pains to capture in its bloodless data. Coming seven years after the existential blow of the 9/11 terrorist attacks, the American condition of 2009 could not be adequately characterized as "the worst recession since the Great Depression." In a much deeper, more encompassing sense, the country was at a loss.

America had been at a loss 220 years before, in the spring of 1789, when sixty-five men arrived by ship and stagecoach to the reeking, war-ravaged streets of New York City to convene the First Federal Congress. Taking up business on the lower floor of Federal Hall, the House of Representatives threw open its doors to the public on April 9 (unlike the Senate upstairs, which tended to its affairs privately for another six years), thereupon securing its reputation as the People's Institution.

The commoners and journalists packing the public gallery of Federal Hall noisily munched on peanuts while bearing witness to America's unsteady embrace of republican democracy. Among the House's stars in 1789 were James Madison of Virginia, the primary author of the Constitution and the Bill of Rights; and, somewhat less famously, thirty-year-old Fisher Ames of Massachusetts, the House's first great orator, who crafted the final language of the First Amendment. But, as Ames wrote of his colleagues in 1789, "There are few shining geniuses." It was instead, Ames noted, a body of "sober, solid, old-charter folks"—parochial, at times shortsighted and short-tempered, prone to grandstanding and with one eye cocked to the next election. Ames would himself later confess to becoming "crazed with the chase" of political adrenaline, but he was not the only ambitious soul among the class of 1789: nine of the first congressmen would later ascend to the Senate, while Madison would serve as the nation's fourth president and Elbridge Gerry as his vice president.

And yet, with ample reason to put their own interests before those of a nation in its infancy, the sixty-five men of the First Federal Congress—northerners and southerners, Federalists and Anti-Federalists—found it within themselves to cohere as a body of statesmen and thereby give America its structural and social coherency. During the spring and summer of 1789, the House of Representatives would lay the foundations for a federal government. After first standing up an executive branch and inaugurating George Washington as America's first president, they established a Treasury Department and a federal bank. They tended to the nation's war debt by levying taxes. They instituted a federal judiciary. They accepted Vermont and Kentucky into the union. And, to round off the House of Representatives' maiden legislative session, they passed the Bill of Rights.

This was the story of the House, back in the day when elected leaders elected to lead.

Two hundred and twenty-two years later, a very different kind of story of the People's Institution would unfold from the deliberations of the men gathered that evening in the Caucus Room. The story of this House, the 112th Congress, the People's Institution in its super-evolved state, may be seen as a parable of how democracy works in a nation beset by postmodern paradoxes—at times purposeful, at other times as boisterously inconsequential as an episode of *Seinfeld,* and at nearly all times infuriating even to its members . . . a tale of many things, but not necessarily one of statesmanship.

The protagonists of this story are a few of the 435 American men and women on both sides of the aisle who love their country and who showed up to the Capitol with every intention of leading, or at least serving, the people who voted them into office. What in fact transpired was an outcome the men in the Caucus Room—also patriots, many of them widely admired public servants—only partly anticipated. Their schemings helped to produce a House that appeared to spring directly from the impulses of an outraged public; a House of passionately iconoclastic newcomers, some of them proudly oblivious to political fallout and others so hyperreactive to their constituents that they followed their Twitter feeds on their iPads while sitting in the House chamber during votes; a House that made an elaborate show of openness and of speedily fulfilling its campaign pledges; a House that, for the first time ever, scheduled half of its workdays away from insular Washington, so that its members would be maximally hot-wired to feedback from the home folks; a House unabashedly grasping for the throwback luster of James Madison and Fisher Ames, to the point of spending much of its first full day reciting aloud the entire U.S. Constitution and the Bill of Rights on the House floor. This was a House of clearly spelled out principles, and of considerable clout. Fulfilling the wildest hopes of the men in the Caucus Room, the Republican-controlled House passed hundreds of bills, threw the Obama White House squarely on the ropes, and dominated a jillion news cycles. In Beltway parlance, the House controlled the narrative.

For all of these exertions, the 112th Congress was awarded by its fellow Americans an approval rating of 9 percent, a depth of loathing for that institution never before seen in the history of public opinion polling—a contempt eclipsing that for car salesmen, revenue collectors, the news media, and the president. This public disgust, principally aimed at the majority party but in no way acquitting the Democrats (especially the Democratic-controlled Senate), plainly bespoke a yearning for the lost art of governance. It was as if Americans, having long forgotten what political leadership looks like, saw in today's House of Representatives an unambiguous portrait of what leadership precisely is not.

Yet something deeper is being expressed when a democracy reserves its greatest hostility toward the elected representatives who most acutely reflect the public mood. Perhaps Americans can no longer decide what it is that they want. Or perhaps—after being bombarded by the Internet, agitated by cable news and talk radio, bifurcated by redistricting maps, and dispirited by homegrown preoccupations—the outcry is in fact simple and plaintive: a plea for one America again.

✦ ✦ ✦

Instead: *You will remember this day. You'll remember this as the day the seeds of 2012 were sown.*

When Newt Gingrich spoke those departing words at the Caucus Room, the others traded looks of doubt. On January 20, 2009, hope was in the air, but the fifteen Republicans were not yet feeling it. They stepped out into the cold. It was nearly midnight, and the other side was still out dancing.

They needed reinforcements.

PART ONE

REINFORCEMENTS

CHAPTER ONE

Tea Party Freshman

"Mr. Duncan from South Carolina . . ."

A few of his new buddies in the Republican conference of the U.S. House of Representatives hollered out "Yeah!" at the sound of his name. Duncan stood up. He was forty-four, big-shouldered with thinning hair, and his round face radiated a kind of pastoral bashfulness. With the rolling gait of an ex-football player, he walked down the aisle toward the lottery box. One hand was behind his back, fingers crossed. With the other hand he pointed ceiling-ward, lifting his gaze as well so as to petition the Good Lord who had brought him this far. Directly in front of him, engraved on the wall of the House Administration Committee room in the Rayburn House Office Building, was a scripture from Proverbs: *Where there is no vision, the people perish.* His meaty hand dove into the box. He retrieved a slip of paper and handed it over to committee chairman Dan Lungren.

"Mr. Duncan drew . . . number twenty-one."

He lifted his arms in triumph and his jowls reddened as his freshman pals cheered. The twenty-first pick among eighty-seven freshmen! Guaranteed one of the better soon-to-be-vacated House offices! Already Duncan was breaking out of the pack.

Two days earlier, on November 17, 2010, Congressman-elect Jeff Duncan sat in the Capitol with the entire House Republican conference for the first time. Before the election fifteen days prior, there had been 198 of them. Now there were—or would be, after all the recounts were completed—242. They were the majority. They were the one sector of the federal government that the Republicans controlled outright, making the House their spear point against the Obama White House. That day Duncan and his new colleagues voted to select John Boehner as the new Speaker-designate. *All those in favor say . . . AYE!* Duncan had nearly fallen out of his chair. In the South Carolina state legislature, where he had previously served, there were seventy-four in the GOP caucus. Reacting to that sonic boom of affirmation, which of course included his own voice, Duncan thought: *What a true majority we have.*

He did not yet think: *How the hell will* my *voice ever be heard?*

Boehner had hosted a dinner for the freshmen in the National Statuary Hall of the Capitol. The members of the Republican leadership were profuse in their gratitude that the freshmen had restored the GOP to the majority. "We've been holding down the fort, like the guys in *Saving Private Ryan*," one of the leaders declared. "We've been the guys shooting at the tank—and now all of a sudden, the plane comes flying in. We've finally got help."

Duncan had arrived at Statuary Hall early. It was a Sunday evening; a ghostly quiet enveloped the marble corridor. Walking by the statues of his fellow South Carolinians John Calhoun and Wade Hampton—both of them nineteenth-century statesmen and slaveholders—he paused instead to study the newest figure in the Rotunda: the bronze, five-hundred-pound likeness of his hero, Ronald Reagan. Then he stopped. Two other freshmen were with Duncan. They all stared up at the dome together. No one said a word. Duncan could feel his knees go weak. He was part of all this now. This was his pantheon.

Not knowing what else to do, he pulled a camera out of his pocket and took a picture that would never come out and would never be of interest to anyone—just the heavenly roof of democracy hovering 180 feet above Jeffrey David Duncan.

Along the campaign trail, Duncan the candidate had always carried a copy of the U.S. Constitution in his pocket. *I believe in the Constitution,* his campaign website declared—adding for clarity's sake, *I believe in the Second Amendment. I believe in States Rights.* And then a twenty-first-century conservative's elucidation: *I believe illegal immigration is a national security problem . . . I believe we should reject amnesty . . . I believe in limited government . . . I believe that the economy prospers when we lower tax rates. I believe in a Balanced Budget Amendment to the Constitution. And I believe in term limits for all politicians.*

But at the very top of his "I Believe" list, the candidate had stated unambiguously: *I believe in God. Our nation was founded on Christian*

*values and principles. I believe that life begins at conception. I believe tradi-
tional marriage is the foundation for society. And I believe that Washington
will never be the solution to man's problems, therefore we must reject the political correctness that has driven God from the public square.*

Jeff Duncan was a Tea Party freshman. That's what he called himself.
The origins of the "TEA" (Taxed Enough Already) party movement
were revenue-centric, but before long the rallying cries ranged from
a deep distrust of the sitting president to a (seemingly corresponding) outrage over the federal government's spending habits and overall godlessness—the latter two of which were Jeff Duncan's animating
principles. There were eighty-seven freshmen in all, and some had benefited from the Tea Party wave, while others had won in spite of it, and
others still had embraced the movement but would be edging away
from it as soon as no one was looking. Not Duncan. *As a Christian,
Husband, Father and Small Business Owner, I know what I believe in.*

He'd spent the previous day, November 18, roaming the halls of
the three House office buildings, each named after former Speakers:
Rayburn, the newest and closest to the Capitol across the street, with
the most spacious offices and the House gymnasium in the basement;
Longworth, a neoclassical building and thus more stylish than Rayburn, with the biggest cafeteria; and Cannon, the oldest and smallest of
the three, a Beaux-Arts creation completed in 1908, and which had the
added benefit of being a few feet from both a Metro subway station and
the Republican Party's national headquarters. Each building contained
from 85 to 251 offices, many quite different in size, shape, and view. As
in the corporate world, office space on Capitol Hill conveyed its occupant's station in the political food chain. Representatives with the
greatest seniority clung tenaciously to their sprawling real estate. Those
of middling tenure traded up whenever one of the old warhorses departed by retirement, defeat, or death. The offices abandoned by them,
and by the recently defeated, constituted the pool from which Duncan
and the other incoming freshmen chose their new habitats.

Duncan surveyed the buildings with two of his young staffers,
who directed him to this or that soon-to-be-vacated space so that the
congressman-elect could study his options. The least desirable of these
was the fifth and uppermost floor of the Cannon Building, a forlorn
former attic that later housed, among others, a California freshman

named Richard M. Nixon. Next door to Nixon's haunt in Room 511 was Republican Congressman Louie Gohmert, a bald and hawk-eyed former judge who had just earned a fourth term representing the 1st District of Texas, and who possessed a gift for finding his way in front of TV cameras. Up until now, Gohmert had remained on the top floor for six years—and by choice, for the simple reason that he could park his barbecue grills on the ledge just outside and cook ribs for his buddies.

"The architect of the Capitol sat me down," Gohmert explained to the visiting freshman, "and he told me about the OSHA restrictions, and we cleared through all the baloney. And that left only one fire code violation I had—which is no fire within ten feet of the wooden window frames. I'm moving to the Rayburn Building. There's a window I'm gonna work to get open."

He asked Duncan, "Are you thinking about the RSC?"

That was the Republican Study Committee, the GOP's in-house conservative policy coalition. Duncan said that he had already signed on.

"And you heard about the dinner Heritage is having?" Gohmert shook his head reverently. "Just a great group."

In another Republican congressman's office, Duncan ducked in and noticed a Bible on the shelf. "A Christian," he observed. "That's good." But for the most part Duncan's encounters that afternoon were with soon-to-be-departed Democrats. In the office of defeated New York Democrat Michael McMahon, a couple of staffers slouched vacant-faced in their chairs, drinking Sam Adams beer. The office of Tennessee Democrat Lincoln Davis was a jumble of boxes and—on top of a lone file cabinet—a plastic statue of the R&B singer James Brown. One of Duncan's entourage pushed a button on the statue. It responded with a miserable tape loop of "I Feel Good." Davis's staffers glowered and the Republicans mumbled their goodbyes.

At one office in the Cannon Building, the receptionist was crying. Amid the stacks of file folders and hollow office rooms, the main switchboard in front of her now lifeless, she seemed both overwhelmed and bereft. The woman asked Duncan if he would come back some other time. The congressman-elect said he understood.

His voice became brittle, however, once he was out in the hallway. "They had a chance to choose right and vote right on behalf of America," he said. "And they didn't. I wouldn't wish it on anyone, but," he corrected himself, "I wished it on those guys, so we could get our majority and get some things done."

Duncan was one of four freshmen to win seats from South Carolina. *The Four Horsemen*, he had helpfully mentioned to a couple of local reporters. (Thus far, the moniker hadn't taken hold.) His rural district bordering Georgia and North Carolina was a Republican shoo-in. All he'd had to do was prove to voters in the primary of South Carolina's 3rd District that he was the truest conservative in the field and at least as conservative as his predecessor, Gresham Barrett, who had vacated the seat to run (unsuccessfully) for governor. The other three Horsemen had stories that wrote themselves. Tim Scott from Charleston was one of only two blacks in the entire House Republican conference. Trey Gowdy was a lawyer with not a day's worth of political experience who had mustered enough Tea Party support to demolish not-conservative-enough incumbent Bob Inglis in the Republican primary. As for Mick Mulvaney, in winning he had delivered to the GOP the prized scalp of John Spratt, a fourteen-term Democrat and chairman of the House Budget Committee.

By comparison, Duncan could seem like something of a country plodder, the kind of fellow you ran into so many times in the course of a day that he became as familiar and forgettable as wallpaper. He made no apologies for his steadiness. After emerging from the bottom of the heap to prevail in a four-man Republican primary, Duncan aimed to make a nice little career out of defying expectations. He would seek to get on the powerful Energy and Commerce Committee, where he could strut his oil and gas expertise. He would introduce a balanced budget amendment to the Constitution. He would slash away at the federal budget like a reaper.

Most of all, he would represent his district, which was among America's most conservative. In his pre-political life, Jeff Duncan had been a real estate auctioneer. To him, the 3rd District was now his business and its 750,000 or so constituents his customers. He intended to run things like a business. Before ever setting foot in the Capitol, Duncan had already decided that he would cut his designated budget by 10 percent. He did not know exactly what he would cut or what effect such cuts would have on his office's overall performance. He just knew that it would set the right tone, as Jeff Duncan came to Washington to curb its appalling spending addiction, to begin his tenure by handing over to the U.S. Treasury a check of the taxpayers' hard-earned dollars. And so he instructed his new chief of staff to figure out the cuts. *Get 'er done.*

And lo and behold, Speaker Boehner was now himself making noise about reducing the House's overall administrative budget back to 2008 levels. The Republican leader was following the freshman! Already he was making a difference!

But just to show everyone how sincere he was about his small businessman's approach to governance: on the day of his swearing-in, January 5, 2011, Jeff Duncan was going to have a ribbon-cutting ceremony, right there in his new office doorway. That office would, like its inhabitants, be accessible to all his visiting customers. It would be on the first floor of the Cannon Building, less than a block from the Metro subway. Not the biggest office he could have chosen with his twenty-first pick of the lottery, nor the fanciest. But the best for his customers.

It would be Cannon 116, the office where the Democrat woman had been crying.

✦ ✦ ✦

The woman's boss and the office's current occupant was a thirty-six-year-old Virginian named Glenn Nye, a freshman just as Jeff Duncan would be. Nye had endeavored to represent his district, which included the naval base in Norfolk. He fought to keep the nuclear aircraft carrier there and he lobbied aggressively on behalf of military families. But it didn't matter. The economy was foundering, and the Democrats seemed preoccupied with anything but. After passing a $787 billion stimulus bill at Obama's behest, House Speaker Nancy Pelosi had devoted much of the 111th Congress to passing energy and health care legislation. Nye voted against both. He couldn't understand why, with so many Americans out of work, the House Democrats were fixated on cap-and-trade legislation—especially when the controversial measure stood no chance of making it through the Senate.

By 2010, a volley of attack ads twinned Nye with the House Speaker, whom the Republicans had invested a fortune in demonizing. *Glenn Nye votes with Nancy Pelosi 83 percent of the time.* Which was true, if you counted procedural votes, like whether to adjourn for the day. But try explaining that to the voters. Nye did his best to do so. They either didn't listen or didn't care. Following the precise message prescription used by Jeff Duncan and hundreds of other Republican candidates—repeal Obamacare, fire Pelosi, choke off the spending, cut the taxes—a car dealer and Republican neophyte named Scott Rigell whipped Nye the incumbent Democrat by 10 points.

A couple of days before Jeff Duncan selected Glenn Nye's office for his own, the House Democrats met in HC-5, the conference room in the Capitol basement, to rehash the midterm shellacking. Pelosi, now deposed as Speaker, had recently announced that she intended to run as the House minority leader. Nye was astounded by this news. He talked to several of his colleagues who had also lost on November 2. Pelosi's decision was crazy, he told them—they had to speak up. Some agreed to do so. Others saw little point in complaining. Who in the Democratic caucus could beat Pelosi? She had all the votes she needed: the liberals, the Californians, the women, the Congressional Black Caucus. And the Democratic members most likely to oppose Pelosi's bid were those who had just been beaten and therefore wouldn't have a vote. The losers could bitch about it, but what good would it do?

At the caucus, Nancy Pelosi did something unusual. She barred staff members from sitting in, because she wanted her colleagues to be able to speak frankly. "I'd like for us to hear from those who lost on November second," the Speaker said.

A long line formed at the mike stand. Some of the defeated blamed the economy. Others cited the intransigent Senate and the detached Obama White House. Still others recognized that they may well have been done in by the health care bill that had been so extravagantly vilified by the Republicans—but that they were proud to go down for such a noble cause.

When it was Nye's turn, he began by thanking the Speaker for leading the Democrats through difficult times. But, he went on, "You clearly became the face of the election in a way that harmed a lot of us. Fair or not, the Republicans were able to paint you with an image that dragged us down.

"It's up to me to win my race," said the defeated freshman. "I get that. But this is a moment where we have to be honest with ourselves. We have to accept your role in these defeats. And it's going to be much harder for someone like me to run again if you're the party leader. Because instead of running a race where it's me against the other guy, I'll be dealing with the same ads. The same framing I can't get away from."

When he was finished, Nancy Pelosi nodded and said nothing. Another defeated member stood up to talk, then another. The caucus lasted nearly five hours.

Glenn Nye didn't stay for the end of it. Instead, he went back to Cannon 116 and began packing up.

CHAPTER TWO

The Dean

At a weeknight party for the ninety-six incoming freshmen (including nine Democrats) in the solarium of a Washington hotel, an old man materialized from the sea of fresh faces. He made his way to an open area by means of a walker—a bald and bespectacled yet not quite frail figure who with his stooped posture was still taller than most of the others in the crowd. He leaned into a microphone and in an arid voice began to talk to the guests about the House of Representatives, where they would soon be serving, the place where he had served the past fifty-five years, longer than any other United States congressman in its history.

"It is an institution that is often demeaned," said the old man. "Usually during campaigns."

Through his glasses, the blue eyes glared meaningfully at the much younger men and women fresh off the campaign trail.

"But it is an institution composed of people who pride themselves on being public servants," he went on. "And I'm pleased to tell you that most of the members who come here do so to serve and look after people and do important things."

Without benefit of notes, the old man proceeded to bless them with a quote from Daniel Webster's famed discourse at Plymouth: *Let us rejoice that we behold this day. Let us be thankful that we have lived to see the bright and happy breaking of this auspicious morn* . . . He spoke of the great House Speaker Sam Rayburn, with whom the old man had once worked, a half century ago—how Mr. Sam had once been asked how many presidents he'd served under, prompting the reply, "Not a damn one. I served *with* presidents."

And then the old man shared with the gathering a joke that he had once been told "when I was a young fella." He said, "A fellow was once very impressed with this institution he'd come to work for. And an older colleague said to him, 'My friend, for the next six months you're going to be wondering how the hell you got here. And then one day you're going to come out onto the House floor, look around—and wonder how the hell all these *other* fools got here.'"

The old man permitted himself a tight smile and waited until the laughter died down. Then he said, "At any rate, it is a wonderful institution, one I've been very proud to have the privilege to serve in. Something like ten to fifteen thousand Americans, out of the two billion who've been part of America, have had such a privilege—to be part of the most humanly perfect . . ."

His eyes seemed to become watery as he looked out into the crowd. "Most humanly perfect," he repeated, "institution on this planet."

He welcomed them to the House, finished with a terse "Thanks," and then the old man with the walker took off with surprising velocity.

Though the eighty-four-year-old man, whose name was John Dingell, had a not-undeserved reputation for being cantankerous, he got along with almost everybody. He got along with Mr. Sam and his fellow Democrats, of course, but he also got along with Ronald Reagan and counted Newt Gingrich as a friend. He got along with big business—particularly the American auto industry, which was the chief employer of his Michigan district—and equally so with labor unions. He got along with consumer groups and the National Rifle Association, with all the ethnics, with young and old, urban and rural. The only folks he'd yet encountered with whom he simply could not get along were the tea partiers—"but then again," he would invariably add, "I don't think the good Lord will get along with them, either."

Tea-baggers, he preferred to call them. Over time it became clear to his (significantly younger) staff that Mr. Dingell (as they called him) was unaware of the term's alternate meaning. This had been a source of private hilarity, until March 2010, when Dingell was invited to be a guest on *The Daily Show with Jon Stewart* to discuss the recent passage of the Democrats' landmark health care legislation, which had been Dingell's legislative raison d'être not only throughout his career but also throughout that of his father, John Dingell Sr., whose congressional seat the son was elected to after the elder died in office in 1955. To say "tea-bagger" on the comedian Stewart's much-viewed show would ... well, no one on his staff could envision an upside to it.

Dingell was surprisingly nervous about going on the show as it was. The congressman had been studying past episodes as if preparing for a confirmation hearing—relishing the way Stewart had verbally undressed TV stock tipster Jim Cramer, yet dreading such a fate himself. Staffers took turns playing the host in mock Q&A sessions with the boss. After maybe the third or fourth mention of "tea-baggers," Michael Robbins—Dingell's chief of staff at the time—finally spoke up.

"Sir," he said carefully, "do you know what that actually means?"

By the look on Mr. Dingell's face, it was clear that he did not.

Because Mr. Dingell was hard of hearing, Robbins knew that he would have to speak loudly and enunciate. *Well, sir, I guess you could say it's a kind of sex act, when a man places his testicles onto the face of another person ...*

One of the four other staffers in the room turned the color of a fire engine.

Then, from the old man: *"Hah!"*

Followed by: "That's disgusting."

Followed by: "But it's funny, and I'm going to keep using it."

(He refrained from doing so on the show, which went well.)

John Dingell first encountered the Tea Party phenomenon on August 6, 2009, when he held a town hall in Romulus, Michigan, to defend Obama's health care legislation. He was booed and heckled from the moment he entered. A man wheeled in his son, afflicted with cerebral palsy, and stood about ten feet in front of Dingell and proceeded to assert, earsplittingly, that the new bill would end his son's life. "Fraud! Liar!" the man hollered as Dingell calmly tried to assure the man that he was incorrect. Dingell's answers to nearly every question were met with catcalls of "Bullshit!" and "You haven't even read the bill!" Dingell had quite a temper but kept it in check. He held a second town hall immediately after the first one was over and then informed his staff that he would not be doing any more in the near future.

Dingell had faced a Republican cardiologist with stout Tea Party backing in the 2010 midterm election. It was by far the toughest of his twenty-nine general election campaigns, though he still won by 17 points. Shortly after the midterms, the entire fifteen-member Michigan congressional delegation—including Dingell and three newly elected Tea Party freshmen—convened for the first time. Speaking at the event was Daniel Akerson, a prominent Michigander who happened to be the CEO of General Motors Company. One of the freshmen, a surgeon named Dan Benishek, arrived late and promptly announced that he would be leaving in five minutes.

"Sit down, Dan," growled Dingell. "This is important to Michigan. You've got nowhere else more important to be."

Dingell had once been an obnoxious freshman himself—a radical liberal in the eyes of Speaker Rayburn, who had a glare that, as Dingell would say, "damn near melted your cuff links." He had been, as Dingell liked to say of anyone new at anything, "as green as grass."

The difference, of course, was that Dingell had grown up in the institution. While his father, John Dingell Sr., was passing New Deal legislation on the House floor, the younger John was a House page, spending afternoons in the Capitol basement with a terrier and an air gun, shooting rats. He'd grown up in the presence of political giants. He'd seen what was humanly perfect. And therefore he could recognize that as a young freshman he was something of a jackass and had better shut up and absorb the wisdom of Mr. Sam Rayburn.

But these damn fools? They were going to come in and immediately start running down the House. And then wonder why Americans hated the institution!

Dingell felt sorry for Speaker Boehner, almost.

Still, it was his own party, not the Tea Party, that had dented Big John Dingell's armor back in 2008.

After he had spent twenty-seven years as the Democrats' leader on the Energy and Commerce Committee—which Dingell himself had built into one of Washington's great fortresses of power—Nancy Pelosi and her close friend, Dingell's nemesis, Henry Waxman of Los Angeles, had conspired to take away his chairmanship. The man responsible for the Clean Water Act of 1972 and the Endangered Species Act of 1973 had been deemed insufficiently progressive to move the Democrats' legislative agenda for 2009. Waxman became the new Energy and Commerce chairman. Dingell was pushed to the margins.

Tom DeLay, the House Republicans' whip, majority leader, and resident enforcer from 1995 until 2006, always said that there were three types of congressmen. There were leadership congressmen who, like DeLay, aimed to spend their careers governing the House and their colleagues. There were committee congressmen who took up residence in a particular outpost—Agriculture, Transportation, Appropriations, Armed Services—and made it their fiefdom. John Dingell had done precisely that with Energy and Commerce.

Now he fell into the third category—he was a district congressman, his energies largely consigned to Michigan's 15th District. Now he was 1 of 435, just another voice in the cacophony.

Except that this voice was John Dingell's. Even as the 111th Congress marked the undoing of the Democratic majority, the old man enjoyed one of the most productive legislative sessions of his career. He established America's newest national park, in his own district. He authored a rare bipartisan food safety bill that the president signed into law. He beat back the Tea Party candidate.

And for an encore, John Dingell intended to begin the 112th Congress in January 2011 by announcing his intention to run for an unprecedented thirtieth term.

Hah!

CHAPTER THREE

Bayonets

The 112th Congress was due to begin its work at noon on January 5, 2011. That morning, a swearing-in ceremony for the members of the Congressional Black Caucus took place in the Capitol Visitor Center. Accompanied by the swelling fanfare of horns and strings, the forty-three African-American representatives filed onstage in order of seniority—beginning with John Conyers, a CBC cofounder in 1971 and the original House proponent of the Martin Luther King federal holiday. Then another cofounder, Charles Rangel, war hero and legendary Harlem congressman, whose failure to pay taxes had led six weeks ago to his being censured on the House floor by a vote of 333 to 79—though with only a single CBC member, departing Alabama Congressman Artur Davis, voting against him. Then Edolphus Towns of Brooklyn. The civil rights icon John Lewis. James Clyburn, the House's third-ranking Democrat. And slowly cascading into relative youth as six black freshmen joined their seniors on the auditorium stage.

"Ladies and gentlemen," concluded the announcer, "the representatives of the Hundred-and-Twelfth Congress of the Congressional Black Caucus!"

And as the crowd applauded, one of the members seated in the back row onstage responded with a crisp salute. His graying hair was cut in the style of a flattop, and he wore wire-rimmed spectacles almost identical to those of Donald Rumsfeld, the former defense secretary and thus his former civilian commander, whom he happened to despise. His name was Allen Bernard West. He was a retired lieutenant colonel in the U.S. Army, a month shy of fifty, and, had fate turned against him a few years earlier, he might very well be winding down an eight-year prison term rather than beginning his first day as a United States congressman serving the 22nd District of Florida.

While Jesse Jackson Jr., a congressman and CBC member for the past fifteen years, fiddled with his BlackBerry, West the freshman sat at ramrod attention throughout. Among the forty-three CBC members, he was its only Republican. When Steny Hoyer—still the House majority leader until noon—stepped up to the podium, he described those seated onstage as "critical members of the Democratic caucus." *Typical,* thought the freshman. And when Hoyer applauded the black members for being such a positive force "in a country that . . . enslaved some citizens because of the color of their skin," West thought, *I never been nobody's slave.* But his expression remained stolid, unfazed.

Only when the new CBC chairman, a Missouri congressman and former Methodist pastor named Emanuel Cleaver II, spoke did Allen West's heart begin to quicken. "Well, my friends," the chairman declared in preacherly cadence, "the wall of protection for the unemployed is down. The wall of summer job security for young people is down. The wall of Middle East peace is down. The wall of civil discourse is down . . . But good news—we've got forty-three wall builders, standing ready! And we're gonna rebuild the wall!"

That was Lieutenant Colonel West—that signified his brothers in arms, he thought: *We stand on the wall, guarding this country's foundations.*

Before the 2010 elections, the House Democrats had forty-two black members. The Republicans had zero. Now there were two of the latter. The other African-American freshman, Tim Scott from the old slave market town of Charleston, South Carolina, had made it clear during the 2010 campaign that he had no interest in joining the Congressional Black Caucus with its liberal agenda. West hadn't discussed the subject with Scott. In Scott's view, politics was beside the point. Allen West was beside the point. West's parents had spent most of their young lives in south Georgia, where society's tenets were inalterably color-coded. Raised in Atlanta less than two miles from Ebenezer Baptist Church, West could still remember the primal wailings of his mother and his aunts the night Martin Luther King was shot. To honor the perseverance of his forebears, West knew what he had to do.

"My parents were Democrats," he told Jim Clyburn when they met and shook hands. "I think they'd be proud of the decision I made to join."

The seventy-year-old Democrat replied, "And my parents were Republicans. Welcome."

John Lewis welcomed him as well. "We're looking forward to working with you," the Georgia congressman said.

"My parents used to vote for you," said West. "I'm from right near your district at Grady High School."

"I get my laundry done at the dry cleaner's right over there!" exclaimed Lewis.

Thought West: *Yeah, so don't come down to my district anymore and campaign against me like you did last October!*

"Never see your color as a crutch," his father used to tell him. Herman West was an Army corporal who had helped liberate Rome in World War II. His older brother was wounded in Vietnam. His mother worked for the 6th Marine Corps District headquarters in Atlanta. West joined the ROTC at the age of sixteen. Instructed the father: "You make yourself so good that you can't be denied."

The Corps became his world. He did not fraternize or smoke or drink or do drugs—not then and not to this day. At jumpmaster school in 1984, he blew out his knee on a night jump from an aircraft and attended graduation on crutches. His first tour of duty was with an airborne battalion unit in Vicenza, Italy. At the conclusion of Operation Desert Storm in March 1991, Captain Allen West stood beside the tent in Safwan where Iraqi generals signed on to the terms of the cease-fire agreement—and he thought to himself, *We've left a dictator's military intact.* He strongly suspected that he would be back in Iraq one day.

A dozen years later, Lieutenant Colonel West was commanding a 4th Infantry Division battalion in the central Iraq town of Taji when he learned of a plot to assassinate him. After a roadside bomb hit his unit, he decided to take the report seriously. On his orders, an Iraqi police officer named Yehiya Kadoori Hamoodi, who supposedly had knowledge of the plot, was detained and brought back to the base for interrogation.

Hamoodi insisted, through several hours of questioning, that he knew nothing. Then West entered the room. The lieutenant colonel sat down in front of the detainee, on a stack of MRE boxes, and placed his 9mm pistol on his lap, with the barrel facing Hamoodi. "You're either going to tell us what we need to know," said West, "or I'll kill you."

Hamoodi repeated his denials, and one of West's soldiers punched him in the face. They dragged the Iraqi policeman over to a weapons clearing barrel and shoved his head down into it; West held his pistol against the back of Hamoodi's head. He counted backward from five. Hamoodi still offered nothing. West then fired off a shot, purposefully missing the detainee by maybe an inch. Hamoodi promptly collapsed, invoked Allah, and proceeded to rattle off names and locations. Arrests were made. Nothing of substance was uncovered. No more ambushes occurred. West immediately reported what had taken place to his superior, who did not relay the information up the chain of command. The information got out anyway, and in October 2003 Allen West was relieved of his command and choppered to the base in Tikrit to await further discipline. At minimum, his Army career was finished. Just as likely he would be court-martialed and sentenced to prison at Fort Leavenworth.

West testified at his Article 32 hearing in November 2003. He acknowledged that his actions were in violation of Army rules. He pled that no action be taken against his subordinates, who were only following his orders. He told the court about a promise he had made to his soldiers' families at a pre-deployment gathering: "I'm going to bring your guy back alive." Their safety was worth his breach of regulations, he contended—adding, "I'd go through hell with a gasoline can for my men."

After the hearing, West's attorney, Neal Puckett, could barely contain his awe. "Your life's going to be totally different.," he said. "The nation's going to see you as a leader who stands up for what's right."

Puckett added, "Allen, you should run for Congress."

"I just don't want to be in jail," said West.

The "I'd go through hell with a gasoline can" quote made its way back to Washington. Republican congressmen wrote letters to the secretary of the Army asserting that West should be commended for his actions rather than disciplined. A pro-West petition collected 130,000 signatures. Enough donations poured in to more than cover his legal fees. In the end, the military fined him five thousand dollars and permitted him to retire with full benefits. A martyr of the right was born.

West, his wife, Angela, and their two daughters relocated to south Florida in 2004. He taught history at Deerfield Beach High School but only lasted nine months. It astonished him that his students knew nothing about the Constitution or why the Civil War was fought. When one of the kids took a swing at him, West knew that there would be serious trouble if he remained. He decided that he would be better off in a war zone. For the next two and a half years he worked as a military contractor operating out of Kandahar. As it turned out, Neal Puckett was not the only one with ambitions for his former client. Some individuals in Florida contacted him after the Republicans lost the House in 2006. Would he consider running?

Allen West returned to the Fort Lauderdale area in May 2007 to begin plotting his campaign. But he was unknown and underfunded, running against an incumbent Democrat in the hope-and-change election cycle of 2008. The Democrat, Ron Klein, beat him by double digits. November 4 was an evening of tangled emotions for the West family. Many of his relatives had voted for Obama, with great enthusiasm. West caught some of the man's victory speech. What he felt was not pride but skepticism. They had a term in the Army for a slick-talking media darling like the president-elect: *spotlight Ranger.*

Three months after his defeat, West was knocking on doors again. A movement was beginning to brew, with CNBC correspondent Rick Santelli challenging viewers on February 19 to show up in Chicago for a "Tea Party" in July to protest the government's ill-advised mortgage lending policies. What the crusade lacked was a warrior.

On October 21, 2009, at a Tea Party rally in Fort Lauderdale, congressional candidate Allen West stood onstage, dressed in khakis and a white cotton shirt with the sleeves rolled up to mid-forearm, watching two performers in colonial attire play the fife and drums. West's assignment at the rally was to recite the Pledge of Allegiance, nothing more. Just as he was about to begin, he noticed a gentleman standing off to the side, costumed as a Revolutionary War soldier, complete with musket and bayonet. West got his cue, took the microphone, and decided that he would make the most of his moment.

He briefly sketched his life as an inner-city Atlanta boy given America's promise of opportunity, and how that was all he needed and all anyone should have the right to expect. Then he said, "We cannot live in a country where the government sits around and tries to engineer and design results and outcomes. Every time they try to do that—'Everyone has a right to own a home'—how does that end up? 'Everyone has a right to health care'—how does that end up? The Constitution says, 'Promote the general welfare'—not 'PROVIDE the general welfare!'"

After the cheers died down, West picked up steam. "We've got a class warfare going on. You've got a producing class, and you've got an entitlement class. If we're not willing to take our country back"—the candidate jabbed a finger at the crowd—"then you're complicit. It's your fault."

Said the lieutenant colonel, "You'd better get your butts out there and fight for this country!"

The cheering grew.

"This 2010 election is a defining moment for the United States of America . . . If you're here to shrink away from your duties—there's the door. Get out. But if you're here to stand up, to get your musket, to fix your bayonet, and to charge into the ranks—you are my brother and sister in this fight. You need to leave here understanding one simple word.

"That word is: *bayonets*.

"And charge the enemy—for your freedom, for your liberty. Don't go home and let your children down! You leave here today—CHARGE!"

The Democrats scoffed at Allen West. They painted him as the most off-the-beam of the extremist Tea Party candidates. They basked in the conventional wisdom that an African-American ultraconservative Christian could not possibly poach on Ron Klein's Jewish constituent base. They did not know how to account for West's own adoring followers or his astounding talent for fund-raising. The triumph of a man like Allen West seemed every bit as unthinkable as the viability of a ragtag movement that seemed more akin to a primal scream than anything of electoral significance.

The unthinkable occurred. He beat his opponent by 8 points.

On December 30, 2010, at six in the morning, Congressman-elect Allen West kissed his wife goodbye, hopped into the front seat of a U-Haul truck, and drove out of Plantation, Florida. The following morning, as he passed over the Potomac River, he reflected on Caesar crossing the Rubicon to save his beloved Rome. And he thought as well about the last time he drove a U-Haul, seven years ago, when the freshly discharged lieutenant colonel and his young family headed east from Fort Hood, Texas, to begin a new life in Florida—then to teach history. And now, to make it.

He spent New Year's Eve drinking sparkling grape juice at the Alexandria, Virginia, home of his lawyer and friend Neal Puckett. By January 1 he had already moved in to the basement apartment of an Army buddy near McPherson Square, walking distance from the White House. Congress would not be in session for another four days. None of the other freshmen had yet arrived. And that was the idea.

Because his foray into Washington was, in a sense, a paramilitary operation. Let the others stumble in on January 5 with their thousand-yard stares. West intended to get a jump on the rest. And so on New Year's Day he was jogging on the Mall, standing before the great statue of the seated Lincoln, all pores open. Then back to his man-cave to spend the day absorbing budgetary data and parliamentary procedures. On the morning of the second, he and his chief of staff, Jonathan Blyth, visited the Capitol when no one else was around. He wandered the bowels of the Capitol basement and a couple of times got lost. Blyth had worked on the Hill before, but his boss's instructions were to let West figure his own way out. He intended to learn every corridor, game out every shortcut. He'd drawn a low number in the office lottery, which consigned him to the seventh floor of the Longworth Building. West didn't give a crap. He was used to living out of a tent.

On the morning of the third, when the freshmen got their office keys, West marched up to Longworth carrying a book about blacks in Congress and various other documents in his old helmet bag ornamented with the myriad postings of his twenty-two-year military career. He convened a meeting with his new staff. His instructions to them were in fact his standing orders as a battalion commander, written on a three-by-five index card that he had laminated because he carried it with him on the campaign trail:

Keep your bayonet sharp. Keep your individual weapon clean.
Be the expert in your lane, and knowledgeable in another.
Be professional.

Not on the list was: *Blindly follow commands.* The freshman had already staked out his contrary position back in October, a month before he was even elected, when Boehner flew in for a campaign appearance with West at the Gun Club Café in West Palm Beach and quietly advised him to go easy on the rhetoric about tax reform and the flat tax. "Try to avoid talking about that," the Republican leader told the candidate, who ignored the counsel.

A month later, the congressman-elect appeared on NBC's *Meet the Press* and responded to a question about potential budget cuts by saying, "Everything has to be on the table ... We need to look at our Defense Department." As soon as the show was over, the incoming chairman of the Armed Services Committee, Buck McKeon, called West on his cell phone. How could West—who was vying for a seat on McKeon's committee—say that the defense budget ought to be cut?

"You're talking to a guy who's been on the ground," the freshman coolly replied. "There's waste, and I know where the low-hanging fruit is."

And shortly after learning of the House's new working calendar, which would involve fewer days in Washington and more time back in their congressional districts, West fired off a letter to the man who designed the new schedule, incoming House Majority Leader Eric Cantor. They should be spending *more* time in Washington, not less, the freshman wrote. How could they possibly contend with all the issues on their plate "when, among other things, we start off being in session only ten days the entire month of January?" West then circulated the letter in the form of a press release. Cantor's spokesman responded with his own statement: "What matters is who's in charge and the process put in place, not the number of days in session." The majority leader himself did not contact West—which, of course, was a statement of its own.

Fine, thought West. He saw the matter as he always did, through a military prism. Any private on a rifle range can call a safety violation without the permission of the Officer in Charge. Otherwise someone could get hurt. The private is showing initiative and care. He's thinking. He's not a Soviet-style robot. The OIC should be grateful.

And anyway, his bayonet was sharp. Now it was January 5, 2011. Time to charge the enemy.

PART TWO

✦

SHUT 'ER DOWN

CHAPTER FOUR

Citizens in the Devil's City

On the morning of his swearing-in, Jeff Duncan held a prayer breakfast in a reception room of the Republican National Committee headquarters, across the street from the Cannon Building, where he now worked. In previous months, there had been a banner affixed to the RNC building's façade. FIRE PELOSI, it had read. Now there was a new banner, hailing the politically radioactive Democrat's commitment to stay on as their minority leader: HIRE PELOSI.

A hundred South Carolinians were there to join Duncan. Most of them had traveled eight hours in a bus caravan from the 3rd District, and with few exceptions they wore Carolina (or Republican) red. One of his buddies led them in prayer: "We know that the Lord installs kings, princes and leaders, and we thank him for our brother Jeff Duncan ..."

When it was Duncan's turn, he closed his eyes and began: "God— you are so good ..."

The freshman choked up briefly. Taking a breath, he continued: "I thank you for this opportunity to serve my country and serve you ... I am focused on getting back to what was inspired by you, this form of government ... Shine your face on this nation once again. Turn it from its wicked ways ..."

Then he led the procession over to Cannon 116—where, as promised, a ribbon barricaded the doorway. One of his young sons held the ribbon taut while Duncan applied the scissors.

"This is the grand opening of a business," he told his constituents. "We are open for business, starting today!"

For two centuries, Washington, D.C., has sustained itself with intrigues. "May this Territory be the residence of virtue and happiness," President John Adams had declared on November 22, 1800, five days after the Sixth Congress officially relocated to America's permanent seat of power, the Congress having been based for a year in New York, followed by a decade in yellow fever–plagued Philadelphia. Major Pierre-Charles L'Enfant's newly designed metropolis took a while to achieve its grandeur, if not its virtuelessness. Too squalid for family life, Washington in its first few years was a city of men who lived and dined together in coarse boardinghouses—the New Englanders in one, the southerners in another, the westerners in another still. Their shared workplace stood at an elevation of eighty-eight feet above the Potomac River, on land acquired from the wealthy farmer and slave owner Daniel Carroll. The Capitol's earliest incarnation was so stifling that its inhabitants nicknamed it "the Oven." A half-century later came its ornate dome, and then a succession of House and Senate office buildings— and not only families but whole colonies of Washington professionals, from the partisan wordsmiths who scribbled for Thomas Jefferson's and Alexander Hamilton's rival newspapers to the sly female "spider lobbyists" who drew the hapless congressmen into their webs by means of "pleasant parlors" and "Burgundy at blood heat."

Now it was January 2011. Two years after a desultory cell of Republicans licked their wounds in the Caucus Room, the streets and hotels and reception rooms were exultantly theirs. Correspondingly, the K Street lobbyists and consultants and Republican job seekers were out in force. Above all, they sought out the eighty-seven new arrivals like Jeff Duncan and Allen West. That so many of the freshmen had achieved victory by denouncing John Adams's "residence of virtue and happiness" only meant that they were due a suitable orientation to how Washington works.

The educating went both ways, of course: the Washington establishment sought to disaggregate this great blob of newness and take its measure of them one by one. After all, this was hardly the first time that the town had seen a large freshman class. There had been a whopping 94 incoming Democrats following the referendum on the corrupt Grant administration in 1874; a class of 86 Democrats following the Panic of 1890; an unprecedented 131 Democratic freshmen riding the FDR wave in 1932; the 49 Watergate Democrats in 1974; the 52 so-called Reagan's Robots in 1980; and the 73 Gingrichites in 1994.

Each outsized freshman class rode into Washington confident that it had received an unambiguous mandate to change how business was done here. None was terribly successful at doing so.

For it was never all that hard for the Washingtonians to break down a brawny yet tender freshman class into its constituent parts. The Republican class of 2010 was not by any means monolithic. Nearly a third of them had never before held public office and were instead "citizen-politicians" from the fields of medicine, law enforcement, farming, auto sales, football, roofing, or pizza making. Others, however, were seasoned state legislators, two had been congressional senior staffers, and another was a well-known Republican opposition researcher. Occupying a category of his own was the unsinkable Charlie Bass of New Hampshire, who first was elected to Congress on the Gingrich wave of 1994, then rolled out to sea on the anti-Bush wave of 2006, only to return on the Tea Party wave four years later.

Beyond individual background, each representative, in the end, answered to his or her peculiar country-within-a-country. A dentist from Arizona named Paul Gosar now represented the state's 1st Congressional District—sent here by the Tea Party, except that Gosar now had to figure out how to respond to the needs of the Navajos who occupied vast swaths of his constituency. County prosecutor Sean Duffy, a former lumberjack and reality TV show star, had won a Wisconsin seat that had been in Democrat hands for four decades—and now came the hard part: convincing blue-collar union workers that the Tea Party sensation was one of them. Mo Brooks of Huntsville, Alabama, ran against the evils of Obamacare but now had to find a way to protect his district's missile defense interests. Allen West was now the duly elected defender of the Florida coastline; Jeff Duncan, the overnight guardian of the U.S. Department of Energy's Savannah River Site, a major nuclear facility.

Even among Republicans, America could be interpreted 435 different ways.

For these newcomers in the company town, there was an avalanche of names, customs, and vocational minutiae to reckon with. But all of them had a jump on Renee Ellmers and Blake Farenthold, who showed up to Washington like naked orphans on the doorstep of power.

Ellmers was a registered intensive care nurse from Michigan with a teenaged son, married to a surgeon whose practice had relocated them to North Carolina in 1999 and ultimately to the small town of Dunn, forty miles south of Raleigh. Her political involvement had been marginal until October 2008, when Barack Obama had his famous exchange with Joseph "Joe the Plumber" Wurzelbacher about the candidate's desire to "spread the wealth around." As Ellmers would say two years later, "I knew at that point that things were going to change for me. And either I could be a victim of it and yell at the TV every time I heard a speech or saw a story, or I could become involved."

The ex-nurse felt that Obamacare had it all wrong—that the emphasis should be on decreasing health care costs, and that the best approach to this (she believed, as a surgeon's wife) was to enact tort reform. She and her husband attended a town hall of local congressman Bob Etheridge, a seven-term Democrat. The crowd was rowdy, Etheridge was testy, and Renee Ellmers decided that he could be beaten.

No one in Washington thought she stood a chance. That included Kevin McCarthy, the two-term Californian who had been among the forlorn schemers in the Caucus Room on Obama's inauguration night. As the House Republicans' chief candidate recruiter, McCarthy had visited Etheridge's district in search of a viable opponent during the summer of 2009, just as Ellmers was making plans to run. McCarthy decided no Republican, including Ellmers, was worth throwing his weight behind and wrote the district off. After managing to secure the nomination the following summer, she visited with National Republican Congressional Committee chairman Pete Sessions in Washington but got the distinct impression that he had better things to do.

Ellmers caught a huge break in June 2010, when two NRCC interns who were following Etheridge to a fund-raiser got under the skin of the Democrat. The videotape—"Please let go of my arm, Congressman"—went viral. Oddly, Ellmers's consultant, Carter Wrenn, advised her not to fan the flames, which further convinced Washington Republicans that the nurse wasn't ready for the big leagues.

Wrenn did, however, commission a poll that summer to determine hot-button issues in Ellmers's district. The most significant—"overwhelmingly," Ellmers would recall—concerned the desire by a Muslim organization to erect a mosque two blocks from Ground Zero in lower Manhattan. "We were having a discussion about the poll numbers," Ellmers would remember. "My point, and this is from a historical standpoint and my own personal knowledge, is that when Muslims would conquer areas, they would erect a mosque—I guess you could call it a Victory Mosque."

Ellmers's political ad termed it precisely that—followed by the narrator's skeptical, "Where does Bob Etheridge stand? He won't say." The ad got her a slot on Anderson Cooper's CNN show. When Cooper suggested that the people building the mosque "are not terrorists," Ellmers interjected, "Do you know that, sir?"

Ellmers became ridiculed by the left and embraced by the Tea Party movement. Sarah Palin endorsed her. Ellmers pulled off an astonishing upset—though not until after a recount that lasted seventeen days, which on the congressional learning curve put Renee Ellmers well behind the other Republican freshmen . . . with one exception.

Blake Farenthold's recount took twenty days. Farenthold was a shy and roly-poly forty-nine-year-old trust fund beneficiary from Corpus Christi, Texas. According to congressional analyst David Wasserman, Farenthold was a "fluke winner." Possibly Wasserman had understated the matter. Texas's 27th Congressional District, which included the border city of Brownsville, was 70 percent Hispanic. The incumbent, Solomon Ortiz, had represented the district for twenty-eight years. Ortiz had done no polling whatsoever and was sitting on a hefty war chest. What did he have to worry about? His Republican opponent was a conservative talk radio sidekick who didn't speak Spanish and whose only claim to fame was that his grandmother, Sissy Farenthold, had been the state's liberal icon three decades ago.

Ortiz clearly had not taken stock of Farenthold's listenership on *Lago in the Morning*. They were angry that the Democratic incumbent had not hosted a health care town hall, that he used earmarks both to reward and to punish, that in a variety of ways he fulfilled the stereotype of the political fief who had overstayed his welcome. Even so, it was hard to take Blake Farenthold's candidacy seriously. Farenthold himself was anything but self-serious—a good-natured, clever bon vivant whose grandfathers (businessman George Farenthold and attorney Hayden Head Sr.) were two of Corpus Christi's wealthiest citizens. (Blake Farenthold's father, Randy, was murdered when Blake was eleven.) After working eight years as a radio disc jockey ("It was a great way to meet girls at the time") followed by another eight years in his wealthy grandfather's law firm, and then creating and eventually selling a Web design company, Farenthold seemed content to spend his semiretirement throwing rocks at politicians from the air-conditioned confines of a radio studio.

Then a day came when he found himself giving a five-minute pro-growth speech in front of two hundred cheering strangers. "I could do this," he decided. On the filing date deadline, Blake Farenthold hopped on an airplane, flew to Austin, and called his wife along the way to tell her, "You've got ten minutes to talk me out of filing." She thought he meant "filing for divorce."

Farenthold enlisted $100,000 of his own money. He made it into the Republican primary runoff, where he beat an opponent whose candidacy was doomed when it was learned that his wife worked for Planned Parenthood. Seven different Tea Party groups fell in behind the Farenthold insurgent campaign. The National Republican Congressional Committee had eyeballed the candidate but showed little interest until early October, when Farenthold spent $10,000 on a respected pollster whose findings showed the Republican ahead of Ortiz by 8 points. Suddenly Blake Farenthold had an NRCC staffer flying down from Washington to assist him in debate prep and Pat Boone doing a robocall on his behalf. Meanwhile, the 27th District's Hispanic voters stayed home on November 2. After a manual recount that finally came to an end on November 22, Blake Farenthold emerged with even fewer votes than the previous Republican whom Solomon Ortiz had *beaten* in 2008.

But in 2010, Farenthold's tally was just enough. Having defeated Solomon Ortiz by 799 votes, he was the Tea Party David who slew the Hispanic Goliath, and was now occupying the very office formerly inhabited by the vanquished, albeit with a tiny and woefully unprepared staff. The reception buffet in his congressional office on January 5, 2011, was the only one in the Rayburn Building to include beer and wine (along with tacos and quesadillas)—as if Blake Farenthold had still not yet caught up to the fact that he was no longer just an affable big fish on the Gulf Coast but a federal officeholder whose every blurt and quiver would be thrust into the blogosphere.

In a sense, he was all too aware. Farenthold was prone to anxiety dreams. One night he dreamed that he was a newly elected congressman, standing cluelessly alone in an office that was bare except for a telephone that would not quit ringing.

Still: Blake Farenthold and Renee Ellmers were present among the eighty-seven Republican freshmen who would soon become the great animators of the 112th Congress—which, apart from a single tragic interruption, quickly and inalterably became an ideological contest that at times would join the freshmen and their colleagues to the ageless national quarrels personified by America's greatest statesmen . . . but which at other times would resemble nothing so much as a professional wrestling match wherein, despite spasms of epic brawling, the outcome was preordained.

At 2:03 P.M. on January 5, 2011, Speaker Nancy Pelosi officially relinquished power by handing over to John Boehner an almost comically oversized gavel that he had chosen for the occasion. He wiped his eyes during the applause. After both he and Pelosi spoke to the chamber, the dean of the House, John Dingell, stood in the well and administered the oath of office to the new Speaker, just as Dingell had done to Pelosi four years prior. After Boehner declared, "I do," and the chamber erupted in cheers, the eighty-four-year-old Michigan congressman made his way up the stairs to the Speaker's chair, assisted by a gnarled wooden cane. He offered his hand to the Republican.

"Hey!" said Boehner in apparent surprise, then shook Dingell's hand.

Boehner swore in the new members. Clapping and handshakes were general throughout the chamber.

Only a few minutes later, the new House majority leader, Eric Cantor, called up the new rules package that would govern the House for the next two years—"a different and better way" that would include repealing the previous Congress's most significant achievement, the Affordable Health Care Act.

The bipartisan applause ceased. For the next hour, Democrats took to the floor to blast the new majority for "hypocrisy" and "discredited old tricks." The 112th Congress was officially under way.

The following afternoon, for the first time ever in the recorded history of the House of Representatives—and at the suggestion of veteran

Republican lawmaker Robert Goodlatte, though likely inspired by the sentiments of the Tea Party movement that had returned the GOP to power—the body's 435 elected members stood on the House floor to read sections of the U.S. Constitution. Jeff Duncan had made a point of arriving early and was among the first five in line. But then the House leaders from both parties were permitted to cut in front of him, and other latecomers saw their chance and edged in as well. Before Duncan knew it, he was thirtieth.

But the freshman still felt an overwhelming thrill as he stood at the podium for the first time and, with his own pocket Constitution in hand, read in a noticeably quavering voice from Article I, Section 8, relating to Congress's enumerated powers: "To declare war, grant letters of marque and reprisal, and make rules concerning captures on land and water; to raise and support armies, but no appropriation of money to that use shall be for a longer term than two years."

A few minutes later, a congresswoman—a Democrat from Arizona named Gabrielle Giffords—read the immortal words of Fisher Ames: "Congress shall make no law respecting an establishment of religion, or prohibiting the free exercise thereof; or abridging the freedom of speech, or of the press; or the right of the people peaceably to assemble and to petition the government for a redress of grievances."

CHAPTER FIVE

Gabby

Two weeks after the midterm elections had wiped out more than half their membership, the fiscal conservative Democratic coalition known as the Blue Dogs hosted a wake at Charlie Palmer steak house. The group's administrative cochair, Stephanie Herseth Sandlin, asked each member to toast another. When it was Gabrielle Giffords's turn, the forty-year-old Arizona congresswoman stood, smiled, and raised her glass.

"I want to toast all of the lady Blue Dogs, since there aren't that many of us," she said. Giffords proceeded to praise each of her fellow female moderates: Herseth Sandlin, Betsy Markey, Kathy Dahlkemper, Melissa Bean, Jane Harman, and Loretta Sanchez. She did not have to add that among this meager list, only three—herself, Harman, and Sanchez—would be coming back for the 112th Congress.

"Well," said Herseth Sandlin when her friend was done, "if they're really set on trying to figure out how to come back in 2012, you and Donnelly"—referring to Indiana Blue Dog Joe Donnelly—"are the ones that should be at the table. They need to hear how you managed to survive this."

After raising $4 million in contributions and outspending her Tea Party opponent three to one, Giffords had survived by 4,156 votes out of nearly 284,000 votes cast—and it wasn't until three days after the election that her victory was made official. She was down in the polls going into the final week of the campaign. During one low moment, a dismayed Giffords told a colleague, "My constituents don't like me anymore."

The hard, abrupt swing against her in Arizona seemed unfathomable after so many years of mutual infatuation. Her boomerang trajectory could have been diagrammed by a Hollywood screenwriter: brainy, beautiful, free-spirited local gal becomes New York financial planner, only to spurn the skyscraper world and return home to rescue her family's struggling tire business . . . and later, marry an astronaut! She drove a pickup truck and a Harley, had been restoring Vespas since she was fifteen, was fluent in Spanish, and, as the great-granddaughter of a Lithuanian rabbi, was herself a practicing Jew. In a highly transient southwestern state of asymmetric social hierarchy, Gabrielle Giffords won over her constituents by not pretending to be a square peg. After one term in the Arizona House followed by a single term in the state senate, in 2006 she ran for the 8th District seat, being vacated by a Republican. Assisted by blue-ribbon donors like Emily's List and the Sierra Club, by helpful campaign plugs from John Dingell and then-Senator Barack Obama and by an ad campaign that promised an unyielding stance on border security, Giffords walloped her opponent by 12 points, and then won a second term by the identical margin in 2008.

What made 2010 different was a rising tide of economic distress, coupled with the growing belief that the Democrats were only making things worse. Unlike many of the other Blue Dogs, Giffords had voted for the complete unholy trinity: stimulus, cap-and-trade, and health care. The latter vote set off an ugly conflagration of attacks—the very least of which were snarky ads featuring a Pelosi double instructing a Giffords stand-in who would bleat, "Whatever you say, mama Nancy." More ominously, an anonymous assailant blew out the windows on her district office. Sarah Palin's PAC website showed a map of congressional districts with crosshairs covering twenty of them, representing Democrats who had voted for health care. Arizona's 8th District was one of them. Giffords went on MSNBC to warn Palin that "there's consequences to that action." Already an attendee at one of her health care forums had dropped a loaded revolver on the ground. Now her Tea Party opponent, a twenty-eight-year-old Marine named Jesse Kelly, was posing in campaign ads brandishing an M-16 assault rifle. "Send a Warrior to Congress," Kelly's ad said.

Giffords herself was more of a survivor than a warrior. She navigated the fault line between her conservative voters and her party's progressive agenda with acrobatic expertise—which did not mean that her footwork escaped notice. The Republicans in the Arizona delegation

felt that her efforts to secure her district's porous border lagged behind her tough talk. During one breakfast with her Arizona colleagues,
Giffords described a recent trip she had taken to get to know ranchers
along the border and then chidingly added, "All of you were invited, too.
How come you weren't there?"

"Listen, young lady," growled Senator John McCain. "We know a
little bit about the border, and I won't be lectured by you about it!"

While staking out territory as a centrist, Giffords departed from
other Blue Dogs by cultivating a relationship with Speaker Pelosi—
believing that, for all the Speaker's shortcomings, she was a strong advocate for women in Congress, and believing further that most of the
attacks on Pelosi had their basis in sexism. Pelosi, for her part, saw star
potential in the freshman and therefore awarded her choice committee
assignments for her district (Armed Services and Science and Technology). A year later, Giffords became the only sophomore handpicked by
Pelosi to join the twenty-member congressional delegation to the Co-
penhagen climate change summit. That same year, the Speaker invited
her to a weekend of rubbing elbows with big donors at Pelosi's Napa
Valley cabin.

Giffords had district-specific reasons for supporting most of the
Democratic agenda—especially the energy bill, which would have been
a boon for Arizona's solar power industry had it passed the Senate. But
she also voiced sharp disagreements with the party, particularly during
the 2010 election cycle. Along with other Blue Dogs, she emphatically
told then–Budget Committee chairman John Spratt that she could not
vote for Obama's $1.4 trillion budget—and as a result of such objec-
tions, the Democrats never introduced a budget for the next fiscal year.
That spring, shortly after the shooting death of a well-known rancher
in her district, Giffords had lunch at the White House and spoke forcefully to Obama about the administration's insufficient efforts on the
border.

Her opponent Kelly had proclaimed himself "absolutely the Tea
Party candidate," leaving Giffords a wide swath of running room in the
middle. "Gabrielle is not like other politicians," her press statements
unfailingly asserted. "She takes an independent view on the issues and
was rated Arizona's most moderate member of Congress by the *National Journal . . .*" Her campaign ads—at least the ones that weren't

excoriating her opponent as "dangerous"—touted endorsements by Arizona Republicans, veterans, senior citizens, small businessmen, and local law enforcement agents. She buttressed her advocacy of seniors by introducing a resolution that would oppose an increase in the Social Security retirement age—though no such policy was under active consideration that legislative session. Above all, both on the House floor and on the campaign trail, she delivered multitudes of speeches on border security—including a tart critique of the president's claim that the border was "more secure today than at any time in the past twenty years."

Still, Giffords never equivocated in her support of the much-demonized stimulus, energy, and health care bills. While calmly explaining her votes during a debate with Kelly two weeks before the election, she was drowned out by boos.

The catcalls Giffords could handle. If representing her constituents in the legislative process meant shouldering some political grief, so be it. But, as she confided to some of her colleagues, Pelosi's domineering reign had taken some of the joy out of public service. Giffords saw herself as a legislator. During her first term, seven bills and amendments that she introduced were signed into law. In four years, she had introduced fifty-nine bills and amendments.

But her contributions had, like that of most other House Democrats, slowed to a crawl in 2009, when Speaker Pelosi began to stifle amendments and limit debate so as to prevent the Republicans from throwing the Democratic agenda off course. And in the meantime, Giffords told associates, the party had been far too deferential to seniority, and discouraging its younger members from aspiring to leadership roles.

Adding to her doubts was her desire to start a family with her husband, Mark. The astronaut lived in Houston; the congresswoman, in Arizona and Washington. One night over dinner at the Democratic Club a few blocks from the Capitol, Giffords asked her friend Diana DeGette—a seven-term Colorado representative who had two teen-aged children—just how a young mother could make it all work. DeGette offered encouragement. Her friend Gabby wasn't convinced, however. The two agreed to continue discussing the subject some other time.

• • •

Tears ran down Gabrielle Giffords's face on election night when she heard the news that nearly every one of her friends in the House had lost. On January 5, 2011, the day of her swearing-in, Giffords joined her depleted Blue Dogs in voting against Nancy Pelosi for minority leader—though she discussed the matter with Pelosi on the floor that morning, saying that it wasn't personal but instead a reflection on how effective the Pelosi-bashing had been in her district. Giffords then proceeded to support not the Blue Dog candidate Heath Shuler but instead civil rights legend John Lewis. The next day, just after reading the First Amendment to the Constitution on the House floor, Giffords introduced legislation to cut the salaries of all congressional members by 5 percent—an effort she had cosponsored the previous year, but which then-Speaker Pelosi had not permitted to come to the floor. Under a Republican majority with its budget-slashing Tea Party freshmen, she figured that the bill stood a better chance.

The following day, Friday, January 7, Gabby Giffords accosted one of the freshmen, David Schweikert, on the House floor. She took the fellow Arizonan on a tour of the Capitol. That same day, her staff announced that she would be attending her premiere "Congress on Your Corner" event of the year, on Saturday the eighth at a supermarket in northwest Tucson.

Giffords had told her staff that life in the congressional minority would mean concentrating more on district issues. She expressed the desire to get to it right away. The Safeway event would be the beginning of her up-tempo, localized focus—and would also be the 8th District's first opportunity to embrace Gabrielle Giffords's message, verbalized in her victory speech back in November, that "there's a big difference between a crowd and a community. When you're in a crowd, you're pushing. You're shoving. You're jockeying for position. But when you're in a community, you stop for a second, and you acknowledge one another . . . and you can disagree, without being disagreeable."

The next morning just outside the Safeway supermarket, the congresswoman and her constituents renewed their acquaintance. They lined up and chatted amiably with her, in the civil manner of community. It did not feel like a crowd until all of a sudden someone pushed forward. A moment later came the act that defied all agreeability.

CHAPTER SIX

The Institutionalist

Boehner had been at his home in West Chester, Ohio, that Saturday afternoon when he picked up the phone and heard from his chief of staff, Barry Jackson, that Gabrielle Giffords and three of her staffers had been shot and possibly killed.

He called his Democratic counterpart, Nancy Pelosi, who had been taking down her Christmas tree at home in San Francisco when she got the news. Then the Speaker released a short statement. "I am horrified," it read, "by the senseless attack on Congresswoman Gabrielle Giffords and members of her staff. An attack on one who serves was an attack on all who serve . . . This is a sad day for our country."

That evening, Boehner's staffers back in Washington urged him to hold a press conference. *People needed to see the House leader, not just hear him*, they said. *You can deliver it in West Chester. You're the Speaker. The cameras will come to you.*

Boehner had been at his job only three days. He of course understood the Speaker's traditional duties: controlling the House's legislative calendar, overseeing the majority party's committee assignments, and standing second in the line of succession to the presidency. Still, he was not yet accustomed to the full power it conferred on him. Sure enough, a phalanx of reporters awaited him on Sunday morning at the West Chester township office, where Boehner had begun his political career as a township trustee nearly three decades ago. He took no questions and read from a prepared statement that again included the sentiment that "an attack on one who serves is an attack on all who serve." That same morning, Boehner's staff wrangled the entire House membership for a conference call. Boehner led off with remarks—which were again written down and included the same verbiage as his other two statements—before passing the call off to Pelosi.

This was Boehner. Like his immediate predecessor, Pelosi, he did his best work behind the scenes. But this, too, was Boehner: he ordered the flags flown at half-mast on the House side of the Capitol in honor of Giffords's staffer Gabe Zimmerman, who had died on the scene. He and Majority Leader Eric Cantor agreed to postpone next week's business in the House, which would have included efforts to repeal Obama's health care act (which Republicans had heretofore described as "job-killing").

"And frankly," he told his House colleagues on the conference call, "we need to rally around each other. This is a time for the House to lock arms . . . We must rise to the occasion for our nation and show Congress at its best."

Two days later, on the House floor, Boehner gave a more poignant speech in honor of the Arizona congresswoman who was now fighting for her life in a Tucson intensive care unit. He choked up and tears ran down his face. This, unmistakably, was John Boehner.

The body closest to the people, and to their passions, was ever susceptible to unruliness and thus to violence. At times the congressmen themselves were the instigators. In 1808, New York Representative Barent Gardenier denounced President Jefferson's sweeping trade embargo on the House floor with escalating obnoxiousness, to the point where House Ways and Means chairman George Washington Campbell challenged Gardenier to a duel. Campbell was the abler marksman. The gravely wounded Gardenier, it was later said, "escaped with his life; and when he returned to his seat he assailed his opponents with more violence than ever."

On an afternoon in February 1857, as the *New York Times* breathlessly reported it, "The vulgar monotony of partisan passions and political squabbles has been terribly broken in upon to-day by an outburst of public revenge"—referring to New York Congressman Daniel E. Sickles gunning down the District of Columbia's district attorney, who was the son of Francis Scott Key, after learning that the younger Key was enjoying liaison with Sickles's wife. The jury ultimately found the congressman not guilty—telling a reporter later that the murdered adulterer "deserves his doom"—and overjoyed spectators carried Sickles out into the streets.

In 1978, California Congressman Leo Ryan became the first U.S. representative to be killed in the line of duty when he was gunned down in Jonestown, Guyana, while investigating the mass suicide of the Jim Jones cult there. Two decades later, a man suffering from paranoid schizophrenia entered the Capitol with a .38-caliber handgun and shot two policemen to death before being subdued. In the days following the 9/11 attacks, a package mailed to the office of Senate Majority Leader Tom Daschle was found to contain a deadly strain of anthrax. In both 2009 and 2010, a man carrying a firearm in the vicinity of the Capitol was chased down and killed by police.

That members had largely managed to avoid danger all this time did not mean they were unaware of the risks. Implicit in their job description was contact with constituents, without security, and their workplace was open to anyone who walked in. In town halls they often encountered belligerence or worse. The calls that came into their offices were at times hostile, at other times plainly nuts. Most of them had received threats of varying severity, only a few of which were passed on to the Capitol sergeant at arms. Everyone seemed to have a story. One California Democrat had been tailed in a pickup truck loaded with weapons and driven by some unhinged former high school classmate. In early 2009, Heath Shuler's office received a call from a disabled Vietnam vet threatening to kill the Blue Dog Democrat. Federal authorities arrested the man, who was heavily armed and readily admitted his intent to kill his congressman.

During the final voting on the Affordable Health Care Act in March 2010, Blue Dog Democrat Betsy Markey's office received a death threat by telephone. Her fellow Coloradoan, Senator Mark Udall, had also been threatened for having voted aye. Then–Minority Leader Boehner went before the cameras on March 25 and said, "I know many Americans are angry over this health care bill, and angry at Democrats here in Washington for not listening. But as I've said before, violence and threats are unacceptable."

Boehner himself had never received any serious threats in all his twenty years as a congressman. Now the new Speaker was beginning to grasp the full responsibility of his office. He was the custodian of the lower body's welfare. It was not the sort of thing that you prepare for.

✦ ✦ ✦

He had prepared for everything else.

During the summer of 2011, a dinner was held in Kentucky marking the two hundredth anniversary of the great Henry Clay's inauguration as House Speaker. Three of the attendees were Boehner, Pelosi, and her predecessor as Speaker, Dennis Hastert. Each of them spoke at the dinner. Hastert had been well down the leadership chain in early 1999, when scandal brought down Gingrich and Bob Livingston and suddenly thrust the Republican deputy whip into the Speaker's chair. Listening that night to both Pelosi and Boehner describe the elaborate plans they had made for the day when each of them ascended to the Speakership, Hastert thought to himself: *Wow. These two people were thinking about all this for a* long *time.*

Boehner had never bothered to conceal his ambitions. But they were limited to the institution of the House. Boehner was a bartender's son from Reading, Ohio, and it seemed plausible to draw a straight line from his upbringing behind the bar at Andy's Café to the contentment he derived from the House's raucous confines. Many if not most congressmen didn't share his contentment with being one among a body of 435. It was a given that just as the Senate was composed of one hundred self-regarded presidents-in-waiting, the House functioned for many members as a senatorial way station.

One House Republican harboring such ambitions was Jason Chaffetz, an aggressive conservative sophomore from Utah who was publicly contemplating a 2012 primary challenge against Senator Orrin Hatch. Chaffetz came to Boehner for advice on the matter. The Speaker made his preferences plain. "You'll enjoy it more over here," Boehner told Chaffetz. "There's action. If you're a serious legislator, you can really dive down into an issue—you can really own it on this side. And we need more specialists." The Speaker reminded Chaffetz that there was greater turnover in the lower body. An ambitious fellow could move upward in a hurry.

It was the most persuasive argument Jason Chaffetz had heard for staying in the House. Ultimately, and to the surprise of many, he took Boehner's advice.

Over the course of his career, various Republicans would sidle up to Boehner and suggest that *he* make a run for the Senate. He assured them of his disinterest. Upon latching on to Newt Gingrich's coattails, he and a few other class of 1990 Republican upstarts known as the Gang of Seven helped Gingrich engineer a revolution that drove the House Democrats out of power for the first time in forty years.

Boehner didn't want to break out of the pack. He just wanted to be leading it. From 1995 onward, he was riding the leadership escalator. And though the chain-smoking, merlot-slurping, perma-tanned, and ever-golfing Republican conference chairman was not the type to out-work or outthink his fellow GOP leaders Gingrich, DeLay, and Dick Armey, Boehner's steadiness had a way of growing on people. He refrained from the kind of risk-taking that might make him a lightning rod. (Among the Gang of Seven, it was always someone like Jim Nussle or Rick Santorum insulting President Clinton or putting a paper bag over his head—while Boehner sat behind the back rail, smoking and observing the antics of his colleagues.)

Of course, in Washington, the road to endearment is the fund-raising trail. Fortunately for Boehner, he loved to drive. Every summer he would head out of West Chester in his RV, which he nicknamed Freedom One, and would amble across America, district by district, from one fund-raiser to the next—smoking and crooning to cheesy music with the country whipping past him, occasionally spelled behind the wheel by his next-door neighbor Ron. Boehner was well aware of the Washington verity that the most powerful politicians are the ones who distribute money to other politicians. It suited his backslapping manner to talk up his colleagues to wealthy Republican donors. In this way he made friends, and they stayed his friends.

He also made a few enemies. Boehner's alliances with powerful lob-byists became embarrassingly apparent in 1995, when the conference chairman materialized on the House floor and proceeded to dissemi-nate campaign contributions from tobacco lobbyists to fellow Repub-licans who were about to vote on a tobacco subsidies bill. And yet one thing differentiated him from the backroom dealmakers on the Hill: he didn't like earmarks. He just thought designating taxpayer dollars for a particular congressman's local college or airport wasn't the right way to do business. Even before Gingrich became Speaker and routinely sent over to the Appropriations Committee lists of federal projects to fund for Republicans in vulnerable districts, Boehner as a freshman took to the House floor to excoriate the 1991 Highway Bill, which bore the fingerprints of eventual Transportation Committee chairman Bud Shuster: "I stand opposed to this legislation because spreading pork around to secure enough votes to pass this turkey is wrong!"

As GOP conference chairman, Boehner continued to criticize Chairman Shuster's earmarking antics. He was warned by colleagues, "This could be trouble for you." It was. After Gingrich had worn out his welcome and skulked off in 1998 following a poor performance by Republicans in the midterms, the conference reckoned that more changes in leadership needed to be made. J. C. Watts of Oklahoma ran for Boehner's job. Some thought Watts, at the time the party's only black House member, would be a fresh messenger. Others, like DeLay and Hastert, believed that Boehner had botched his job overseeing the House Republican communications apparatus. Then there was Shuster, who had a long memory and a formidable bloc of indebted colleagues.

On the evening after he was pushed out of leadership, Boehner went out with about thirty allies to Sam & Harry's, a Capitol Hill steakhouse. He blubbered a bit that night, but he also declared bravely to his disheartened staffers, "Look, sometimes blessings come in a form where they're not immediately obvious." It was the kind of thing someone's grandmother would say. It was also common Boehner-speak. He seemed to actually believe it.

Following a script carefully plotted by his chief of staff, Barry Jackson, the deposed conference chairman reestablished himself as a legislator. He took over the chairmanship of the Education Committee's most desolate backwater, the Subcommittee on Employer-Employee Relations. Showing a surprisingly aggressive streak, Chairman Boehner won a few turf wars and steered important legislation through his bailiwick. He became the full committee chairman in January 2001 and immediately caught a big break when the new Republican president, George W. Bush, decided to lead off with the No Child Left Behind education initiative. Boehner's work on the bill with Bush, Senator Ted Kennedy, and California Congressman George Miller won glowing reviews.

His fellow Republicans appeared to be developing a case of seller's remorse. One night at a party banquet, a longtime ally, Indiana Congressman Steve Buyer, stood up and began to praise Boehner's comportment after having been rejected by his colleagues. "You're like that first-string quarterback who's asked to come to the sidelines," Buyer said as he faced his friend. "And when you did, you didn't just sit on the bench. You grabbed a clipboard and a headset, and you started helping the quarterback on the field. That's the kind of guy you are!"

The attendees leaped from their chairs and awarded a standing ovation to Boehner—who, being Boehner, proceeded to weep.

In January 2006, Tom DeLay was collared with a federal indictment for illegally transferring campaign contributions to fellow Republicans and was forced by Speaker Hastert to vacate the post of majority leader. John Boehner lunged out of the wilderness. FOR A MAJORITY THAT MATTERS, read the title of his majority leader campaign document. "We seem adrift, uncomfortable with our ability to reach big goals," he wrote. "America needs more from us ... My goal is to create a *confident* majority ..." Deftly turning his aversion to earmarks to his advantage, Boehner reminded his colleagues that "I cut my teeth here as a reformer," suggesting that he was uniquely qualified to lead the party out of the brewing scandal involving GOP lobbyist and DeLay friend Jack Abramoff. The Education Committee chairman now proclaimed that "the lifeblood of the House runs through the Committees and their members" rather than through leadership. And, in a veiled swipe at the autocratic DeLay, Boehner argued that the House majority should "make consideration of bills more open— and always guaranteeing the Democrats the right to offer a substitute amendment, *even when they don't want to offer one*, so that voters can size us both up and see which philosophy and which proposal they support."

On February 2, 2006, the Republican conference met to consider three candidates: Boehner, who had cast himself as the reformer; the majority whip, Roy Blunt, who was next in line for the post and thus heavily favored; and conservative favorite John Shadegg. Testimonials attesting to Boehner's leadership skills were given by two Army veterans, Steve Buyer and South Carolina Congressman Gresham Barrett. But the most surprising endorsement came from House Ways and Means chairman Bill Thomas, who had tangled with Boehner over committee jurisdictional matters. The famously crusty Thomas professed his admiration of his former adversary.

Boehner prevailed on a secret ballot vote, 122–109. He was now second in command to Speaker Denny Hastert. After the Republicans were stomped in November 2006 and Hastert decided to retire, Boehner ascended to minority leader. Then came November 4, 2008, and the GOP lost even more seats.

The clock was ticking fast for the John Boehner Era.

Fretful of the locomotion that the Democratic majority's agenda was gathering, his colleagues said it to him over and over: "John, we've gotta be more aggressive!"

Boehner's reply, through a cumulus cloud of cigarette smoke, was more or less the same: "Relax. We're gonna be fine."

It drove his fellow Republicans a little bit nuts, the way Boehner stabbed languidly at the ashtray, shrugged his shoulders, moseyed on over to the Capitol Hill Club or Alberto's with his cycling pals and in general acted as if the rise of Nancy Pelosi and Barack Obama was all part of the plan. He was never going to be an advocate of uptight discipline like his lieutenant Eric Cantor, a forty-eight-year-old former Richmond, Virginia, lawyer who was taut with calculation and poised as a cobra. During his January 5, 2011, speech on the House floor to introduce the rules that would govern the body throughout the 112th Congress, Cantor would proclaim that the Republican-controlled House would "hold ourselves accountable by asking the following questions: Are our efforts addressing job creation and the economy? Are they cutting spending? Are they shrinking the size of the Federal Government while protecting and expanding individual liberty? If not, why are we doing it?"

Subsequently, a sign with that very litany of questions and the heading CANTOR RULE would be sitting on several desks throughout the majority leader's Capitol suite.

Boehner wasn't ever going to encourage a personality cult in his workplace. Nor was he ever going to inhabit the cutting edge like the third-ranking Republican, Kevin McCarthy, himself not lacking in ambition. McCarthy was from Bakersfield, California, and often flew to

Silicon Valley so that he could trade ideas with high-tech CEOs. During the doldrums of early 2009, McCarthy used GOP funds to start a graphically jazzy website, AmericaSpeakingOut.com, where anyone could register their disgruntlement over the Obama agenda and propose agendas of their own.

Boehner often communicated with other members via highly abbreviated text messages. But that was about as sophisticated as he got. During one Republican conference, the Speaker gamely exhorted the members to use their Twitter accounts to convey the House GOP's themes of the week. "And," he added, "uh, don't forget to, when you're, uh, tweeting, to, uh, type in a, uh . . ."

The next words seemed to come out of his mouth sideways, like a Czech adjective: ". . . er . . . *hash . . . tag!*"

McCarthy had brought Boehner along to a Bakersfield Tea Party rally on tax day, April 15, 2009. Boehner had never seen anything like it—an outcry of anti-Washington vitriol bordering on the elemental—and immediately recognized that he could either board this train or be flattened by it. He deputized McCarthy to oversee the drafting of a Pledge to America, a riff on Gingrich's Contract with America, which Boehner's staff had commandeered sixteen years prior. As a sop to Cantor, they unveiled the Pledge in the latter's district in September 2010. The promises contained in the forty-eight-page Pledge—repeal Obamacare, halt all tax increases, cut federal spending by at least $100 billion in the first year—were an unmistakable paean to the Tea Party movement. (Only a passing wink was given to social conservatives in the Pledge's introduction: "We pledge to honor families, traditional marriage, life and . . . faith based organizations . . .")

Meanwhile, Boehner heated up his own denunciations of the president and the Democratic Speaker. For this task it was clear that he was not the ideal messenger—this pronouncedly retro, Naugahyde-skinned Beltway lifer suddenly spouting maverick claims about how the White House was "out of touch" and that "Washington's not listening" to the average American.

He had greater worries, however. By October 2010 it had become increasingly evident that the Republicans would retake the House. But would Boehner be their leader? It was hardly guaranteed. He had appointed McCarthy his chief candidate recruiter for the election cycle. The Californian had built intimate bonds with the new candidates. Boehner hadn't. One of the highest-profile candidates McCarthy was advising, Kristi Noem of South Dakota, had told her local paper that she wasn't ready to commit to Boehner. Another Tea Party recruit, Missouri auctioneer Billy Long, would loudly drawl to a couple of lobbyists at a reception that "John Boehner and Roy Blunt are what's wrong with Washington."

Though McCarthy was unlikely to take a run at the Speakership, he was tight with Cantor, whose ambitions were undisguised. In 2008, it had been leaked that the Virginia congressman was on the short list to be John McCain's vice presidential candidate. This amused McCain's senior staffers, who had each been asked to contribute their recommendations and who therefore knew that Cantor had not been recommended by *any* of them. No doubt the leak had come from Cantor's inner circle, which was every bit as loyal as Boehner's.

Boehner had vowed in the fall of 2010 to "end earmarks as we know them"—employing that measured construction because there were many in the GOP caucus who supported earmarks. Two weeks later, Cantor, who himself had requested a $7 million flood control earmark in the past, had managed to get to the right of Boehner on his signature issue by declaring in an op-ed that "the next Republican conference should immediately move to eliminate earmarks." Cantor played offense, and his lieutenants rivaled Nancy Pelosi's as the most aggressive on the Hill. The mutual distrust between Boehner's and Cantor's staffs was at times toxic.

Still, Cantor had been the Republican whip. He knew how to count votes. Boehner had more of them—for now.

And so it was John Boehner who rapped the monstrous gavel on January 5, 2011; Boehner who received a unanimous vote from his Republican colleagues that same afternoon; Boehner who led the reading of the Constitution the next day; Boehner who spent his first weekend as Speaker talking with FBI Director Robert Mueller and House Sergeant at Arms Bill Livingood about the security of Gabby Giffords's 434 colleagues. It was John Boehner who treated his conference early and often to the Boehneresque mantra, "Let the body work its will." He would not dictate in the manner of Gingrich or Pelosi.

Instead, he would at times lead—as another former House and Senate leader, Trent Lott, would say—"by being led." A ferocious wind had blown him into power. The wind was still out there. He was going to hold on. He was going to relax. Things were going to be fine.

CHAPTER SEVEN

State of the Weiner

At the House Democrats' annual retreat in Cambridge, Maryland, on January 22, 2011, a Texas communications specialist and longtime friend of the Clintons with ruddy cheeks and a bouffant of sandy-blond hair named Roy Spence stood before his audience and challenged them to rethink their purpose for being congressmen.

"The American people have left the building," Spence told the Democrats. "They can see it. You're in the reelection business. You're not in the make-a-difference business. They know it, and so do you. The test for the American people is, are you in it for us—or for *you*? You passed all these laws, but you didn't pass the test."

Pacing while he glared defiantly at his audience, Spence continued, "We're not in a recession. We're in a winter. The last winter was World War II. Before that, the Civil War. Before that, the American Revolution. The difference is that in the previous winters, we knew what we were fighting for. The American people have left the building because they don't know what we're fighting for. And in a democracy, if you don't know what you're fighting for, you fight each other. That's what's happening now."

The audience was absolutely quiet. Roy Spence had them spellbound—all except for one congressman, who got up out of his seat and, with a haughty glare, stalked out of the conference room. It was the representative from Brooklyn, Anthony Weiner.

What was unusual about this was not the show of attitude—Weiner's colleagues widely viewed him as insouciant in the extreme—but rather that he had expressed his disapproval for once without actually moving his mouth. In a chamber replete with self-regarded descendants of

Demosthenes, Anthony Weiner was straight-outta-Brooklyn mouthy, orating with all the gentility of a human threshing machine.

January was shaping up to be a busy month for him. After spending the 112th Congress's first full day reading from the Constitution and later lapsing into somber tribute to their wounded colleague, Gabrielle Giffords, the House Republicans were now proceeding full tilt with their legislative agenda. Speaker Boehner's House promised to be a paragon of openness and frugality. Mainly, however, it would be the GOP's spear point against Obama. Anthony Weiner could not wait to gird for battle.

Two days after Boehner rapped the 112th Congress into session, Weiner gleefully charged that the Republicans had already violated one of their new rules by failing to post a minor piece of legislation online three days before considering it on the House floor. When the Speaker pro tempore ruled that the rule applied only to bills and joint resolutions, not this simple resolution, Weiner howled, "Am I to understand that under the rules that were just passed . . . that the new rule requiring three days is *already being waived*?"

Ten days later, as the Republicans set to work repealing the Obama health care bill, Weiner stepped up his lacerating game. "And just a word on this whole government takeover thing," he said in his nasal near-shout. "I mean, I love you guys, and I know you are caught up in the rhetoric of the campaign . . . Now, what's your solution? Well, they don't have a solution. We know what they are against. They are against health reform. We don't know what they are for. Welcome to the Republican majority."

After listing several Republican misrepresentations of the Obama health care plan, Weiner said from the House floor, "You know, I want to just advise people watching at home playing that now-popular drinking game of you take a shot whenever the Republicans say something that's not true: please assign a designated driver. This is going to be a long afternoon."

He stuck out in the House chamber like an extended middle finger. During floor debate, Weiner would saunter in, his face already wrenched in irritation, and flop down into one of the seats near the back, far from the other Democrats. He would check his BlackBerry, then yawn and stretch his arms extravagantly in the manner of a spoiled prince. When it came his turn to speak, he would invariably bypass the microphone at the committee table where Democrats frequently gave their floor statements, instead proceeding to the well, so that he could face the full panorama of onlookers—Democrats, Republicans, visitors in the upper gallery—and they in turn could see him.

His jeering, sneering, and frequently hilarious rants were delivered off the cuff, without benefit of any notes—though now and again he brought with him a poster from the House graphics department, or on one occasion a book he had acquired from the House gift shop (*House Mouse, Senate Mouse*, to showcase the House Republicans' seeming refusal to recognize the legislative role of the Senate).

But his work was hardly done upon leaving the House floor. Oh no: the cable TV cameras beckoned, and Weiner was more than obliging. As recently as early 2009, the congressman would enter his office in the Rayburn Building screaming at the top of his lungs, *"Why the fuck am I not on MSNBC?!"* When the health care debate kicked in, Anthony Weiner became the one-man standard-bearer for the single-payer system. He was now on MSNBC every week, sometimes every day—to the point where he was carrying his own makeup kit. (Or rather, his press guy was.) But because he believed that a fighter should also go into the enemy camp, he was also the designated liberal brawler on Fox. He rather enjoyed his screaming matches with Fox hosts Sean Hannity and Megyn Kelly. It burned bile, he liked to say.

Neither Pelosi nor anyone else deputized him to speak for his party. But as the ultimate freelancer in a body of 435 legislative entrepreneurs, Anthony Weiner had discovered that if you go on TV often enough and say something catchy, two things happen. First, your point of view, through repetition across each network, can actually become the conventional wisdom. During the health care debate in August 2009, Weiner had predicted on CNBC that a health care bill without a public option would lose the support of one hundred Democrats. That number had just popped into his head. He'd uttered it without any reason to believe it was accurate. And yet it soon became a widely quoted number.

Second, by speaking for the party, you are a de facto party spokesman. But not just perceptually: as if to fulfill the prophecy, Pelosi and Steny Hoyer were now actually turning to him to issue points of order on the House floor! They'd seen he was quicker on his feet than most of his other colleagues, not to mention an obliging slasher. And of course he loved the performance art of it, going back to his days in the mid-1980s as a young aide to then-Representative Chuck Schumer. Weiner had learned from the master how to vault one's self into prominence without asking anyone's permission. Freighted with pop culture references and leavened by the self-awareness that this was, on a certain level, pure shtick, the high-wire act of Anthony Weiner offered a postmodern road map of how 1 out of 435 could become first among equals.

Fellow Democrats weren't always amused. On January 24, 2011, he told a *Politico* reporter that Obama was not going to gain any points with the new Republican majority by being conciliatory: "I don't think he should have this tone that if he rolls on his back the new Congress is going to rub his belly." The following morning, Weiner got an angry email from White House political director Patrick Gaspard, saying words to the effect of, *Don't compare the president of the United States to a puppy.*

Okay, so he'd been a little inartful. Still, the White House senior staff's enthralled view of their boss's superiority ate at him. He thought Obama should have done a lengthy rollout of the health care bill, touring the country to explain its contents and objectives to American audiences. In September 2009, after spending a day with Obama in New York to promote a financial reform bill, Weiner hitched a ride back to Washington on the president's private plane—and, being Weiner, couldn't resist giving the leader of the free world some advice on how to achieve health reform.

"Mr. President, I think you're looking at this entirely the wrong way," he said. "You need to simplify it. Just say that what we're doing is gradually expanding Medicare."

Weiner was advocating a single-payer system. "We don't have the votes for that," said Obama.

"Mr. President," said Weiner, "you only have votes for something when you go out and fight for them."

At least Obama had a sense of humor. "Well," he'd said with a grin after their conversation was done, "enjoy your last ride on Air Force One."

Needless to say, the president had ignored his advice. He and his colleagues in the House weren't always on the same page, either. During Boehner's opening statement as new House Speaker, he announced that as one of the Republicans' first acts of frugality, they would be putting their money where their mouth was by reducing every congressman's office budget by 5 percent. Every Republican stood and clapped. So did Weiner—and no other Democrat. He'd turned around: *Uh, guys?*

It was fine to be progressive. But tone deaf? Some of the progressives in the caucus had actually been against the Democrats participating in the January 6 reading of the Constitution—as if a show of patriotism was beneath them. Not Weiner. He wore a flag lapel pin. A Democratic consultant had told Weiner one day, "You really shouldn't be photographed wearing a flag on your lapel. Our base doesn't like that."

Weiner was apoplectic. *So we're handing the flag over to the Republicans now? Are we really that dumb?*

And at the same time, it astonished him how, in the Democrats' abiding zeal to govern—to tinker, to legislate, to compromise—they would so willingly back away from a fight. Obama's debt commission put Social Security on the chopping block. The president himself caved in and preserved Bush's tax cuts for the wealthy during the lame-duck session. Frank Luntz went around bragging that he relabeled the Dodd-Frank financial reform bill "the bailout bill" when the legislation in fact *prevented* bailouts—and who, besides Weiner, refused to take this shit lying down? For that matter, when health care reform foe Dr. Betsy McCaughey insisted over and over that the Democrats' bill made "death panels" the law of the land, Weiner didn't just cry foul—he debated McCaughey for two hours, at one point calling her "a pyromaniac in a straw man factory." Someone had to counter the lies (and of course enjoy precious airtime doing so).

The Republicans, at least, seemed to appreciate his chutzpah. A number of freshmen had come up to him since the beginning of the session. Eyeing him at first like a zoo exhibit, then grinning and saying: *I've been wanting to meet you. I see you on TV. I use you as a dirty word sometimes.* They meant it as a compliment, he'd decided.

The Democratic caucus lacked Weiner's appetite for alley fighting. Seeing that the Republican freshmen were already making noise, Weiner had approached Pelosi and Hoyer and said to them, "Here's what we should do. We should get a hundred and fifty of us and agree not to raise the debt ceiling—that's the Republican majority's job. That gives us negotiating position."

This is too serious an issue to be demagoguing, they had told him. But in Weiner's view, the Republicans were only going to be having conflicts if Democrats *drove* the conflict.

During a caucus in late January, Pelosi and one of her top messaging deputies, Representative Debbie Wasserman Schultz, were exhorting the Democrats to hammer the Obamacare-killing Republicans for not focusing on jobs. Weiner stood up and told the others that there was a better counterthrust available.

"These eighty-odd Republican freshmen don't even know what's in the bill!" he exclaimed. He reminded them that one of the freshmen had claimed that senior members of Congress were exempted from the health care bill. "They've been spouting lies so long, they don't even know what's in the bill! So why don't we read it to them on the floor? Every time they lie, one of us goes down to the floor and says, 'If they'd read the bill they'd know that' and then you read the relevant part. Then TV commentators would start asking them, 'Well, did you read the bill?'"

The Democrats didn't think that was so hot an idea—perhaps because several of them hadn't read the bill, either.

Weiner had read the bill. They could say that he was disengaged, easily bored, not a team player, overly focused on his singular ambition to become mayor of New York in 2013—but they couldn't say he was lazy. Weiner worked fifteen-hour days. He expected his staffers to work approximately twice that. They nearly wept with gratitude whenever his wife, Huma Abedin, the longtime aide to Secretary of State Hillary Clinton, showed up at the office to take him away. Weiner behaved differently around his wife. She had a sedating, even humanizing influence. This was known as "the Huma Effect," and it was an affirming spectacle for those who otherwise had cause for doubting that Anthony Weiner cared about anyone other than himself. When the Clintons hosted an engagement party for the couple in July 2010, Weiner gave a toast to his bride-to-be and broke down in tears as he described his love for her.

The only other times he showed any degree of vulnerability were the inevitable moments when staffers would come into his office and say

that they had to quit because they couldn't take the hours and his yelling anymore. Then his tone would become beseeching.

"Could you not say anything to the press about this?" he would ask.

Weiner spent much of the morning of January 25, 2011, the day of
Obama's State of the Union address, on the second-floor balcony of the
Cannon building, making a succession of stops at the various TV crews
haloing the area. That evening, a phalanx of cameras cluttered Statuary
Hall in the Capitol—set up in preparation for the on-the-air opining
that dozens of congressmen would engage in immediately following
Obama's speech. Anthony Weiner did not want to wait that long. He
arrived in Statuary Hall early and offered himself up for pre-speech interviews. Sidling up to a couple of reporters, he confided, "I'm gonna
sit next to two Republicans tonight—one I like, and one I can say 'fuck
you' to. Just for ballast."

Then a host of security agents descended on the room, preventing
anyone from leaving. A procession of dignitaries streamed out of the
Senate side of the Capitol, heading toward the House chamber. Among
them were Supreme Court justices, cabinet members, senators, and the
president of the Senate, Joe Biden.

"Hey Mr. Vice President!" hollered Weiner—his voice cutting
through the din like a rotary blade. "Big fan! *Big fan!*"

CHAPTER EIGHT

Madam Minority Leader

Nancy Pelosi was not in the TV frame as Barack Obama delivered his State of the Union address: a call to "win the future" by spending more federal dollars on education, research, and clean energy technology—the president's attempt to counter the new budget-cutting ethos, and one that the White House would soon abandon. Rather, Pelosi took her place once again among the rank and file—albeit at the front and on the aisle, a prime location befitting her status as minority leader. Obama did not mention her tonight as he had in the previous two addresses, and as he did the new Speaker. This was Boehner's chamber now. Pelosi was relegated to playing defense.

Everything that she had achieved during the past two years, at great electoral expense, Boehner's Republicans now endeavored to obliterate. The Affordable Health Care Act, Pelosi's single greatest legislative accomplishment, was their primary target, but hardly their only one. Scores of progressive federal programs would be targeted for severe cuts. The environmental, food, and drug safety regulations that had multiplied on her watch were destined for evisceration. The Republicans even intended to defund the ex-Speaker's pet project, Green the Capitol, with its energy-efficient lightbulbs and recyclable utensils in the House cafeterias. It was as if they sought to annul the very fact of Nancy Pelosi's historic Speakership. A lesser woman—or man—would have lost all resolve.

Not Pelosi. She spent her mornings and her evenings tirelessly raising funds so that her party could take back the House and return her to the Speaker's chair in 2012. During the day, she was a ubiquitous presence on the House floor, a self-styled messaging coach to the minority party. Sitting next to each Democrat before they spoke, leaning into their faces, waving her hands and exhorting them to focus their message, she cut a figure of manic determination: *Jobs, jobs, jobs. The American people want to know what they're going to do to create jobs—and all* they're *talking about is taking health insurance away from pregnant mothers and throwing children out of Head Start. JOBS!*

On January 5, the opening day of the 112th Congress, Nancy Pelosi sat and watched as all 242 Republicans voted for Boehner as the House's new Speaker. She maintained a lacquered smile as nineteen Democrats voted for someone other than Pelosi as minority leader. One of the Blue Dogs' leaders, former Washington Redskins quarterback Heath Shuler of North Carolina, had received eleven of the votes.

Shuler had called her two days after the midterm elections. They spoke for forty-five minutes. "I just want you to understand that every single Blue Dog who lost, one hundred percent of the attack ads that were run associated you with them. You have a very low approval rating in our districts.

"Now, I can relate to this," he went on. "As a football player, I was successful in high school and in college. When I went to the NFL, things didn't go the way I wanted them to. They replaced me as starting quarterback. And I had two options. I could say, 'I'm not the problem—it's everyone else.' Or I could support the other guy taking my place. I decided to be a team player. And I'm asking you to be a team player."

"I totally understand," she had replied when Shuler was done. "But you need to understand, Heath, that there are a lot of other members who are calling me and asking me to maintain the leadership role."

What she told her other colleagues was, "I'm the person to lead." Pelosi had returned them to power in November 2006. She would do the same again. The Democrats had lost power because of the economy. Who else was going to hold the base together and raise the sums of money needed to return them to the majority, if not Nancy Pelosi?

She knew, of course, that moderate Democrats had been beaten senseless by a cudgel that had Pelosi's face on it. In the past, Republicans had sought to wrap liberal Democrats like Speaker Tip O'Neill and Senator Ted Kennedy around the necks of their colleagues. Democrats had done the same with Tom DeLay and Newt Gingrich—and Pelosi herself had been a part of such efforts. Never before, however,

had a party spent $65 million in an attempt to emblazon a gross cari-
cature of a House member into the minds of the American electorate. *Sixty-five million dollars.* And zero dollars spent by the Democrats
defending their leader. Instead, the most vulnerable House members
did all they could to distance themselves from her. In some cases, they
openly criticized her.

"Do what you have to do," Pelosi would tell them. "Hit me if you
have to."

She was an exquisite target: a San Francisco liberal who lived in a
mansion and flew around on a taxpayer-funded private plane; a woman
of a certain age whose trim and strangely unmarred physical appearance
spurred conservative pundits to deride her as a Botox Frankenstein; and
a specialist of the inside game who did not fare as well under the light
of day. When the Speaker memorably said, two weeks before final passage of the health care bill, that "we have to pass so that you can, uh,
find out what is in it," the context of that remark—that voters had been
misled about the bill's contents but would eventually come to understand its true benefits—was forever erased from memory. "They understand what I was saying," she had insisted to her staffers, who knew
better—and so, surely, did she.

Her aides had devoted enormous effort throughout 2006 to promoting the incoming Speaker, Nancy Patricia D'Alesandro Pelosi, as
America's quintessence—a child of Baltimore, granddaughter of Italian
immigrants, daughter of Mayor and Congressman Thomas D'Alesandro
Jr., devoted Catholic and grandmother. That entire backstory was also
forgotten. It hadn't stuck, in part because the benign image failed to
capture not only her shortcomings, but also her greatest strengths. She
could be charming, witty, reasonable, and deferential when the situation
called for it. But most of all, she was tenacious.

"I know how to win elections." That was her self-assessment, and
also her impetus to lead the House Democrats. For the 2000 elections,
her caucus had only needed to gain seven seats to retake the House
majority. Pelosi herself promised that she would deliver four of those
from races in her home state of California. She did—and it still wasn't
enough. The Democrats managed a net loss of one House seat in 2000
and remained in the minority. How could Nancy Pelosi keep going
back to her donors and asking for more resources without anything

positive to bring back to them? *Someone needs to teach these people—these men—how to win!*

In truth, fully two years before the 2000 elections, Pelosi had set her sights on the party leadership by deciding to run for minority whip, the second-highest post, as soon as David Bonior made good on his vow to vacate it. The problem was that someone else was already in line for the job: Steny Hoyer, with whom she had worked back in the mid-1960s, in the office of Maryland Senator Daniel Brewster. They were friends. But this wasn't personal. It was about winning. She informed Hoyer that she intended to run against him. He was, to put it mildly, taken aback.

Pelosi aided her cause by distributing $964,000 in campaign donations to members who would be voting in the whip race. Hoyer didn't have the funds to match Pelosi's effort. She beat him by twenty-three votes on October 10, 2001, thereby becoming the first woman whip in the history of Congress.

Two years later, when Dick Gephardt resigned from the House to run for president, Nancy Pelosi became the House's first-ever female minority leader. In January 2007, she became America's first U.S. representative ever to be addressed as "Madam Speaker."

On January 20, 2009, George W. Bush left the White House. Pelosi commented that his departure "felt like a ten-pound anvil had been lifted off my head." Now she had a Democratic president and a Democratic majority in the Senate alongside her.

But she and her Democrats were living on borrowed time. At the House Democratic retreat just days after Obama's inauguration, party pollster Stan Greenberg—who was married to one of Pelosi's closest friends in the House, Connecticut liberal Rosa DeLauro—gave a sobering presentation to the victors. The Democrats had benefited from consecutive "wave elections" in 2006 and 2008, Greenberg reminded them. Their power now extended into traditionally Republican districts. And yet the number of voters who identified as Democrats had barely grown at all during the same time frame. History and the odds were sure to catch up to them in 2010.

"Look at the person to your left, and then to your right," Greenberg intoned. "One of them is likely to be gone after 2010."

To many of the members, Greenberg's numbers amounted to a

strong argument for going slow and sticking with the mainstream. But this was not the Speaker's way. She was just getting started.

No one in the House knew how to get to 218 votes better than Nancy Pelosi. As the House Democrats' leader and as their preeminent fund-raiser, she doled out both money and committee assignments, and she was not the least bit shy about reminding recipients of her largesse whenever she needed a vote. But she also possessed an acute understanding of the Noah's Ark that was the House Democratic caucus.

The progressives uniformly disliked the fiscally conservative Blue Dog coalition. "I'm tired of bending over for you Blue Dogs!" John Tierney of Massachusetts had snapped at Oklahoman Dan Boren during one caucus. Another liberal, Pete Stark of California, had referred to them as "brain dead," while Henry Waxman mused to a reporter that the loss of a few Blue Dogs might purify the caucus. (At Pelosi's behest, he placed a call to an enraged Allen Boyd and assured the Florida Blue Dog that his words had been taken out of context.)

Then there was Sanford Bishop of Georgia, a Blue Dog but also a member of the Congressional Black Caucus, which had brawled with the Blue Dogs over welfare reform in the mid-1990s. The CBC was thoroughly progressive, but with particular causes—such as the *Pigford* discrimination lawsuit, brought by black farmers—in which the rest of the Democratic caucus had little investment. Their insistence on standing by William Jefferson of Louisiana (after federal authorities found $90,000 in his freezer) and Charles Rangel (after the Ways and Means chairman failed to declare to the IRS some property that he owned in the Dominican Republican) gave the House Democrats, and their leader, considerable heartburn.

In short, the House Democrats were cursed by diversity. The devoutly Catholic Speaker at times sought to unify them by reminding them of Jesus Christ's admonition to his disciples during the Last Supper: "Love one another as I have loved you."

If necessary, Nancy Pelosi would wash her disciples' feet—at least until she got to 218.

✦ ✦ ✦

Never was her relentlessness more apparent than on the American Clean Energy and Security Act of 2009. Pelosi viewed energy as "my signature issue." Her highest-end donors were ardent environmentalists; she had promised them that the Democrats would address climate change, and she aimed to deliver. Shortly after assuming the Speakership in January 2007, Pelosi paid a visit to the Bush White House to discuss a bill that would promote fuel and home energy efficiency. Bush's aides found it telling that the Speaker had not brought Energy and Commerce chairman John Dingell with her. Eyebrows were also raised when Pelosi formed a Select Committee on Global Warming and installed liberal Massachusetts congressman Ed Markey as its chairman. Dingell and his nemesis on Energy and Commerce, Henry Waxman, didn't agree on much, but they both saw the new committee as a threat to theirs and demanded that Pelosi strip it of legislative authority.

On the latter she acquiesced. But her thumbs-on management of energy legislation irked Dingell, who one day snapped to Pelosi, "Nancy, maybe you shouldn't be Speaker. Maybe you should be chairman of Energy and Commerce instead."

Pelosi did the next best thing: she allowed her friend Waxman to challenge Big John's chairmanship. When Waxman won, she and her "signature" energy bill were off to the races.

Without consulting with anyone else on her leadership team, Speaker Pelosi announced in February that the House would proceed with the bill, which would include a provision that capped greenhouse gas emissions. Blue Dog Democrats protested that their constituents were concerned about the economy, not climate change. One of the most prominent Blue Dogs, Tennessee's John Tanner, collared Majority Leader Hoyer on the House floor and, with a sweeping wave of his arm to encompass some of the more electorally vulnerable newcomers, said, "Steny! You are *killing* these freshmen! They're not gonna come back after this!"

Hoyer agreed with Tanner's sentiment but knew Pelosi's determination from painful experience. For her part, the Speaker responded that at bottom, the bill was about "four things: jobs, jobs, jobs, and jobs."

Obama's then–chief of staff, Rahm Emanuel, was among the unconvinced. He begged Pelosi not to introduce energy legislation before health care, which would by itself be a heavy political lift.

Pelosi replied, "I've got the votes."

Meaning: she would *find* the votes, eventually. After the Energy and

Commerce Committee produced a "discussion draft" of the energy legislation in late March, Democratic chief deputy whip Diana DeGette's office tallied the bill's supporters as a meager eighty Democrats and no Republicans. Pelosi continued to work her caucus, cutting deals that would thread the needle between the opposing concerns of the Sierra Club and more conservative Democrats. The number moved into triple digits. Pelosi kept pressing her colleagues. When the whip count exceeded two hundred, Pelosi scheduled a vote on the House floor for June 26, 2009.

The day before the vote, Obama threw a Hawaii-themed congressional picnic on the White House lawn. One by one, undecided Democrats with their leis and their cocktails were escorted to the Oval Office by White House legislative liaisons to be subjected to the president's persuasions. But Obama was unable to turn anyone. A whip staffer approached DeGette and told her that Pelosi was going to make a final decision at ten that evening on whether to bring the energy bill to the floor.

"By my count we've got 208, maybe 209," sighed the chief deputy whip. "It's her decision, but we don't have the votes."

What the Speaker had not told DeGette, or apparently anyone else, was that Pelosi on her own had quietly met with a group of moderate Republicans and had procured eight of their votes. The bill went to the House floor on June 26, passing by a vote of 219 to 212.

It was a remarkable victory—but for whom? When the final tally was announced by the House clerk, several Republicans began chanting, "BTU! BTU! BTU!"—referring to the controversial 1993 bill that taxed the heat content of fuels, or BTUs, and which House Democrats had passed at the behest of President Bill Clinton. That bill had subsequently died in the Senate, serving only as a political millstone for the Democrats during the 1994 midterms. Numerous colleagues had pled with Pelosi not to "BTU" them with an easily demagogued cap-and-trade bill that stood little chance of passage in the upper body.

Pelosi had not budged. Promoting clean energy and reducing greenhouse gases were fundamental progressive values, she would remind them. This is why they were here, to do big and difficult things. If not now, then when? Perhaps their actions would spur the Senate to action—but regardless, the House couldn't wait around to see what their colleagues on the other side of the building would do. They had to move the agenda.

And so they did, after which Nancy Pelosi's "signature issue" was dead on arrival in the Senate. Meanwhile, 467,000 Americans lost their jobs during the month of June 2009. The unemployment figure now stood at 9.5 percent.

And between the $780 billion stimulus and the "cap-and-tax bill," the suddenly energized Republicans had arrived at a winning narrative: *The Democrats don't care about jobs. They just want to shove a liberal, over-regulatory, Big Government agenda down your throats.*

Next up: the health care bill. Or, as Republican pollster Frank Luntz helpfully renamed it after first hearing the term from a middle-aged St. Louis woman in one of his focus groups: "the government takeover of our health care system."

On the evening of January 19, 2010, the House Democrats caucused at the Capitol Visitor Center. The atmosphere bordered on riotous. It had just been announced that in Massachusetts, Republican Scott Brown had won the Senate seat previously held by the late Ted Kennedy—effectively ensuring that the Senate Democrats would no longer have the sixty votes needed to overcome a Republican filibuster. This meant, among other things, that the health care bill that the House Democrats had sent over to the Senate stood no chance of passage in the upper body. Many in the room believed that the Affordable Health Care Act, with its divisive provision of a "public option," or government-run health insurance program that would compete with private insurance companies, was dead—or that it should be dead.

Speaker Pelosi quieted the members. "We came here to pass a health care law that will really change this country," she said. "And we're not blinking." Pelosi promised them that she would fight to keep the public option in the health care bill. Then she left the caucus to meet with Senate Majority Leader Harry Reid.

Even some of the progressives in the caucus were astonished by her words. One of them was Massachusetts Congressman Mike Capuano, who represented Cambridge, but also the working-class city of Chelsea, with a poverty rate exceeding 20 percent. Capuano kept on his office wall a large framed photograph of a meaty-handed Italian-American from his district. He had recently come off the campaign trail in a failed bid to be the Democratic candidate for the Senate seat that Scott Brown had just won. "They're telling us, 'Slow down,'" Capuano warned his colleagues that evening. "They don't trust Washington. They don't understand what we're doing here. And this is a message they've sent us, and we'd better pay attention to it."

Gene Taylor, a Blue Dog from Mississippi, was even more emotional. He stood before the microphone and told the House Democrats about how, in the aftermath of Hurricane Katrina, Taylor and his son were touring the devastation by boat when they happened upon a man who refused to believe that his home had been destroyed. "They were telling him, 'Your house is gone,'" said Taylor. "And he kept saying, 'No, no, it's still there, you just can't see it from the water.' He was in denial!

"And if the Speaker were still here," Taylor declared sharply, "I would tell her: 'Madam Speaker, face the facts! We haven't listened to the people—and now our House is gone!'"

The moment represented an astonishing turnaround from the year before, when the House Republicans seemed paralyzed by the new president's ability to find support from among private insurers, the American Medical Association, and doctors for a comprehensive solution to the nation's health care problems. But by August 2009, the health care debate had ceased to be an earnest disagreement over policy. It was now an ugly snarl of fear, loathing, and cynicism blaring through a Tea Party megaphone.

Pelosi's task was a hopeless one. The progressives wanted universal coverage. The Blue Dogs wanted lower health care costs. Rural members wanted higher Medicare reimbursement rates for rural hospitals. Bart Stupak of Michigan wanted a stipulation that none of the federal funds would be used to pay for abortion. President Obama wanted at least one Republican vote from the Senate.

And these were only the major demands. Pelosi had countless others to contend with. Her most poignant dissenter was John Tanner. The Blue Dogs' cofounder had served with Pelosi for over two decades and was on good terms with her. During the health care debate, when Tanner and others were hosting town halls that degenerated into screaming matches, he dropped by the Speaker's office to share with her a theory he had been nurturing.

"There's a lot of anger, but people don't know what they're angry about," he told her. "You know, from the end of the Vietnam War all the way up to 9/11, for the most part everyone was fat, dumb, and happy. Then 9/11 happened and shattered all that. People became scared and anxious and out of control. They'd go to Wal-Mart and realize that everything they've been buying says 'Made in China.' They see the complete ineptitude of the federal government during Hurricane Katrina. They see some guy [investment advisor Bernie Madoff] within the shadow of the SEC run a $50 billion scam—and who the hell is watching out for *their* $10,000 IRA? And then the banks melt down, the auto industry is taken over, and we pass this huge stimulus. All of this builds up and they're saying, 'What the hell can *I* possibly do about a $14 trillion national debt?'

"But then it gets to health care," Tanner said. "And they're saying: 'That's me. That's *mine.*' It's the first big issue that's personalized. And that's why we're getting all this pent-up frustration and anger. Because when you explain the bill to 'em, they say, 'Well, that doesn't sound too bad.' But it doesn't matter. All their anger is focused on this, because it's personal.

"Madam Speaker, what you need to do is break the bill down. Have a bill that covers preexisting conditions. Pass that—or make the Republicans vote against it—and then move onto another part. But you do this omnibus approach, they won't know what the hell's in it. And they'll keep yelling at it."

Pelosi had been listening politely, until now. Crisply she informed John Tanner that the health care bill would stay big—and that it would pass.

The Speaker achieved an initial victory on November 7, 2009, when the bill passed the House by a margin of five votes. The Senate then passed its own health care bill six weeks later. But before the two versions could be merged, Scott Brown took the sixtieth Senate seat away from the Democrats.

Gene Taylor was both right and wrong. For Nancy Pelosi's House was not gone just yet. The Speaker and Harry Reid agreed to reintroduce the bill under a reconciliation rule that would permit passage under a simple majority. Even so, the Senate, in its post–Scott Brown victory state of jitters, could no longer muster the vote for the public option.

Nancy Pelosi then did what only Nancy Pelosi could do. In a Nixon-goes-to-China moment, she convinced the Democratic Party's progressive backers that even without their prized provision, a bill without the public option amounted to a legislative milestone and deserved their support. And so they gave it.

Pelosi had run the table. Every major legislative initiative she or the president had sought had passed the House: fair pay in the federal workplace, expanding health coverage for children, the stimulus, energy, hate crimes, federalizing student loans, financial regulatory reform, health care.

After all that, her House was gone.

The day after the midterm elections, when Pelosi had not yet announced her future intentions, Majority Leader Steny Hoyer had said to her, "Nancy, you're the leader. What are you going to do?"

She did not say just then. But she already knew.

Exactly two weeks after that, the Democrats caucused and returned Nancy Pelosi to power by a vote of 150–43, defeating Heath Shuler. One of Shuler's votes had come from Dennis Cardoza, the Blue Dog intermediary on Pelosi's leadership team. Pelosi promptly removed Cardoza from the job—installing in his place Henry Cuellar, who had given one of her nomination speeches that day.

Winning with a team of rivals might have been Abraham Lincoln's way. Nancy Pelosi's way worked for her.

CHAPTER NINE

Continuing Resolution

In March 1902, early into Teddy Roosevelt's dynamic presidency, a reporter found something newsworthy about the House's freshman class—who, as with all innocents, were expected to spend their first several years in Washington being seen and not heard. "The 48 new Republican members of the House," this reporter wrote, "having discovered what an inconsiderable figure they cut in the general scheme of national legislation, had a dinner the other evening and amid much merriment organized the Tantalus Club." The Republican freshman caucus was named after the Greek god who was condemned by Zeus to spend eternity grasping for fruit and water just beyond his reach.

Their exasperation over not being given adequate floor time and committee assignments was apparently sincere. But their outlook was one of jolly fatalism. That first night, undoubtedly with substantial lubrication, the freshmen dashed out several House resolutions they pronounced worthy of consideration. One was to make the state of Iowa an independent republic. Another was to establish a federal bureau for cutting the hair of Native Americans.

The Tantalus Club met every month or so for dinner at various hotel banquet rooms. Sometimes they would roast ambassadors and other distinguished guests. Often they performed skits, as when a Colorado congressman named Herschel Hogg pretended to be instructing President Roosevelt on the telephone as to whom to appoint to his cabinet. It was a given that the sessions would end with drunken choruses of "For He's a Jolly Good Fellow." Soon the Tantalus Club affairs became as popular as the journalist-sponsored banquets known as the Gridiron Club. The freshmen had achieved relevance, in a sense. They were Washington's new entertainers.

During that first year of the fraternity's existence, House Speaker David Henderson, his designated replacement Joseph "Uncle Joe" Cannon, and several other powerful House members were invited to a Tantalus Club dinner. The dinner menu featured a cartoon of Uncle Joe waiting at the doorstep for the coveted Tantalus endorsement. One of the freshmen stood up and mock-endorsed Maine Congressman Charles Littlefield as "the only man who had located the solar plexus of the octopus, the man who could command the undivided support of 25% of the Maine delegation . . . [and] the man who never sullied his name by attaching it to a majority report." The freshmen loudly feigned disapproval over the Speaker-designate, then just as loudly gave Cannon their imprimatur once he assured them that they would all be awarded committee chairmanships. Eventually they broke into the club's adopted anthem, "Johnny Smoker," and everyone toasted the exquisite powerlessness of the 57th Congress's freshman class.

"The congressional 'colts,'" a reporter wrote, "are wise for not taking their helplessness too seriously. It is the experience of all new congressmen, and they must wait patiently for recognition until they get seasoned."

Jeff Duncan walked onto the House floor shortly after noon on February 10, 2011. The chamber was nearly empty. He strode carefully to the well, and then to the left of the House clerk's desk. He held in his hands a five-page House Resolution, which read at the top: "Amending the Rules of the House of Representatives to establish the Committee on the Elimination of Nonessential Federal Programs." Then Duncan deposited it in the wooden box known as the hopper. He looked around. No one was paying attention. He might as well have been tossing a half-eaten sandwich into a wastebasket.

Still, it was a rite of passage to savor. Jeff Duncan had dropped his first bill. He walked languidly across the well, down the aisle, and then out of the chamber.

The bill's intent was to replicate the so-called Byrd Committee, established in 1941 by Virginia Senator Harry Byrd to identify and slash unnecessary federal expenditures. Everything the committee targeted for cutting would be subject to an up-or-down vote in Congress. While campaigning in the summer of 2010, Duncan had read an op-ed calling for the return of the Byrd Committee by Grover Norquist of Americans for Tax Reform. Norquist had later told the *Daily Caller* that this was a golden opportunity for a House freshman to cosponsor: "I want the person who says, 'This is me, this is mine, when this passes, I'm a star.'"

Intending to be that very person, Duncan moved quickly. He procured the blessings of the staffers of the Republican Study Committee, the House GOP's in-house conservative coalition. The RSC circulated a letter to Republican members soliciting cosponsors of Duncan's initiative. With a helpful nudge, the letter closed by observing, "This common-sense bill is an excellent opportunity for freshmen members to build up credibility on fiscal issues." Duncan and Norquist each sent out letters as well. By the time Duncan had dropped the bill, he had acquired sixteen cosponsors, half of them freshmen.

What he hadn't solicited were the blessings of Boehner and Cantor—and in fact when the majority leader was asked by a reporter about Duncan's spending-slashing committee bill, he seemed momentarily taken aback before replying, "What I can tell you is that committees and their subcommittees are doing exactly that, and that is the oversight function, engaged on a daily basis." Duncan also hadn't checked with the Appropriations Committee, which of course already had the job of determining how federal money was spent. He frankly thought the committee was doing a lousy job of it. Washington's addiction to spending was a big part of why he ran in the first place. America was $14 trillion in debt. This was no way to run a business.

Duncan had other bills in the works—lots of them. A balanced budget amendment to the Constitution. A bill limiting House members to three terms and senators to two terms. And in the wake of the Gabby Giffords shooting, Duncan had decided to work with the NRA on a law that would allow Washington, D.C., residents—including, of course, House members—to carry a firearm. Duncan already had a concealed-weapons permit for South Carolina. But when he left the office at night and walked the half mile to the apartment he shared with his fellow South Carolinian Tim Scott, he would walk under an overpass where the long shadows were frankly unnerving. He didn't want to be the next congressman to be waylaid by a madman.

Jeff Duncan was striving to make his mark. He hadn't gotten assigned to the Energy and Commerce Committee as he had requested. Instead, Duncan landed on three committees: Natural Resources, Homeland Security, and Foreign Affairs. He'd signed on to no less than a dozen caucuses—including the RSC, the Balanced Budget Amendment Caucus, the Tea Party Caucus, the Pro-Life Caucus, the Liberty Caucus, and the Sportsmen's Caucus. Majority Whip Kevin McCarthy had asked Duncan to join his freshman whip team. And one afternoon in mid-January, Iowa Congressman Steve King invited him to accompany King and a few other Republicans out on the sullen little patch of grass on the Capitol's east lawn known as the Triangle, and stage a press conference on repealing Obamacare.

About fifty reporters and a dozen or so tourists formed a ring around the rickety metal podium affixed permanently to the ground. Michele Bachmann, the Minnesota congresswoman and soon-to-be presidential candidate, materialized with her press aide and several reporters.

Duncan was a fan of the congresswoman. He introduced himself. "Ohhh, good to meetcha, Jeff," said Bachmann, who was at least a foot shorter than the South Carolinian even in her heels.

She immediately turned and hugged a lady, saying, "Awww, don't you look pretty in your red hair!"

Louie Gohmert of Texas then arrived. Duncan had met him back in November while touring offices—they'd talked about Gohmert's barbecue grills. The Texan seemed to have forgotten who Duncan was. He was carrying with him a phone-directory-sized copy of the health care bill with dozens of yellow Post-it markers dangling from its pages.

They stood in a somber semicircle before the cameras with Duncan and another freshman, Steve Pearce of New Mexico, positioned behind the marquee players. King and Bachmann spoke first. Duncan had brought with him his well-worn copy of the Constitution. After King introduced him, he said, "Folks, as a freshman congressman, it's humbling for me to stand out here in front of the people's House and defend what I carry with me every day, and that's the United States Constitution." He held out his copy.

Of the health care bill, Duncan said in a rising voice, "Millions of Americans screamed out loudly that they didn't want this. And so one of the first significant votes that I will cast as a congressman will be to repeal Obamacare. As a citizen, Jeff Duncan, I didn't want the government making decisions for me and my family. I felt that I could make those decisions better myself."

Duncan said that he now looked forward to working with these distinguished colleagues to "repeal this unconstitutional piece of legislation—and replacing it with something that's better. We're gonna work on that together."

Having suddenly run out of things to say, Duncan concluded with, "So I'll, uh, turn it back over to Steve," and stepped back as Louie Gohmert expertly lunged forward to the bank of microphones and proceeded to interpret, with outsized stupefaction, the contents of the legislative monstrosity he held with both hands: "It takes control of restaurants, vending machines . . . If you're a friend of the administration, you'll get a waiver and it'll cut your costs dramatically. If you're not a friend of Obama, you'll go out of business . . ."

Jeff Duncan was about to become very relevant—though not by himself, and not as a protégé of the TV-savvy Republican members.

At the end of January, Duncan and several other members of the Republican Study Committee flew to California for what one of the RSC officials would later term a three-day "conservative love-fest." Sponsored by the Heritage Foundation and held at the Reagan Library, the retreat had the unspoken purpose of enabling the RSC's new chairman, Congressman Jim Jordan, to identify those freshmen who were particularly wedded to conservative aims.

In previous years, the RSC had been a small if loud sect of the House's most conservative members. More than a policy shop, it served as the Republicans' ideological conscience—or nuisance—much as the Congressional Black Caucus had historically been for the Democrats since its founding in 1971, two years before the RSC began.

But the 2010 elections had changed all that. Fully 78 of the 87 freshmen joined the Republican Study Committee, overnight swelling its ranks to about 177 of the overall conference's 242 members—more than four times that of the moderate Tuesday Group Republicans. Meanwhile, its new leader, Jim Jordan (a two-term backbencher and former Ohio State wrestling coach), was about to become a major player on Capitol Hill.

Jordan immediately took a liking to several of them: Steve Southerland, a former funeral home owner from Florida; Andy Harris, previously a Maryland state senator and before that an anesthesiologist; Mike Kelly, a Pennsylvania auto dealer in his prior life; Steve Pearce of New Mexico, who had actually served three terms in Congress before being defeated in 2008 and returning two years later; Tom Graves, an experienced Georgia legislator who had won in a special election, five months before the rest of them; Raul Labrador, an Idaho immigration lawyer who happened to be both Puerto Rican and Mormon; and Jeff Duncan.

All of them—and indeed most of the Republican freshmen—had run on the Pledge to America, which promised to roll back non-security-related discretionary spending to 2008 levels, or before Obama took office. The savings, based on Obama's requested fiscal year 2011 budget, was estimated by House Budget Committee staffers to be $100 billion. Thus the Pledge became a vow to whack $100 billion.

The problem was that the Democrats had never passed Obama's budget—and further, that by January, four months of fiscal 2011 had already gone by. Appropriations staffers informed Boehner's and Cantor's surrogates that reducing federal discretionary spending over an eight-month period by $100 billion couldn't be done—not without cutting into the bone. They suggested a significant but still much smaller spending cut package. It would be $32 billion in actual reductions, or $61 billion from what Obama had requested—the latter of which, when annualized, amounted to $100 billion.

That would be quite a mouthful to explain to the folks back home. Jim Jordan and his fellow RSC retreat buddies were not happy with the new proposal. Already the Democratic Congressional Campaign Committee was ridiculing the Republicans for backpedaling on their much-publicized campaign document. Conservative groups like Heritage and FreedomWorks were outraged. Jordan's group concurred unanimously that they should push leadership to stick with the original $100 billion. The RSC leader asked the seven of them if they would call all of the other freshmen over the weekend and find out where they stood. They did. Everyone they spoke with wanted to stick with the unqualified $100 billion figure.

And so they went to conference.

• • •

The conference room known as HC-5 lies at the end of a serpentine corridor in the basement of the Capitol. Until 2011, both Republicans and Democrats held their member meetings there. (The minority party later claimed meeting space in the Capitol Visitor Center and named it in honor of Gabe Zimmerman, the aide to Gabrielle Giffords who was killed in the Tucson shooting.) The room is drab and painfully overlit, its only hint of significance being the Capitol police who stand outside guarding its closed doors while a few reporters slouch in the hallways, waiting to pounce on any member who leaves early. Unlike their genteel counterparts in the Senate, who work out their intraparty differences over crab cakes and salad in the Capitol's chandeliered Lyndon Baines Johnson Room, the House conferees in HC-5 line up before one of two microphone stands, much as their constituents do at town halls, and in one minute or less say to the leadership team whatever is on their minds. During 2009 and 2010, as the Democrats struggled to pass a health care bill, their caucuses in HC-5 at times resembled a reality show hair-tugging match between progressives and Blue Dogs. Meanwhile, the Republican minority's conferences were largely rancor-free—a short, straight line to a collective "No." The roles would reverse in 2011.

As a rule, Republican conferences, like Democratic caucuses, were numbingly predictable and thus frequently avoided by the more senior members. Those who lined up to speak tended to be "frequent fliers" like Steve King, Louie Gohmert, and Michele Bachmann who also gravitated to the House floor and the cable TV cameras. Among the GOP leadership, Pete Sessions—the National Republican Congressional Committee chairman and frustrated football coach—could be counted on to spew out a few motivational homilies (or "Pete-speak"), like "Winners do things losers don't do" and "Let's make the big deal *the big deal!*"

The freshmen had not yet been assertive in conference. Boehner knew how to count: they constituted more than one-third of the Republican membership. He was well aware that the force that had blown them into Washington still gusted in the near distance. He had originally awarded the new arrivals one seat at the leadership table and two on the Steering Committee (which doles out assignments to other committees). When the freshmen asked for an additional seat at each post, Boehner relented the same day. Majority Whip Kevin McCarthy also advised Boehner to hold weekly meetings with the freshmen in the Speaker's office. Boehner agreed to that as well. After all that, he resumed his position as laissez-faire CEO of the lower body, while the class of 2010 spent its initial month on Capitol Hill preoccupied with parliamentary procedures, committee briefing books, staff training, and a locust storm of lobbyists.

By the time Boehner and the rest of his leadership team had arrived in HC-5 on the morning of Thursday, February 10, 2011, they had already been hearing plenty from Jim Jordan of the RSC and from conservative watchdog groups. The issue at hand was the Continuing Resolution, or CR, that Congress was now obliged to pass to keep the government funded through fiscal 2011, since last year's politically skittish Democratic majority had chosen not to bring a budget to the floor. The GOP majority had until March 4 to pass a CR before the government ran out of money. The CR that the study committee had in mind entailed the aforementioned $100 billion in nondefense cuts. Now leadership was going to hear what the caucus thought about the $32 billion alternative.

Raul Labrador rushed to the open microphone. Labrador had won in November with significant help from local Tea Party groups and none whatsoever from Washington Republicans. "This new number is not going to go over well with the people who elected me," Labrador told the Republican leaders. "To me, $100 billion isn't the ceiling. It's the *floor*. And $33 billion . . ." He shook his head. "That's under the floor."

The funeral home operator Steve Southerland was the last of the members to speak. "I want you to know," the big, bald man said slowly, "there is a limit to how far I will follow. I may lose in 2012—but I will not lose *me*."

The freshman stared directly at the House Speaker and said, "I will hold you accountable to the promises that you made to the American people."

Within twenty-four hours, the Appropriations Committee had drummed up a CR containing $100 billion in cuts. The freshmen had won.

• • •

Later that week, the freshmen met to discuss what and how to cut. Everything, they agreed, should be on the table. No sacred cows.

Then Jeff Duncan spoke up. "Look," he said, "as we're going through these possibilities, I think it's imperative that the United States stands with Israel, and we exclude them from any cuts."

All but one freshman concurred. They moved on.

A number of freshmen who had formerly been state legislators argued that the best way to go about budget-cutting was an across-the-board rather than targeted approach. Better to share the pain, not pick winners and losers—it was a lot easier to explain back home than to justify each and every reduction.

It was then that Lieutenant Colonel Allen West spoke up for the first time. "That's the coward's way out," he snapped. "The people sent us here to make tough decisions."

That was the last word on the matter. A number of people in the room left the meeting believing that West—the Tea Party favorite son who had joined the CBC and always walked around with his papers in a helmet bag and military pendants on his jacket lapel—should perhaps be taken seriously.

The second week of February was shaping up to be a terrible one for Majority Whip Kevin McCarthy. It had begun with a vote to extend the Patriot Act, which had first been enacted as a domestic counter-terrorism tool in the wake of 9/11 but had engendered some criticism for sanctioning potentially invasive surveillance techniques. Republican members were notified over the weekend that the bill would be brought to the floor right when they got back on Tuesday the eighth. McCarthy's whip office had disseminated almost no information on what extending the Patriot Act would mean. He had also assumed that the senior members who had voted for the original bill back in October 2001 would do so again a decade later. He was wrong. The bill was defeated on the floor.

The next day, another bill (though a minor one) failed to pass, and a trade bill was withdrawn when some conservatives threatened to vote against it. Now it was Thursday the tenth, and Boehner was hearing directly from the freshmen what McCarthy had already been telling the

Speaker: they didn't have the votes in their own conference to pass the CR with $32 billion in spending cuts.

McCarthy knew the freshmen better than any other Republican on the Hill did. Some of them he had personally recruited, like a folksy but canny farmer and gospel singer named Stephen Fincher from Frog Jump, Tennessee. Others he coached actively throughout the election cycle. One such protégé was Sean Duffy, the Wisconsin county prosecutor and former star in MTV's proto-reality show, *The Real World*. Another was Kristi Noem, the South Dakota state legislator and rancher, who was running on an anti-Washington theme while receiving ongoing messaging advice from McCarthy back in the Beltway. Still another was Rick Berg, a respected North Dakota state representative who had been planning to retire from politics, until McCarthy begged him to run for Congress, saying, "I'll come to Fargo in January—that's how passionate I am about you."

They were giant-killers in the making. Noem would be going up against Stephanie Herseth Sandlin, one of the Democratic Party's rising stars and the head of the Blue Dogs. Berg's Democratic opponent, Earl Pomeroy, had held North Dakota's at-large seat for nine terms. Fincher's adversary, John Tanner, was the eleven-term cofounder of the Blue Dogs. Duffy's particularly quixotic goal was to beat David Obey, the chairman of the House Appropriations Committee, and representative of Wisconsin's 7th District since 1969.

With McCarthy's active support, the energetic campaigns waged by Duffy and Fincher helped spur the retirements of Obey and Tanner, respectively. All four Republican neophytes won—as did Scott DesJarlais, a Tennessee physician who was bald and wore a goatee, until McCarthy advised the candidate to shave it.

"Do you think that's important?" DesJarlais asked doubtfully.

"Michael Phelps shaves his entire body to get one-tenth of one second faster," McCarthy replied, referring to the Olympic swimming champion. "I think that goatee is costing you five percent of the vote. Do *you* think it's worth it?"

The next time McCarthy saw Scott DesJarlais, he had shaved off his goatee, and McCarthy decided that he was serious.

Now that the eighty-seven freshmen had arrived in Washington, McCarthy offered himself up as their resident big brother. He regularly took them out for dinner on his political action committee's dime. He played a weekly game of basketball with Jeff Duncan, Steve Fincher, and a few other freshmen. Nineteen of them slept in their offices, both as a symbolic commitment not to become Beltway fixtures and as a means of saving money. McCarthy also slept on his office couch, and in the morning he would go cycling or work out in the House gym with Paul Ryan and a few of the newbies. He gave them tips on running their offices. He organized get-togethers between them and the older members. And his Capitol office suite, H-107, became the freshman class's unofficial flophouse, where they would go to filch a granola bar, have an evening glass of wine, or duck away momentarily from the demands of their own offices across the street.

The freshmen found it easy to connect with McCarthy. That he had spent the past year nurturing their political growth only partly explained the bond. The whip was informal (no one, including his junior staffers, called him anything other than Kevin), almost absurdly sunny, and far more proactively attentive than the ever-calculating Cantor or the amiable but oft-sequestered Boehner.

He was practically one of them. McCarthy had himself served only two terms thus far, and he liked to emphasize his entrepreneurial past— that of a Bakersfield fireman's son who at the age of twelve was making money sorting bottles at the neighborhood convenience store, using the proceeds to pay for a vacation to Lake Tahoe for his entire family. (He tended to omit from his narrative that he had been born with a speech defect—that for the first ten or so years of his life, he could not pronounce the first letter of the party he now helped lead. McCarthy's brother Mark had been born with glaucoma, necessitating two dozen eye surgeries before he was two years old. McCarthy's father had quit a higher-paying job to become a fireman so as to be eligible for public-employee health insurance to pay for his children's difficulties— something else McCarthy did not volunteer.)

Just after graduating from high school, young McCarthy had walked into a store, purchased a lottery ticket for the very first time, and won five thousand dollars. With the proceeds he opened a sandwich shop, Kevin O's, where his high school sweetheart and eventual wife, Judy, also worked. Tired of wading through onerous regulations on his small business, he sold out after about a year and pronounced himself a Republican. It was 1984, and another Californian, President Ronald Reagan, was incanting about morning in America. McCarthy got his undergraduate and MBA degrees at California State University Bakersfield, became the national chairman of Young Republicans, and went to work for his local congressman, the notoriously crusty Ways and Means chairman Bill Thomas. After a decade apprenticing under Thomas and serving two terms in the California State Assembly, when his boss decided to retire in 2006 Kevin McCarthy took the path that had been cleared for him.

McCarthy hit the ground in Washington at warp speed. His own race had not been strenuous, so he had spent the summer and fall of 2006 raising money for other incoming freshmen, who in turn showed their gratitude by voting McCarthy to be the designated freshman on the influential Steering Committee. Boehner had encouraged their vote. He had met McCarthy through Bill Thomas years earlier and knew a racehorse when he saw one. The freshman was put on the whip team. What contacts he'd brought with him he now supplemented by requesting lunches with influential Beltway Republicans like columnist Fred Barnes and former Senate Majority Leader Trent Lott. The latter emerged from their meeting and declared to a confidant, "Watch this guy. He's *the* star."

Boehner put McCarthy in charge of the Republican Party's platform for the 2008 GOP convention. The following year, he became Minority Whip Eric Cantor's chief deputy. The year after that, following his critical role as chief recruiter in the November 2010 election, McCarthy's colleagues unanimously elected him to be majority whip—which came with a large office suite, Capitol security, and the distinction of being the third-ranking House Republican. He had leapfrogged other leadership aspirants with far greater seniority, most notably National Republican Congressional Committee chairman Pete Sessions and Intelligence Committee chairman Mike Rogers of Michigan. More senior members did not altogether trust the unctuous, upwardly mobile whip. McCarthy worked hard to ingratiate himself with them. He played paddleball with old bulls like Alaska's fourteen-term congressman Don Young, and continued to raise money and give speeches in the districts of lifers like Hal Rogers, now the House Appropriations chairman.

"You can't have too many friends," was one of the peppy McCarthy's two favorite sayings. The other: "Continuing education!"

He was getting an education now, on the fly.

The term *whip* is British, referring to the foxhunting aide tasked with keeping the hounds in the pack. It implies coercion and in recent years has called to mind the chest-to-chest backroom persuasions of Republican whip Tom "the Hammer" DeLay. The former Sugar Land, Texas, pest exterminator thoroughly enjoyed his reputation as a bone-breaker, but in truth he relied more on deal-cutting. DeLay termed his whipping strategy "growing the vote": finding out what it would take to gain a member's aye, then adding that component—say, a special exemption or subsidy—to the overall package until he had his 218 votes. Relentlessly partisan though he was, DeLay was not above earmarking for a new hospital or a new research center in a Democrat's district in exchange for the latter's vote.

McCarthy wasn't going to be like DeLay. Not that he was a political puritan. Like any other highly successful politician, the whip had done his share of kissing up, had given his blessing to rank attack ads against Democrats, and had happily fudged facts for the sake of a winning narrative. But he distrusted the effectiveness of deal-cutting. What worked for the Hammer might not work for him. First, DeLay had spent fully a decade forging relationships as a congressman before he became whip in 1995. McCarthy was still new on the Hill, his alliances still frail. Second, the earmark ban had removed a crucial inducement from the whip's tool kit.

But the most important distinction between the two whips was this: Tom DeLay's seventy-three freshmen were thoroughly beholden to Newt Gingrich—their Speaker, but also their guru. Kevin McCarthy's eighty-seven freshmen had no particular allegiance to John Boehner, or even to the Republican Party. He had no leverage over them.

A few hours after the freshmen demanded that the CR include $100 billion in spending cuts, Kevin McCarthy was summoned to a meeting with the Cardinals.

The House Appropriations Committee is divided into twelve subcommittees that control funds for federal agencies and cabinet departments. Each subcommittee is its own fiefdom, with billions of dollars under its control. Together the twelve chairmen and the full Appropriations Committee's chairman, Hal Rogers, are known as the Cardinals. McCarthy came to their office in the Capitol that morning. They sat around him in a glowering semicircle.

This is the biggest rescission of a budget in the recent history of the House, the Cardinals told the whip. *The biggest since disarmament after World War II. Thirty-two billion dollars is a lot of money.*

"It won't pass," McCarthy replied.

How do you know it won't? Have you done a whip check?

A whip check was a basic count of where every member currently stood, before any actual persuading, or whipping, had taken place.

"No," said McCarthy.

The Cardinals were stunned. *How do you expect us to craft a bill if you don't know the level at which it'll be acceptable to the members?*

"They all campaigned on the Pledge," McCarthy said. "They told their voters they would cut $100 billion. That's where they are."

The meeting lasted over an hour. Even the Cardinals who personally liked Kevin McCarthy could see that he didn't know much about the appropriations process. He didn't understand how allocations were set. He didn't seem to know the difference between "obligations" (funds allocated) and "outlays" (funds spent). And as a result, he was in no position to educate the freshmen—who, in the view of the Cardinals, had absolutely no clue what they were asking the Appropriators to do . . . had no clue at all, really, what they were doing, other than pulling a huge round number out of the sky and vowing that this was how much they would cut.

But what McCarthy did know, they could see, was where the freshmen stood.

The Cardinals offered up a counterproposal: $54 billion in spending reductions. McCarthy took it back to the conference.

He returned to the Cardinals that afternoon. "It's not enough," he informed them.

The Appropriators finally got the figure up to $61 billion—which, when prorated, amounted to $100 billion over the entire fiscal year. McCarthy's shuttle diplomacy led him back to the freshmen. "This is

$29 billion more that we got for the American people in a single day's work," the whip told them. "This is a huge concession on Hal Rogers's part."

The freshmen were disappointed. But they also knew enough to trust Kevin McCarthy that it was the best deal they could get.

They agreed on the number offered by the Appropriations Cardinals, and House Resolution 1, the Full-Year Continuing Appropriations Act for 2011, was introduced as legislation the very next day, on February 11. The House would begin debating it four days later.

Within the Appropriations Committee where H.R.1 was being crafted, the veteran Appropriators struggled to adjust to the cut-first, ask-questions-later Tea Party ethos.

Boehner's Steering Committee had awarded five spots on the all-powerful committee to freshmen—and an additional seat to Jeff Flake, the Arizona anti-earmarks crusader. The new committee members did not disguise their hostility toward appropriating. One freshman, Alan Nunnelee of Mississippi, had quizzed a Department of Agriculture undersecretary about food stamps recipients during an early sub-committee hearing. Nunnelee wondered if there was a way that they might be gaming the system. "Do we just ask people, 'Is this your income?' Or do we ask them to bring in their income tax statements, their paychecks? . . . What about people that work for cash—that does not show up on IRS or paycheck?"

Connecticut liberal Rosa DeLauro couldn't believe what she was hearing. "Their average net monthly income is $329," DeLauro had snapped when it was her turn to speak. "We want them to bring their W-2 forms? I submit to you that we [should] ask GE to bring in *its* forms and tell us how they have managed to pay *zero* in taxes to the United States of America! And they ship their jobs overseas, and they take their technology and take it overseas! And we do not hold them accountable for anything! But let us make sure that anyone who gets $134 [in food stamps], that they may be buying the right thing or the wrong thing for their families! *Who are we? Who are we in this great nation?*"

The progressives wondered what world the freshmen inhabited. The freshmen wondered the same about the liberals. Kansas freshman

Kevin Yoder's first Appropriations subcommittee hearing took place on February 11, with testimony from the U.S. Postal Service inspector general. One of the other members present was California Democrat Barbara Lee, the past chairwoman of the Congressional Black Caucus. It astonished Yoder to hear Lee say that she deliberately paid extra to buy postal stamps at regular price because "I am trying to support the Post Office," and that when she visited grocery stores, Lee refused to use computerized checkouts "because I know that is a job or two or three that is gone."

Yoder was dizzy with disbelief. Never before had he heard someone say, in effect, "I try to create jobs by promoting inefficiency." When Yoder was a kid, his mother always told him, "Clean up after yourself. Otherwise someone else is going to have to do it." Barbara Lee had stood his mother's admonition on its ear: *Leave a mess, so that someone has a job.* That was practically Soviet!

The chairwoman of that particular Financial Services subcommittee hearing was Jo Ann Emerson of Missouri, who inhabited a world somewhere in between the freshman Republicans and the liberal Democrats. Emerson was a Tuesday Group—meaning moderate—Republican and an Appropriations Cardinal who chaired the Financial Services subcommittee. Her southeastern Missouri district was almost entirely rural and was the state's poorest, as well as the most dependent on Medicare, Medicaid, and veterans' programs. During the spring of 2011, rising waters from the Mississippi River would submerge vast swaths of four rural counties in the 8th District. Emerson had never harbored qualms about the role of the federal government in assisting disaster-stricken locales. Soon she would watch as freshmen representing districts along the flood-swollen Mississippi like Billy Long of Joplin, Missouri, and Scott DesJarlais of South Pittsburg, Tennessee—two political novices who had campaigned on the bloatedness of the federal government—began to take a different view as well. Such freshmen were now begging for federal disaster relief.

The congresswoman was not a passenger on her colleague Jeff Flake's anti-earmarking bandwagon. Rural districts like hers lacked the ability to write competitive grant proposals. A member-directed funding request leveled the playing field. Flake had gone after her in 2007, labeling her request for $50,000 to control feral hogs in her district This

Week's Egregious Earmark on his congressional website. ("This is a rather literal interpretation of 'bringing home the bacon,'" Flake yuck-yucked.) The reality was that an uncontrolled population of thousands of hogs had destroyed hundreds of thousands of dollars' worth of crops in Emerson's district.

It was hard for her to relate to saber-rattlers like Flake or the freshmen. She hadn't ever considered a role in politics—until some time after June 22, 1996, when her husband, Missouri Congressman Bill Emerson, died of inoperable lung cancer. The same afternoon that he was laid to rest in Cape Girardeau, Bill Emerson's staffers confronted the widow. "We have to talk to you," they said. Her husband had left instructions: *Talk Jo Ann into taking my place.*

Up until that time, she had been content as a forty-six-year-old politician's wife, mother of two daughters, and lobbyist for the American Insurance Organization. But the calls kept coming—from Gingrich, from Boehner.

Three weeks after the funeral, Jo Ann Emerson was on the campaign trail. The policy stuff wasn't difficult for her. Giving speeches, on the other hand—she had never been particularly adept at expressing her feelings publicly, and now, after Bill's death ... During one campaign stop in Steelville, Missouri, she faced a huge audience and decided for the first time to pitch her notes and just talk. It was like suddenly comprehending a foreign language. The audience responded. She stopped using notes after that.

In her new workplace, the Capitol, Jo Ann Emerson found a lovely way to grieve. Her new colleagues, Bill Emerson's old buddies, didn't try to dance around her loss. They were grieving, too. They actually *wanted* to talk to her about her husband. They *wanted* to share stories about fishing trips and late-night carousing. Bill Emerson was still present here. Two years later, she flew out to California and campaigned for another congressional widow, Sonny Bono's wife, Mary. That same year, 1998, she also welcomed to the House a Democrat named Lois Capps, whose husband, Walter, had died of a heart attack during his first year in office. She and Capps would soon become close friends and form a bipartisan lecture series named for their late husbands.

Gingrich put Jo Ann Emerson on Appropriations because he wanted a pro-life woman on the committee. (She did, however, favor exceptions in cases of rape, incest, or risk of death. Bill Emerson had disapproved of such exceptions but knew not to discuss it at a dinner table with three females.) She became a reliable conservative—which was not always the same thing as a reliable vote for the Republican agenda. Early in her career, Emerson traveled with a rice farmer from her district to Cuba. It struck her how the nineteenth largest rice market in the world, less than a thousand miles by air from her district, was not permitted to buy her farmers' rice. She decided to challenge America's long-standing trade sanctions against Cuba. Her problem was not Fidel Castro. Rather, it was Tom DeLay—who, as a child living with a father who did business in South America, had a searing memory of a pit stop at the Havana airport and being surrounded by heavily armed, foul-smelling Cuban soldiers. DeLay had concluded that this experience was a fitting snapshot of communist Cuba and vowed to withhold any trade from that country so long as he and Castro remained in office. The Bush administration was similarly determined not to do business with the Cuban dictator.

Emerson decided that her farmers were more important than the preferences of her party leaders. In 2002, she flew to Cuba and had a six-hour dinner with Castro. She came back to Washington confident that Cuba's leader wished to do business with American farmers. A Washington state congressman, George Nethercutt, wanted his district's pea farmers to have a cut. Together they slid a proviso easing trade with Cuba into an appropriations bill one late evening. DeLay arrived too late to prevent it from passing.

These were the kinds of maneuvers a veteran Appropriator routinely undertook to help her constituents. Could a congresswoman cut a similar deal with a communist dictator in 2011? Jo Ann Emerson had reason to be doubtful.

✦ ✦ ✦

Boehner had vowed that his would be an open House. And so H.R.1 was brought to the floor under an "open rule"—meaning any member, Republican or Democrat, could offer amendments to it, so long as the cost of whatever was being proposed was offset by a corresponding cost reduction. Each amendment would be debated on the House floor for ten minutes and subsequently put to a vote.

"Transparency and openness is a wonderful process," Minority Whip Steny Hoyer wryly commented to a group of reporters after Boehner's intentions for H.R.1 were announced. Nancy Pelosi and the previous Appropriations chairman, David Obey, had tried the open-rule approach shortly after taking power in 2007. Then the Republicans employed a series of parliamentary delay tactics on a Homeland Security appropriations bill, dragging what should have been a six-hour debate into four rancorous days. The Speaker and the chairman concluded from that experience that the Republicans had proved themselves unworthy of the privilege and thereupon shut down the amendment process. Even fellow Democrats who disapproved of the opposition party's obfuscations found Pelosi and Obey's remedy to be repressive. It meant, among other things, that the thirty-two Democratic freshmen from the class of 2008 had thus far been denied the fundamental legislative experience of offering an amendment.

They were going to get that opportunity now.

House staffers celebrated Valentine's Day 2011 by spending the evening conjuring up spending amendments for their bosses to add to the Continuing Resolution, putting the ideas into legalese and marching them over to the House clerk's office in the Capitol. By the end of the night, 403 of them had already been filed. There would be 583 amendments in all—228 of them authored by House Democrats.

Anthony Weiner had submitted seven amendments. Some of his colleagues had argued that the Democrats shouldn't participate in the whole process. At best, they said, it was a sham, since the House Republicans' proposed Continuing Resolution—with its draconian cuts in beloved programs like Head Start—would be dead on arrival in the Senate. At worst, the entire exercise was immoral. "Why buy into their construct?" Rosa DeLauro asked her colleagues. "Why put us in a situation where we're robbing Peter to pay Paul, where we're having to cut from an education program to pay for a health program?"

Weiner was amazed that some Democrats didn't get it. *You engage in the process precisely* because *none of this is gonna become law! You get to score points for free! Why can't progressives own some of the waste-cutting turf, too?*

Other Democrats seemed to be in denial altogether, preferring to believe that this whole program-slashing Republican orgy was Boehner's way of indulging the freshmen until the grown-ups declared an end to playtime and tucked them into bed. Norm Dicks, who was now the Democrats' ranking member of the Appropriations Committee, had told Weiner, "Let's just get to the end of this, and when we get into conference we'll work all of this out." Weiner thought: *What part of Wonderland are you living in? You've got the same blind spot the Obama people do! These people really do want to slash all this stuff we care about!*

One of Weiner's amendments would restore $300 million to the Community Oriented Policing Services (COPS) program that the CR had cut; it would accomplish this by reducing NASA's budget by the same amount. The aspiring mayor of New York saw this as a twofer. He could ingratiate himself with the law enforcement community while daring Republicans to vote against funding the police.

One of the Democrats' best strategic thinkers, Chris Van Hollen of Maryland, warned Weiner that the opposite could occur. "You're giving Republicans a chance to clean up their record," Van Hollen said. "They can vote for your amendment and then say, 'See? We're not cutting programs for cops.'"

Pelosi was also concerned. She had been discouraging any amendments that might muddy the waters of the Democrats' message—which, in her view, was: *The American people want us to be talking about jobs. And instead, the Republicans are throwing firemen and policemen out of work!* The minority leader wanted every speaker to hammer home that argument—or at the very least, to not dilute it.

Weiner decided to file the amendment anyway. It went to the floor at 10:25 in the evening on Tuesday, February 15. He couldn't resist a jab at the Republicans as he introduced the amendment. "What are we doing here?" he said. "We're figuring out which diminished amount we're going to take to restore another diminished amount. This bill [H.R.1] isn't going to become law! The president today said that he is going to veto this bill—as he should. It slashes funding on so many important things to our communities. I bet you most of the authors of the bill are praying that he vetoes this bill.

"But the fact is, we're in this game," Weiner said. And after extolling the COPS program, he concluded by saying, "In a way, I'm playing the game too . . . So I hope you support the Weiner amendment by taking from Mars and putting it in the streets of your district. I think it's late. Let's fold up the rest of the bill. Let's go back. Let's have some bipartisan discussion, and let's try to figure out how to do this in a way that the President won't veto it."

Minority leader Nancy Pelosi was watching the tally board as the members voted. Only when Weiner's amendment crossed the 218 threshold and its victory was assured did she vote for it as well.

Another one of Weiner's amendments sought to strip federal funds from the U.S. Institute of Peace (USIP), a think tank that was set up to resolve international conflict. Whenever he drove to the morose-looking State Department building to pick up his wife, Huma, from work, he would gaze at USIP's gleaming headquarters across the street and wonder where the hell they got their money. It turned out that the late, great earmarking stalwart, Senator Ted Stevens of Alaska, had created the institute with a $100 million earmark. Weiner found two Republican cosponsors—one of them Chip Cravaack, a Minnesota Tea Party freshman who had beaten eighteen-term Democrat James Oberstar—and rigorously defended the amendment on the House floor against the protestations of fellow Democrats.

When the vote was over and Weiner had won again, Rosa DeLauro threw up her hands in disgust and snapped, "Give me a break, Anthony!"

Jeff Duncan also wanted a piece of the action. He sent his legislative director, Joshua Gross, on a mission to find some program to cut so that he could introduce an amendment. Gross came up with a target that for years had been in the sights of the Heritage Foundation, Ronald Reagan, Newt Gingrich, and the Christian Coalition: the Legal Services Corporation, which provides free legal services to the poor at a cost of $324 million to the American taxpayer.

The legislative director described the LSC's function to his boss, as well as the long-standing conservative claim that the organization was a front for left-wing causes. "That's low-hanging fruit as far as I'm concerned," Duncan said.

Gross wrote a draft of the amendment and sent it over to the legislative counsel to obtain the proper wording. At around nine in the evening on Tuesday the fifteenth, Duncan was back at his apartment, wearing his pajamas and writing on his iPad, when an email from Kevin Mc-Carthy's whip office came over alerting him to the fact that they would be getting to his amendment later that evening. He put on his clothes and hustled over to the Capitol.

There were about ten amendments ahead of his. Duncan took a seat on what in recent years had become the customary Republican side of the floor. For nearly two hours, he sat and listened to the debate. Weiner's COPS amendment was pretty sly, he had to admit. Otherwise, it amazed Duncan how much whining was going on from the other side of the chamber. *They don't want to cut anything,* he thought.

His turn came up at 11:27 P.M. Duncan began his speech, but the Republican floor manager, Tom Price, cut him off. "Say, 'I have an amendment at the desk,'" he murmured discreetly.

"Mr. Chairman, I have an amendment at the desk," the freshman began again. He went on, "Folks, let me remind you that we have a trillion-and-a-half-dollar deficit spending and we have $14 trillion in debt," he said. "We can't afford to keep paying for liberal trial lawyer bailouts like the LSC." He quoted from a half-dozen conservative sources as to the program's dubious worth, declared this proposed spending cut "an easy one for us to deal with," and then sat down.

Adam Schiff, a California Democrat, stood in opposition to Duncan's amendment. "I don't think people who go to Legal Services because they can't afford an attorney and desperately want to stay in their home feel like they are giving some sort of bailout to trial lawyers," Schiff shot back. He added, "I don't think it is a left-wing cause when you have veterans coming back from Iraq and Afghanistan who need mental health services and need the help of counsel to get services they are entitled to."

Three other members—one of them Republican Frank Wolf—spoke out against Duncan's amendment. He half-listened to them, thinking: *Any time they don't want to cut spending, they try to justify what the program does.*

Another freshman, Paul Broun of Georgia, leaned over to Duncan. "Do you want to rebut them on anything?" he asked hopefully.

"They're not affecting the vote anyway," Duncan demurred. "Besides, I'm about out of time."

Broun kept pushing. "What we could do," he said, "is I can stand up and ask to change one word in the amendment. Then the chair would give me time to talk, and I could yield that time to you."

Duncan pondered it for a bit.

"I've said what I needed to say," he told his colleague.

Because the hour was late and there were still eight more amendments to consider that evening, the roll call vote on Jeff Duncan's amendment to the Continuing Resolution was postponed until the next day. The House adjourned just after one in the morning. Before going to bed, Josh Gross sent out a "Dear Colleague" letter to every House member from both parties urging them to vote for Duncan's LSC-defunding amendment.

The next day Duncan felt punchy from lack of sleep but otherwise optimistic. Colleagues—including a Democrat, Corrine Brown from Florida—were contacting him and voicing their support. He began to feel less sanguine after the first roll call votes. Four of the eight spending-reduction amendments before his went down in defeat. Duncan was surprised. Why were Republicans not seizing every opportunity to cut federal spending?

The clerk then called out the Duncan amendment. He put his voting card in the slot. Then he looked up at the board to see how the others would vote.

Two of the other South Carolinians, Trey Gowdy and Mick Mulvaney, sidled up to him. "Hey, I'm not sure they wrote your bill right," one of them said to Duncan. Apparently the legislative counsel had failed to include the boilerplate line at the end of his amendment that the amount cut from the LSC would be transferred to the spending reduction account. Duncan winced.

The letter *N* appeared on the board next to Hal Rogers. That did it. Duncan had heard that upwards of thirty Republicans tended to vote as the Appropriations chairman did. Supposedly the LSC did a lot of business in Rogers's Kentucky district.

Jeff Duncan's amendment was defeated, 171–259, with 68 Republicans siding against him. Duncan still felt good about joining the government-slashing fray. The dissenters could feel free to justify their no vote. He knew why *he* was here.

• • •

Blake Farenthold had been one of the sixty-eight Republicans who voted against Duncan's amendment. As a former lawyer, he knew that the LSC could be very antibusiness. But Farenthold represented a very poor district. People there needed legal services.

This constituted his fundamental dilemma. On the one hand, his constituents in Texas's 27th District—many of whom had stayed home for the 2010 midterms but might well vote during the presidential election year of 2012—would be upset if he voted to cut this sort of stuff. And in fact protesters had gathered outside his district office in the border town of Brownsville after learning that H.R.1 would cut two hundred thousand low-income children from the rolls of the Head Start educational program.

On the other hand, the less he cut, the more wrath he would incur from the Tea Party groups who had come out for him in force the previous November. Two Corpus Christi Tea Party activists were already savaging him on his Facebook page. As he saw it, "I could morph into Michele Bachmann and I wouldn't make them happy."

There was no solution in sight—at least not until the Republican-dominated Texas state legislature redrew the map of his district.

Farenthold had actually voted against several spending cuts. Some of these programs—well, he knew nothing in the least about them. Didn't they deserve a fair hearing? The Appropriators who had come up with the Continuing Resolution at least knew about the programs they were cutting. Could the members regurgitating all these amendments say the same thing? You needed at least a half hour on each of these 583 amendments just to hear the pros and cons. Like Weiner's Institute of Peace defunding amendment: some military people had come by Farenthold's office and lobbied him on behalf of that one. It turned out that the outfit wasn't a tree-huggers club, but instead an organization that supported the U.S. military mission in the Middle East. Apparently a number of the Republicans hadn't been made aware of that. Instead, it seemed to Farenthold that a mentality had developed on the floor among his colleagues: *Fuck 'em! Let's cut it!*

He'd meant to offer an amendment. Defunding something or other . . . But he had no one in his office to jump on the matter. Farenthold didn't have a legislative director—it had sounded to him like a middle management job. Nor did he see himself needing a full-time press person. He'd been an attorney and a radio talk show host, after all. No one had to coach him on how to communicate. So he figured he would save the taxpayer some money—though it was a bit crazy-making in mid-January, when the Republicans repealed Obamacare on the House floor and more than one thousand callers besieged the office phone lines to protest Farenthold's vote. Because of the streamlined staff, the phones rang incessantly, and suddenly the Corpus Christi Republican was living out his anxiety dream from several months ago.

It flabbergasted Blake Farenthold how little common sense existed here. Moving into his office, for example: because of the recount, Farenthold hadn't been around for the office lottery and therefore had inherited the Rayburn office of the Democrat he had defeated, Solomon Ortiz. When Farenthold and his staff moved in, he found that all of the office supplies were gone. No stapler, no pen, nothing. What was that about? Staplers were indestructible! Why should he have to go buy a new one? Did this town have any respect whatsoever for the value of the dollar?

A month into his congressional career, Blake Farenthold still hadn't put up his own House website. The issue was personal to him, because he had been in the Web design business for over a decade. In Congress, you were given eight companies who were authorized to work on official House websites. Eight businesses competing for more than four hundred customers—and so naturally they were charging twenty grand to build his website. Farenthold's former company could've done the job for half that. It was maddening, and it stymied him.

So for now he was just using the temporary website that the House Administration Committee was providing him for free. He'd written some of the copy for it himself. Being as how he was Web-savvier than his staffers, Farenthold was half-tempted to remain the in-house content provider.

But he had too many other preoccupations—starting with the visitors who materialized in his Washington office, from a fruit juice lobbyist (apparently there were a lot of grape growers in the 27th District) to the ambassador from Singapore (whose country also had business interests there). Farenthold had also decided to buy a place in Washington, figuring it would be a good investment. He'd looked at a condo in Georgetown. But it had been unclear whether the board of directors would allow him to rebuild the bathroom shower—which, at two and a half feet wide, wasn't going to suffice for a 250-pound man. Ultimately he settled on a place in Chinatown. His twenty-one-year-old daughter, Morgan, had decided to move to Washington and would be sharing it with him. Farenthold's bedroom furniture consisted of a mattress on the floor and a computer box for his nightstand.

Small wonder, then, that the deadline for submitting an amendment to the CR had passed in a flash. And now, for four days running, the House was in session well past midnight, publicly debating hundreds of ways to rein in government spending. Between votes, Farenthold watched the action on C-SPAN from his office couch. Admittedly, he'd drifted off now and again.

Farenthold had developed a new line for when he spoke to industry groups back home in south Texas. "You know how you have that anxiety dream where you go to school and you've forgotten to get dressed?" he would tell them. "I have this anxiety that there's going to be some important bill that I miss, or that I vote wrong on. Your job is to remind me to put my clothes on. You've got to have my back."

He would take information anywhere he could get it—constituents, lobbyists, the RSC, the daily briefing from McCarthy's whip office, the *Drudge Report*. He'd been thinking of buying a subscription to Inter-Prep, a pop culture news service Farenthold had used back in his radio days. Part of connecting with people, he knew, involved using the day's vernacular. How the hell could he find the time to absorb pop culture while drinking out of this legislative fire hydrant?

It would be two months into his job before Blake Farenthold could spend a Sunday at the movies. His choice was a film about a plastic surgeon, played by Adam Sandler, who pretended to be in an awful marriage so that he could win sympathy from beautiful women. Farenthold enjoyed it for the diversion. There were no parallels to his life. The Sandler character kept lying and digging himself a deeper hole. Farenthold was always going to be plain-spoken and truthful.

Yet the Sandler character managed to end up with Jennifer Aniston, while Farenthold was just hoping to make it through the day with his clothes still on.

✦ ✦ ✦

"I go to bed at ten o'clock," then–Minority Leader John Boehner had once complained during a late vote in June 2007. "I don't think good work happens after ten o'clock at night."

But here Boehner's House was, amending and debating and voting until 1:12 A.M. on Tuesday the fifteenth and until 3:41 A.M. on Wednesday the sixteenth. The deadline of Thursday at 3 P.M. that he and Cantor had previously scheduled had been wishful thinking. Thursday afternoon stretched into evening, until the gavel was banged at 1:08 A.M. and the lawmakers prepared for one final day of legislating, beginning at 9:12 Friday morning and concluding at just after four o'clock the following morning. The Continuing Resolution known as H.R.1 would wind up passing on a largely party-line vote of 235 to 189 (and ten days later would be rejected in the Democratic-controlled Senate, also on a largely party-line vote). The House adjourned, and its exhausted members would then head for the airport, after which they would disperse to their respective slivers of America and spend the next week among their constituents, trying to explain what had just occurred and how it accrued to America's benefit.

Amid the bloodshot panorama, eighty-four-year-old John Dingell maintained his customary position near the front of the House chamber—wooden cane at his side, his young aide Chris seated to his right, his eighty-one-year-old longtime Michigan colleague Dale Kildee to his left. Dingell's expression throughout conveyed weary yet active disapproval. He had refused to join what he would call "this outlandish massacre of federal programs" by offering any amendments. His one contribution to the CR debate occurred midway, when he took to the floor to express his disgust after Speaker Boehner had publicly responded to the prospect of federal workers being laid off with a clipped, "So be it."

"Well, Mr. Speaker, it will be so—in fact the Economic Policy Institute estimates eight hundred thousand jobs will be lost," said Dingell from the well. He enumerated several other harmful repercussions to the spending cut bill, which he derided as "a political stunt."

If anything, he was holding back his true feelings. It was one thing to be skilled liars, as Dingell long believed Republicans to be. But the deep anger and bitterness that underlay the ever-coarsening public discourse was now agitated further by a roiling ignorance that truly surprised Dingell, who had figured he couldn't be surprised anymore. He had served with Reagan, whom the freshmen so revered. Well, Reagan was certainly a charming fellow—but Lord was he senile! Dingell had seen it firsthand, during the very first year of Reagan's presidency, when each House committee chairman was ushered into the White House. Dingell and his staff had prepared a damned good report. He'd distilled it all down to a fifteen-minute presentation, including time for questions from the president.

Well, Reagan had no questions. He sat there glassy-eyed, mute as a paperweight. After seven minutes, the Energy and Commerce chairman said, "Mr. President, I've told you everything I can, and I believe that indicates where I can be useful."

"Well, John, I think that's right," responded Reagan with a crinkly-eyed grin. Dingell took his leave.

Later in 1981, during a meeting in the Roosevelt Room of the White House, Dingell was present when the Gipper began to read a speech from a set of three-by-five index cards he was holding in his hands—a speech that had nothing at all to do with the purpose of the gathering. The president carried on cheerfully while the participants sat and tried not to look alarmed. Eventually an aide came into the room, furtively replaced the cards in Reagan's hands with a different set, and without missing a beat the president continued with a new and more appropriate speech.

Of course, the freshmen wouldn't have known any of this. But they should have known—it wasn't ancient history but rather had occurred even in *their* lifetimes—that their hero Reagan had raised taxes eleven times in the course of his presidency, had tripled the debt and grown the federal government, and had granted amnesty to illegal immigrants. Practically a socialist in their eyes! This crowd would have found Reagan as useful (as Dingell liked to say) as feathers on a fish.

Dingell tried to summon clemency. It had been his luck to have met FDR and Truman, to have served during the presidencies of Eisenhower, Kennedy, and Johnson. Most of all, he had apprenticed under John Dingell Sr. Fifty-five years ago, on January 22, 1956, the younger

Dingell had sat in a seat near where he sat now, and for close to an hour he had listened to one congressman after another eulogize his father, their colleague from Detroit, who had been dead not even four months.

And then it came time for the freshman Dingell's maiden speech. He faced his new colleagues for the first time—this erect and earnest twenty-eight-year-old man who the *Washington Post* had said "looks and talks like a youthful Will Rogers"—and he choked back a sob while managing to say, "If I can be half the man my father was, I shall feel I am a great success . . ."

A sweet little moment that was soon forgotten, as freshman Dingell straightaway endeavored to become a pain in the ass to Speaker Rayburn. Haranguing the Rules Committee to bring the Civil Rights Act to the floor . . . introducing legislation to repeal the 20 percent federal cabaret tax . . . seeking to kill the Taft-Hartley provision that allowed state right-to-work laws . . . demanding better food policing by the Food and Drug Administration . . . oh, to be young and obnoxious again!

But he had never been ignorant—not like these crazy tea-baggers.

CHAPTER TEN

Moment of Silence

Each day the House is in session begins with a period known as "morning hour debate." The phrase is not to be taken literally, since the period sometimes begins at noon, sometimes lasts less than an hour, and rarely involves actual debate. It has evolved, in any event, into a peculiarly postmodern custom of the lower body. Morning hour entails a procession of House members standing in the well of the chamber and for five minutes passionately orating to an audience of virtually zero (though really to a C-SPAN television audience, which might number just slightly more than zero at that hour) on topics of almost absurd boundlessness.

The majority of the House's 435 members do not bother with morning hour. They contend that there are far better ways to spend the first hours of an already overscheduled day than futilely exercising one's lungs. But there are others who simply cannot turn down a chance to speak to a (likely sparse) national audience, uninterrupted and unedited, for five full minutes.

The 112th Congress featured masters of the morning hour tradition. Among the hardy perennials was Ted Poe of Texas, a former judge, whose speeches often decried the havoc on America's southern border (despite the fact that Poe's district abutted not Mexico but Louisiana) and reliably concluded with the solemn intonation, "And that's just the way it is." No morning hour would be complete without a surrogate of Minority Leader Pelosi—among the rotating cast, Debbie Wasserman Schultz, Frederica Wilson, and Keith Ellison—conveying the Democratic message that "we've now entered the XXth day when the Republican majority has been in control of the House, and they've yet to introduce a single bill to create a single job for anyone anywhere."

By and large, however, morning hour would maintain its historical charm as a rhetorical grab bag of parochialism and esoterica. Members offered five-minute send-ups to National Engineers Week, the Super Bowl champion Green Bay Packers, and the Arizona State High School Division 4A-1 basketball champion Nogales Apaches. They gave florid tribute to an obscure war hero from Nevada, the economic resurgence of Chattanooga, the hundredth anniversary of the Army Dental Corps, and the hundredth anniversary of the Thomaston, Georgia, chapter of Daughters of the American Revolution. They agonized publicly over the loss of high-speed rail in Florida and the rickety state of California's salmon industry. Then they handed over their texts to the House clerk and shuffled out of the chamber as another five-minute speech began.

Occasionally, however, a morning hour speaker would stand in the well and exhibit the solemnity befitting a nation traumatized by a decade of war. At about 10:30 in the morning on March 1, 2011, the House floor was completely empty and no more than eight high school students sat in the public galleries when a Republican congressman named Walter Jones walked to the well to give the seventh of sixteen morning hour speeches that day. He was a slightly built, gray-haired, sixty-eight-year-old man with the gentle bearing of a Sunday school teacher, and he spoke in the elastic twang that was typical of the eastern flank of North Carolina, where he had in fact spent his entire life, in the town of Farmville. For the past sixteen years, Jones had represented the state's 3rd District, a largely coastal region that also included the Marine Corps base of Camp Lejeune. To hold that seat is to be unerringly pro-military. But in recent years, Walter Jones had developed a surprising interpretation of what this meant.

Gesturing to a large placard he had placed on a stand beside him, Jones said, "I bring a photograph of a flag-draped coffin—it's called a transfer case—being escorted off a plane at Dover Air Force Base.

"Mr. Speaker, it is time to bring our troops home. They have been in Afghanistan for over ten years. I would also say it is time that this Congress met its constitutional responsibility to debate war and whether we should be there or bring our troops home . . .

"How many more young men and women must lose their legs, their lives, for a corrupt government that history has proven will never be changed? Why should they be dying and losing their legs for Karzai, who doesn't even know that we're his friends? It makes no sense."

He read from a letter sent to him by a retired military general, who maintained that the war in Afghanistan "can't be won." He read from another letter, this one by a recently retired Marine lieutenant colonel who viewed the war as having "gone on for too long." He spoke of a recent visit to Walter Reed Army Medical Center to stand beside the bed of a twenty-two-year-old Army private whose body below the waist had all been blown away.

And then he concluded with a kind of prayer, with eyes closed: "God bless the House and Senate that we will do what is right in Your eyes for today's generation and tomorrow's generation. I ask God to give wisdom, strength and courage to President Obama that he will do what is right in the eyes of God.

"And three times I will ask: God, please, God, please, God, please continue to bless America."

Walter Jones walked away from the microphone. The next speaker happened to be Democratic Minority Whip Steny Hoyer. He grabbed the Republican's hand and spoke in his ear for a moment.

Then, when the Democrats' second-ranking leader turned to the microphone, his first words were not from his prepared text. "First I want to congratulate the gentleman from North Carolina," Hoyer said with a stricken expression. "He is a Republican and I am a Democrat, but I will tell you this: We are friends, and we work together. And he is one of the most conscientious members of this House, who follows his conscience and his moral values in making decisions. He gave a very moving and important speech on the floor today. I thank the gentleman, Mr. Jones, from North Carolina."

Jones nodded his appreciation and walked out of the chamber. Hoyer then proceeded into his daily harangue of the Republicans, and a Republican followed to harangue the Democrats, and whatever subtle and plaintive magic had transpired during Walter Jones's five minutes of the morning hour evaporated altogether.

Every Saturday morning at about 9:30, Walter Jones showed up to his otherwise empty district office in Greenville, North Carolina, and followed through on a ritual he had begun a decade ago. He would put on a pot of coffee for himself. Then he would sit at his desk and reach for the letters he had written, and that his staff had then typed and printed out, to the families of the young men and women from his district who had recently died in combat.

My heart aches as I write this letter for I realize you are suffering a great loss . . . In John 15:13 Jesus says, "Greater love has no man than this, that he lay down his life for his friends . . ."

He would sign them slowly, painstakingly, using an ink pen. The signature on each had to look just right. If the *e* in *Walter* was closed too tightly, he would print out a fresh copy and redo the signature. He would do them in groups of five, because he wanted to take his time, considering each fallen warrior, thinking about why this had happened and about everyone who had been touched by each singular devastation— and about his weakness that had led him to vote for these terrible wars that had cost so many and for so little in return.

After he had signed those five letters, Jones would slide each of them into its respective previously addressed envelope, unfolded, along with a piece of cardboard. Then he would move on to the next five letters. The Saturday after he had given the Afghanistan speech in front of Steny Hoyer and practically no one else, there had been twenty-seven letters waiting on his desk. It took over an hour. Only then, after he had completed his monastic act of penitence, would Walter Jones then permit himself to move on with his day.

Often the families replied to Jones to thank him for being so considerate. He found such letters very difficult to read. Because Jones had never served in the military, he was not strong enough to vote his conscience, which was telling him that Saddam Hussein did not possess weapons of mass destruction and that the pretext for invading Iraq was therefore false. He felt undeserving of any kind of praise. And it was haunting to read notes like the one he received a few years back but could not forget: *Thanks for your letter. My only regret is that my son was killed looking for WMD's that did not exist.*

The liberal magazine *Mother Jones* had put Walter Jones on the cover in early 2006, a few months after he had turned hard against the Iraq War. Jones's press secretary at the time had told him that she believed *Mother Jones* was a Catholic magazine.

Walter Jones was a Republican. He had never been anything but a Republican—though his father, Walter Sr., had been a Democratic congressman for the 1st District for twenty-six years. The younger Jones had been elected in 1994, as a foot soldier in the Gingrich Revolution who faithfully listened to the GOPAC messaging tapes and gratefully received the campaign support of North Carolina Senator Jesse Helms, at the time the nation's foremost paleoconservative.

And Jones remained a conservative: pro-life, against big government, reverent of God and of family values. When Michele Bachmann formed the Tea Party Caucus after the 2010 midterms, Jones's chief of staff signed up his boss. The congressman had to tell his staffer to remove his name and consult with him next time. He thought Bachmann was a nice person, but her divisive statements unsettled him.

In the view of the House GOP leaders, however, Walter Jones was no longer a reliable Republican. He did not attend the House GOP conferences. On the House floor he sat next to his close friend, libertarian Ron Paul. Together they voted against any bill that furthered the war effort, no matter what else was in it. He was working with Dennis Kucinich and other liberal Democrats to produce legislation that would accelerate the troop withdrawals from Afghanistan. When the Democrats were in power, he requested from Speaker Pelosi that the House engage in a moment of silence once a month to honor the fallen. She agreed to do so. A month into the 112th Congress, Jones sent Speaker Boehner a letter, asking that he continue the tradition.

A *Huffington Post* reporter happened to be talking to Jones, who mentioned that he had sent a letter to Boehner requesting that the House honor America's fallen warriors with a moment of silence once a month. A week later, Boehner's chief of staff, Barry Jackson, accosted Jones on the House floor during votes.

"I understand from the *Huffington Post* that you've threatened the Speaker," Jackson said.

He was joking, sort of. But there was in fact a price to be paid for crossing his party with his antiwar posture. When the Republicans regained power after the 2010 elections, Jones was informed that despite his seniority, Speaker Boehner would not be naming him to chair a subcommittee, because he was "too independent."

He knew it was a fair criticism. Jones was not exactly a team player. In late January, when the GOP advanced a bill that would eliminate public campaign financing, Democrat Chris Van Hollen countered with a "motion to recommit" that would substitute the Republican bill with one that required big donors to disclose their identities. Jones had always supported campaign finance reform. He voted for Van Hollen's motion.

Jones was sitting on the front row talking to a colleague when a Republican leadership staffer bent down and whispered to him, "We need for you to change your vote."

"I'm not going to," said Jones.

Majority Leader Eric Cantor then came to see Jones on the floor. He made the same request.

"Eric, I'm not going to change my vote," Jones said. "I've been a campaign reformer since I started out in the North Carolina state legislature in 1980."

"Walter," Cantor said, "we don't need for the freshmen to see any breaks in ranks."

Jones did not oblige the majority leader—though he, too, was interested in what the freshmen thought. He and two other Republican war critics, Ron Paul and Tennessee Congressman Jimmy Duncan, had invited all of the GOP members to attend a meeting on February 16 to discuss U.S. policy in Afghanistan with Council on Foreign Relations president Richard Haass, retired Major General John Batiste, and Grover Norquist of Americans for Tax Reform. Because that day fell during the protracted amendment debate for the Continuing Resolution, only five Republicans showed up. Two were freshmen—one of whom, Todd Rokita, also voted for the amendment Walter Jones had submitted to H.R.1 that proposed to eliminate the $400 million Afghanistan infrastructure fund. Only thirty-five Republicans had sided with his amendment, which was defeated. He could see that Boehner and the rest of the Republican leadership were reluctant to appear in any way dovish.

Nonetheless, eight of those thirty-five Republican votes were from freshmen. Jones knew that the class of 2010 had come to Washington to slash spending. He hoped that he could appeal to their wallets, if not their hearts.

On February 17, 2011, the eighty-year-old Republican congressman and former Vietnam POW Sam Johnson was escorted by Boehner to the Speaker's chair. The occasion was the thirty-eighth anniversary of Johnson's return to America after spending nearly seven ghastly years in the so-called Hanoi Hilton. The war hero's presence was greeted on the floor with a cacophony of soldierly *Hoo-hah*s and a standing ovation. "He's a great American," Boehner proclaimed amid the swelling applause.

But during Sam Johnson's brief moment as acting Speaker, he said to the House, "The Chair would ask all present to rise for the purpose of a moment of silence . . . in remembrance of our brave men and women in uniform who have given their lives in the service of our Nation . . ."

Walter Jones had succeeded.

And he was gratified. But, he felt, it should be a monthly occurrence, until all the troops were safely home at last.

Gently, he would keep pushing.

CHAPTER ELEVEN

Black Republican Out of Florida

The first African-American congressman to be elected in the Sunshine State was a Virginia native named Josiah Walls, believed to have escaped slavery in 1863 by enlisting as a private in the 3rd Infantry Regiment of the Union Army's Colored Troops division. Walls apparently parlayed his military standing into a successful run for the Florida state legislature in 1868. As the Reconstruction era fell upon the South, the white grandees saw the writing on the wall and gave in to Negro pressure, greasing the path for Josiah Walls to run for Florida's only seat in Congress.

In the 1870 general election he narrowly defeated a former slave owner. The House that Walls joined would soon include black members from Louisiana, the Carolinas, Georgia, and Alabama. But the climate in the lower body was not altogether welcoming to the black new arrivals. "Sir, the Negro is a clinging parasite," declared William Robbins, a Democratic freshman from North Carolina, during Walls's first full term in 1873. Robbins added, "Even here on this floor—and I mean no disrespect to any fellow member by this remark—he does nothing, he says nothing except as he is prompted by his managers; even here he obeys the bidding of the new white masters, who move him like a puppet on the chess board . . ."

The lot of freed African-Americans was hardly Congress's preoccupation during the Reconstruction era. As a freshman, Walls took to the House floor to demand a federal education system so that former slaves could find a foothold in society—and in recognition of the unlikelihood that "their former enslavers would take an impartial interest in their educational affairs." Yet the only bills passed during his tenure would sanction states' rights rather than civil rights.

During his first full term, the hyperactive Josiah Walls managed to divide his time between the House, a budding law practice, the cultivation of a sizable cotton plantation, and a newspaper in Gainesville he had acquired for the purposes of promoting "the wants and interests of the people of color." Apparently all of this was not enough, for during his first term in the House he also served a short stint as mayor of Gainesville. Between his burgeoning workload and his Radical Republican politics, Walls was guaranteed a tough reelection battle in 1874. Again he won by a hair. The results were contested and he was forced to vacate his office.

He ran for the House again in 1884, to no avail—by which time the number of blacks in Congress had dwindled to two, both being of such ill repute that a Negro paper pronounced them demagogues and said that white representatives would have been a better choice. When Josiah Walls died, no newspaper in Florida thought him worthy of an obituary. The "experiment" of blacks in Congress had been deemed a failure. In August 1900, the last of them, George Henry White of North Carolina, announced that he would be stepping down and leaving the state, explaining, "I cannot live in North Carolina and be treated as a man." He advised other blacks in the state to move westward, where they could "go on a farm and own their own homes." Another twenty-nine years would pass before Oscar De Priest from Chicago would take his place among the all-Caucasian body and five years later stage a brave and futile crusade against the segregated House dining room. De Priest lost his reelection campaign that same year, in 1934.

And with that, the House faded to white once more.

"You've gotta put me in, coach," Allen West said to Congressional Black Caucus chairman Emanuel Cleaver back in January on the House floor. "I'm not here just to be window dressing. This isn't just a symbolic thing for me."

The freshman was communicating his desire to be a player in the CBC's activities. Cleaver tended to keep his feelings to himself—he was different from West in that regard—and so he simply said "Sure" and walked away. West thought he looked surprised.

Two months later, at a CBC dinner, the third-ranking House Democrat, James Clyburn, told the members, "We're going to need Allen

West over on the other side fighting for some of the issues that we're pushing for." West sat at his table, emphatically nodding yes.

The opportunity for West to contribute arrived at the end of March, when the CBC celebrated its fortieth anniversary. Among the festivities was a reception in the Capitol's Statuary Hall that Nancy Pelosi and Steny Hoyer both attended. During the reception, a seven-minute video was played that honored the CBC's history. Chairman Cleaver learned shortly after the fact that such performances were against Capitol rules. He dispatched CBC member Lacy Clay of Missouri—whose father had been one of the caucus's founding members in 1971—to ask West if he in turn would get a retroactive waiver from Speaker Boehner. The lone Republican CBC member went to Boehner, who had a good laugh about the matter and then granted the waiver.

West's relations with his black Democratic colleagues remained testy, however. Just before a CBC meeting with White House chief of staff Bill Daley was to begin, previous CBC president Barbara Lee fixed the freshman with an inhospitable glare and said, "So, are you planning to tweet during this?"

At least Lee had spoken to him. One afternoon in March, West stepped into a Capitol elevator that already had an occupant: Jesse Jackson Jr. The Illinois congressman immediately looked down at his Black-Berry and did not say a word.

It would be May before the two men finally conversed. On that day, West and Jackson again found themselves in a Capitol elevator, both heading to the House floor to cast votes while the rest of the CBC was at the White House meeting with the president.

"Why aren't you at the White House?" Jackson asked.

"Why aren't *you* at the White House?" West replied.

"Because I take my voting responsibility very seriously," said Jackson.

"Well, so do I," said West. "Plus, I have a hearing."

"Oh," said Jackson, adding with mock reverence: "A *hearing!*"

"Yeah," said West. "A hearing." Thus concluded their pleasantries.

That Allen West was a Republican was not the main reason for all the frostiness. In late January, he had appeared on a Zionist television program called *The Shalom Show* and had taken an unprovoked swipe at Keith Ellison, a fellow CBC member who happened to be of Islamic faith. West spoke of Ellison as being among those who "represent the

antithesis of the principles upon which this country was established."
Unsurprisingly, Ellison was upset by West's comments.

Emanuel Cleaver paid a visit to West's office in the Longworth
Building. "Keith feels you owe him an apology," the CBC chairman
said.

West refused. "I don't have anything personal against him," he said.
"But he's going around and speaking at fund-raisers for a group that is
not in concert with the principles of this country. And I have some issues with that."

West was referring to the Council on American-Islamic Relations,
or CAIR. According to the FBI, CAIR was linked to the Muslim
Brotherhood's Palestine Committee. West viewed the Brotherhood as
fanatical. He was surprised that Cleaver did not seem to know much at
all about CAIR's nefarious ties.

"Look, I'm happy to meet with Keith Ellison and give him my point
of view," West offered.

Emanuel responded that Ellison's feelings were a bit raw. Absent an
apology on West's part, it might be better to wait awhile.

As the CBC chairman got up to leave, the freshman said to him, "I
just want to remind you: I'm black. I've got some opinions that differ
from you guys. But I'm not what you might think I am."

Cleaver nodded and left. The next time the chairman returned to
West's office, it was in April—and this time it was Cleaver apologizing.
The CBC chairman had issued a press release condemning the Republican budget plan. Its lone Republican member had fired back with a
press release of his own, saying, "The CBC should be a bipartisan body
politic and not the place for emotional rhetoric, nor the platform for the
Democratic party."

"You've got a good point," Cleaver conceded to West. "Henceforth,
we'll make sure that on positions that we send out, we'll have some kind
of asterisk that suggests that this is not reflective of all the members of
the caucus."

With some bemusement, West accepted his status as asterisk.

"You recently told a Marine that the terrorists that attacked the United
States, the people that attack America, are following Islam, are following the instructions of the Koran," the south Florida director of

CAIR said to Allen West during a town hall in Pompano Beach. "So a very simple question: can you show me one verse in this Koran"—the questioner held up his copy of the sacred text—"where it says to attack America, attack Americans, attack innocent people?"

"Well, of course it doesn't say America—the book was written in the eighth or ninth century, so America wasn't even around," West scoffed as the largely conservative audience tittered. Then, as the CAIR representative tried to talk back, the freshman proceeded to run the gutters red with Islam's violent historical interludes:

"The truth is out there! Six twenty-two AD, the Nakhla raid—that didn't happen?! Six twenty-eight AD, the Battle of Khaibar?! Seven thirty-two AD, the Battle of Tours?! . . ."

Competing against near-deafening applause, West hollered at the stupefied Muslim man standing in the aisle, *"Now you explain it to me: the people that flew those planes on 9/11 shouted, 'Allah Akbar!' Now, I've been on the battlefield, my friend—don't try to blow sunshine up my butt!"*

Among the jeering and cheering, a large man stood up and thrust his finger at the CAIR representative, exclaiming: "You have just been *schooled*, my man!"

"Mr. West, may I respond to you?" the Muslim man persisted. "I am ashamed to be here with all of these people when you attack Islam—"

"You attack us! You attack us! I went to Muslim countries to defend the freedom of Muslim people! Don't come up here and try to criticize me!"

Performances such as these, while horrifying to the CBC and others, were catnip to the right wing. In mid-February, the former Army lieutenant colonel and schoolteacher found himself delivering the keynote address before an estimated crowd of ten thousand individuals at the annual American Conservative Union CPAC convention. Listening to the muffled roar while he sat in the greenroom before going onstage, West imagined himself a gladiator preparing for his kill-or-be-killed moment in the arena.

West killed. He lashed out at the "bureaucratic nanny state," warned that "we can ill afford to have a twenty-first-century Sir Neville Chamberlain moment," asserted the necessity of "reclaiming our Judeo-Christian faith heritage," and taunted "the liberal press" by saying: "Continue your attack. Because this is what Abraham Lincoln said: 'Be sure you put your feet in the right place, then stand firm.'"

The outpouring of adulation that day was almost too much for him. His favorite compliment came from someone he did not know: "You said what all of us feel."

One morning at the House gym, West ran into Anthony Weiner. West began to introduce himself, but the New York Democrat waved off the gesture as one of inappropriate modesty.

"I know who you are," said Weiner. "You're a rock star."

The actor Gary Sinise thought so as well. He asked West to come visit him in Los Angeles. Alas, there wasn't an opening in his schedule for months. Ernest Borgnine was also an admirer and had sent the freshman an autographed head shot. Upping the ante, the conservative TV host Glenn Beck had begun a movement to draft West for president—which West found both immensely flattering and asinine, as he had been an elected official for less than half a year.

For a Tea Party icon, Allen West could be full of surprises, some of them disappointing to his base. During the Continuing Resolution debate, the freshman passed on several chances to slash federal funding. A group of mayors from his south Florida district came to Washington to lobby him against the Republican amendment that proposed to eliminate all funding for community development block grants. West looked at the data that the mayors showed him and was convinced. He voted against the amendment. Similarly, the farmers of Belle Meade, Florida, convinced West to side against an amendment that would block Environmental Protection Agency plans to clean up Florida's waterways. And when Georgia freshman Paul Broun introduced an amendment that would defund beach replenishment projects by the Army Corps of Engineers, West buttonholed his colleague on the House floor.

"What's wrong with you?" West demanded. "I come from a state where there's nothing but coastline, Paul. It's our number-one tourist destination!"

The group Heritage Action for America had slapped West with a middling conservative ranking for failing to vote for several spending cuts. But the Florida freshman had not exactly emerged from the CR debate as a Democrat sympathizer. After listening to Barney Frank of Massachusetts on the House floor late one evening mock the Republicans' "orgy of self-congratulation" over the use of the open rule— "You will get to debate whole aspects of the government tomorrow for ten minutes"—West ripped into the opposition with a press release. "I have never seen a greater assembly of petulance and sophomoric behavior as what I have witnessed this week on the floor of the House of Representatives."

"Barney Frank at midnight—I couldn't believe it," he later spat. "The arrogance and petulance—here's a guy who for all practical purposes should be in a pink jumpsuit for what he did."

And yet for all his incendiary rhetoric, it was Allen West whose very first piece of legislation as a U.S. congressman—reducing the Defense Department's printing costs by 10 percent—would gain passage by unanimous vote, 393–0. And it was West who sat during Obama's State of the Union address listening carefully while marking up his copy of the president's speech, with occasional notations of *Good point!* and *Key point* in the margins. (Though most of his comments were negative: *Fiscally irresponsible. Serious class warfare. Wrong premise. Heard that before!*)

West and the president had eyeballed each other for the first time at a White House reception in January. Obama had grinned pleasantly as they shook hands, but West could not help thinking: *Yeah, he knows who I am. Like when you're in a combat zone and you see a bunch of sheikhs and there's one that stands out and you can tell: that guy's the bad guy.*

Allen West—rock star, legislator, the anti-Obama—flew to Atlanta on March 21 to give the keynote address at a Georgia GOP fund-raiser. That day he took a sentimental detour down Kennesaw Avenue where he was raised. No one he'd grown up with lived there anymore. A Che Guevara flag hung from one of the windows.

He dropped by Grady High School. No one there knew that a former student was now a U.S. congressman. West left a card at the principal's desk and headed back to the world where he was famous.

CHAPTER TWELVE

Radicalization

One afternoon in early March, Jeff Duncan was using the tiny private restroom in his Cannon office when it occurred to him: *This is the only time I'm ever alone anymore.*

His committee work on Natural Resources, Foreign Affairs, and Homeland Security was demanding enough by itself. But Duncan was now sitting through more than a dozen meetings every week with lobbying organizations. Some, like Caterpillar and International Paper, did business in his district. Then there were others, like an out-fit called American Modern Insurance, that he'd never even heard of but that had somehow gotten on his schedule. Everyone wanted to meet the freshmen—a class whose probusiness attitude was matched by legislative inexperience. The lobbyists would be only too happy to accommodate.

For days at a stretch Duncan subsisted on a diet of coffee and granola bars. His only real recreation was the weekly pickup basketball game he played in the House gym with other freshmen like Kevin Yoder, Ben Quayle, Stephen Fincher, Jon Runyan, and Tom Graves. Consoling him was the recognition that his roommate and fellow South Carolinian, Tim Scott, had it even worse: he was on the Rules Committee and also had to attend leadership meetings, both of which consumed several hours of Scott's weekly schedule. The two almost never saw each other back at the apartment.

One of the groups that came to Duncan's office represented several small companies in his district. Duncan asked them, "Is there any money that could be used for job creation that's just sitting on the sidelines? Do they have cash reserves?"

"Trillions," was the reply. But, they added, the money would stay on the sidelines until the business climate possessed more certainty. A full repeal of Obamacare, they agreed, would be a good start.

"The way government creates jobs is to get the hell out of the way," Duncan liked to say. It was one of his abiding principles as a small businessman. He marveled at how the Democrats failed to get it.

But even though Duncan viewed his House office as a business, not all of the transactions on behalf of his constituents related to dollars and cents. One concern in particular had been expressed to him by South Carolinians numerous times on the campaign trail: the threat of Islamic sharia law being imposed in America, thereby imperiling the Constitution.

Duncan himself did not represent many Muslims in the 3rd District and counted no Muslims as his friends. There was a single mosque in his district, near Clemson University, Duncan's alma mater. "We've heard from others that it's a little edgy, but I've never been there," he said.

The Islamic Society of Clemson was actually not very edgy at all. The mosque had existed for a decade, attracting two hundred or so Muslims who worked and studied at the university. Some of these were citizens of Palestine, Egypt, Libya, Pakistan, and Jordan. But the mosque's cofounder was a fifty-seven-year-old African-American and lifelong Clemson resident named Darnell Oglesby, who had grown up as a black Christian in a climate of segregated bathrooms and unsolved lynchings, and whose brother had graduated from high school with Senator Lindsey Graham. Oglesby viewed sharia as a spiritual compass that "just deals with day to day life—we don't want to make it the law of this country." He and his fellow Clemson Muslims were baffled that their elected congressman would suspect otherwise. They hoped that Duncan would drop by the Islamic Society of Clemson sometime and see for himself.

But Duncan was heading in a different direction.

In early March of 2011, Homeland Security Committee chairman Peter King announced that he would be holding a hearing on radical Islam in America. King, who often sparred with his fellow New Yorker Anthony Weiner, had a knack for drawing media attention. The Muslim radicalization hearing would be his pièce de résistance, dominating the cable shows and garnering front-page headlines for several days.

While many Democrats charged that King's hearing smacked of racial profiling, and hundreds protested in Times Square, Jeff Duncan saw an opportunity. He dispatched two of his legislative aides to spend three days interviewing counterterrorism specialists in conservative think tanks. They prepared a detailed brief for their boss.

Duncan was less interested in the methods of Muslim radicalization than what he believed to be the jihadists' ultimate goal: to make sharia the law of the land in America. He had been reading a book called *Sharia: The Threat to America.* Its coauthor, Frank Gaffney, espoused alarmist views on "stealth jihad" that were distinctively scattershot—accusing conservative tax activist Grover Norquist, for example, of being a radical Islam sympathizer and the CPAC conference where Allen West gave the keynote of having ties to the Muslim Brotherhood. Nonetheless, Duncan had heard anecdotal evidence to buttress Gaffney's claims. There had been a lower court ruling in New Jersey that a Muslim man who had sexually assaulted his wife was exempted from punishment because sharia law held that the wife should submit to him. (The case was overturned in an appellate court.) To Duncan, the equation was simple: "Sharia butts heads with the Constitution."

The hearing took place on March 10 and began with the testimony of Congressman John Dingell. "I represent a very polyglot and diverse congressional district in which we have all races, religions, and all parts of the world society represented," Dingell said, glaring at the committee members instead of reading from a prepared text. "I represent a very fine community of Muslim-Americans . . . They are, almost without exception, loyal, honorable citizens."

Dingell reminded the committee members that he once ran numerous investigations in his capacity as chairman of the Energy and Commerce Committee. "I kept a picture of Joe McCarthy hanging on the wall," he said, "so that I would know what it is that I did not want to look like, to do or to be." While applauding Chairman King for the hearing's "great potential," he urged that "we do not blot the good name or the loyalty or raise questions about the decency of Arabs or Muslim or other Americans en masse. There will be plenty of rascals we can point at," he concluded.

The King hearing lasted four hours. Like most congressional inquisitions, exchange of information took a backseat to speechifying and, at times, emotional theater. Its six witnesses included the House's first Muslim congressman, Keith Ellison, who sobbed bitterly as he recounted the death on 9/11 of a first responder whose Muslim faith had caused his character to be smeared. Less sympathetic to Muslims was the testimony supplied by two men whose young male relatives had turned to violent jihad, and by an Arizona Muslim named Dr. Zuhdi Jasser, who urged reformist interpretations of the Koran. As a freshman, Jeff Duncan's turn came near the very end. He knew that he would have only five minutes and thus time for only one question. He was grateful when none of the other congressmen touched on the topic that he had intended to broach.

He began by reading from a *Newsweek* story that criticized the left for protecting Islamism and the right for "often wrongly attacking the Muslim faith." Then Duncan declared, "I'm not aware of anyone on this side of the spectrum attacking Islam, nor of anyone wishing to limit anyone's First Amendment rights. But rather I believe we are raising the awareness of Islamism."

Duncan said, "I am regularly astonished and outraged . . ." He rapped his fist against the table and repeated, "Outraged! By this administration's continued failure to single out who our enemy is!" The freshman carried on for another minute about the Obama administration's politically correct aversion to using words like *jihad* and *Muslim Brotherhood*, showing a chart by Frank Gaffney to bolster his point.

"But what I came here today to delve into is a completely different line of thought," Duncan then said. "It is this, an issue of particular concern to me and my constituents, and that is the threat of sharia law to the United States Constitution."

The freshman declared his desire "to seek multiple hearings" on "the role that Islamic doctrine plays in the radicalization process." With his time running out, the freshman finally got out his question to Dr. Jasser: "Do you feel the U.S. government has done an adequate job learning about Islam and how Islamic doctrines affect the behavior and community norms of Muslims residing in America, and how does Islamic doctrine and sharia law shape the responsiveness of local U.S. Muslim communities to law enforcement efforts that target Islamic jihad?"

It was a mouthful. "I think that's a wonderful question," Dr. Jasser replied, before proceeding to spend the final two minutes not answering it—instead expanding on his earlier testimony about the antique nature of sharia and the need to reform it.

Duncan was fine with that. He had been permitted his moment on national television to register his concern with radical Islam. That evening, liberal commentator Chris Matthews would run the clip of Duncan's "outraged—outraged!" moment on his MSNBC show *Hardball*, followed by the observation that Duncan was "a congressman reading nonsense."

Duncan's press release that afternoon cast it differently: DUNCAN DEFENDS CONSTITUTION DURING RADICALIZATION HEARING. "Freshman Congressman Jeff Duncan was a leading voice in today's radicalization hearings . . ."

A couple of hours after the hearing had concluded, Duncan was walking down the aisle of the House floor, feeling rather buoyed by his performance. Then someone threw a shoulder into him. Turning, he noticed a short but solidly built African-American woman walking in the opposite direction. He figured it must have been a mistake.

But then as she returned up the aisle, she did it again. Bumped him hard. Duncan realized he'd recognized her from the hearing—she had gone on and on about how the proceedings were "tainted" and "an outrage," refusing to acknowledge Chairman King's rapping of the gavel. Duncan told a few of his colleagues about what she had done to him, and they laughed and shared some of the many stories about her. Sheila Jackson Lee was her name.

"She and I are gonna butt heads," he vowed.

CHAPTER THIRTEEN

Woman of a Certain Rage

Sheila Jackson Lee represented Texas's 18th Congressional District—the seat, in every meaningful way, of Barbara Jordan.

The legendary Houston congresswoman had actually helped draw her own district map while serving as vice chair of the Texas State Senate redistricting panel in 1971—a post she had secured due to her alliances with Lyndon Johnson. The former president saw his protégé as "the epitome of the new politics in Texas, not the politics that seek to destroy and divide and mess up everything in the way." Likewise, much of the all-white Texas political establishment regarded the heavyset young woman from Houston's Fifth Ward with the searing intellect and regal voice as singular and predestined for this moment. Before her, no black had ever been elected to Congress from Texas. Nor had any African-American since Reconstruction served in the state senate until Jordan was elected in 1966 at the age of thirty. But the time now seemed ripe to fall in behind a black politician who was strong and principled yet also accommodating—whose abiding view was that "militancy is expressed in different ways."

Jordan arrived in Washington in January 1973 as a freshman in a class of her own. Her first choice had been to serve on the Armed Services Committee. But LBJ persuaded her to aim for a seat on Judiciary instead—and then sealed the deal through phone conversations with influential Democrats like Ways and Means chairman Wilbur Mills. (John Dingell, who had taken an immediate liking to Jordan, later asked her if she could help secure *him* a seat on her committee. She demurred, laughing, "I don't think Judiciary is ready for you, John.") The chairman, Peter Rodino of New Jersey, curried favor with Jordan rather than the other way around, seeing her popularity as something that might help him gain favor with his own black constituents. It was not long before Washington reporters were referring to the thirty-eight-year-old freshman as "the brightest member of the Judiciary Committee."

On February 6, 1974, the House Judiciary Committee began its impeachment inquiry of President Richard Nixon over the Watergate scandal. Jordan had been a lawyer before she entered politics, but her clients were largely poor and black. Now she endeavored to become a constitutional scholar on the fly. Twice she visited the National Archives and took her place among tourists staring at the Founders' document. By night she immersed herself in legal texts and testimony transcripts. Jordan had quickly formed the conclusion that the president was guilty of obstructing justice. But she had not decided how she would express this opinion until just a few hours before July 25, 1974, when the House Judiciary Committee would convene before a nationally televised audience to discuss articles of impeachment.

Being a freshman, Jordan's turn to give her fifteen-minute statement came near the very end. Leaning into the microphone, she began, "Earlier today we heard the beginning of the Preamble to the Constitution of the United States. *We, the People.* It is a very eloquent beginning. But when that document was completed on the seventeenth of September in 1787, I was not included in that *We, the People.* I felt somehow for many years that George Washington and Alexander Hamilton must have left me out by mistake. But through the process of amendment, interpretation, and court decision I have finally been included in *We, the People.*

"Today, I am an inquisitor. I believe hyperbole would not be fictional and would not overstate the solemnness that I feel right now. My faith in the Constitution is whole, it is complete, it is total. I am not going to sit here and be an idle spectator to the diminution, the subversion, the destruction of the Constitution."

Late that evening, an immense crowd had gathered outside the Rayburn Office Building, where the hearings had taken place. Jordan's administrative assistant, Bud Myers, suggested that they take another route to get to her car.

But the freshman knew that she had become part of history. There was no sense running from it. "Are you kidding?" the congresswoman snapped. "We're going to get out there and be with the people!"

Two days later, Barbara Jordan voted to impeach the president. Nixon resigned less than two weeks after that, on August 9, 1974.

Then, in December 1977, it was Jordan's turn to announce that she, too, would be stepping down from office. She did not say why, beyond the oblique observation that "Congress was not, I believe, intended to be a haven for life." In fact, she had been afflicted with multiple sclerosis for some time. Her face had been swollen from medication that very day in 1974 when the strong black woman from the Fifth Ward became an inquisitor on behalf of the Constitution.

No one had noticed then, just as few would recall later, that her tenure in the House had been a scant three terms. Barbara Jordan had found her moment in history—and from those fleeting fifteen minutes she achieved a state of permanence.

It was in 1978, during Barbara Jordan's final year representing the 18th District, that she received an office visit from a recent law school graduate named Sheila Jackson Lee.

The younger woman was thrilled to be in the famed congresswoman's presence. But she did not behave like a starstruck postgrad. She possessed a deep, enunciating manner of speech not unlike Jordan's, and she used it to ask a very basic question: *How do I gain a foothold in Houston the way you did?*

The young woman was actually from Queens, New York. Sheila Jackson Lee's mother was a vocational nurse and her father drew horror comics for Eerie Publications. But her husband, Elwyn Lee, had just taken a job as professor at the University of Houston, in the city of his birth, and the boomtown openness of the Bayou City was appealing to the plainly ambitious Yale and University of Virginia graduate. She lacked her role model's ability to impress higher-ups. Yet it's likely the congresswoman saw something of herself in this hustling, intense young woman who now sought to succeed in a southern community still dominated by white males.

"The way to become relevant," Jordan told her visitor, "is to go meet the icons of the community. Let them tell you what needs to be done in the community. Find out what that is, and do it well."

It was good advice that Sheila Jackson Lee took, more or less. She did in fact seek out Houston icons, beginning with Jordan's friend, the former Watergate special prosecutor Leon Jaworski, who hired her at his law firm. And after an unsteady decade of attempting to find a toehold in local politics, Jackson Lee at last managed to parlay her seat on the Houston City Council into a primary challenge against the 18th District's officeholder in 1994, Craig Washington, and steamrollered the incumbent Democrat. Amid the tidal wave of the Gingrich Revolution, Sheila Jackson Lee arrived in Washington in 1995 as one of the Democrats' few success stories, much as Barbara Jordan had been twenty-two years earlier.

What she did not follow was the part of Jordan's advice that entailed her doing one thing and doing it well. To the consternation of her Democratic colleagues, Sheila Jackson Lee set out to do everything, all the time—a study in ubiquity, a generalist on steroids.

The congressional aide's eyes were pleading as she approached a staffer from the House Rules Committee. "I'm new here," she said. "Could you please come up with three amendments for this bill? *Anything*."

The Rules staffer did not have to ask. This had to be an assistant to Sheila Jackson Lee, the Empress of Amendments.

It was widely believed on both sides of the aisle, and even by Jackson Lee herself, that no one during her sixteen-year tenure could match her sheer volume of amending. To many, this compulsion on Jackson Lee's part was obnoxious. It bogged down and trivialized the craft of legislating. When the Democrats held the majority, they brought bills to the floor that had been fully hashed out by the relevant committee, with no need for further tweaking. To amend it was to concede the bill's imperfection. And now that the Democrats were in the minority and striving to cast the Republicans as extremists, to participate in Republican legislation by amending it was to confer on the bill an imprimatur of bipartisanship.

Jackson Lee took a different view. Something could always be made better. A bill of national scope might often require an added nuance here or there that would benefit her constituents. (Or, in her grandiloquent phraseology: "I should not deny a corner of the world the opportunity to be heard on an amendment.") In an institution of 435 independent contractors, the Houston congresswoman had determined her own way to stay in business as the 18th District's officeholder. Any opportunity to speak on behalf of her constituents (75 percent of whom were black or Hispanic), on any subject, she would lunge at. Clearly they did not care whether she irritated her colleagues in the bargain: Jackson Lee's margin of victory in each election ranged from 30 to 80 percent. She kept winning, and amending.

Indeed, after the famishing year of 2010, when Speaker Pelosi had shut down the amendments process, Sheila Jackson Lee intended to make a banquet out of H.R.1's Continuing Resolution. She offered sixteen amendments, more than any other Democrat. Virtually all of them simply restored programs being cut by the GOP's Continuing Resolution, without offering a cut elsewhere to offset the cost, as was required by the Republican rules. In other words, the amendments were a waste of everyone's time. None was debated or voted on.

In part her serial-amending ways reflected a driven woman's larger quest for exactness. She spoke with exquisite diction and expected the same of her aides. In her office, she demanded that letters be typed just so, that certain documents be printed in particular colors. To dine at a restaurant with her was to witness a legislator amending every dish: *That's not well done like I ordered. The soup is not hot enough. I'd like some olives on my plate, too. And some chili peppers. And a chopped onion.*

But her demands extended well beyond the objective of getting things right, instead suggesting a desire for omnipresence. Jackson Lee belonged to a staggering fifty-two different congressional caucuses and task forces, ranging from the obvious (CBC, Progressive Caucus) to the decidedly esoteric (Friends of Norway Caucus, Songwriters Caucus, Interstate 69 Caucus). She was a reliable presence on the cable TV political broadcasts, whose producers (if no one else) saw the virtue in a congresswoman who would happily speak on any conceivable subject of the day. On the morning of each State of the Union address, Jackson Lee could be counted on to grab a seat on the House floor and hold it all day long, so that she could be seen for a few seconds in the camera frame with whomever the president of the United States happened to be that year. She managed to materialize at nearly every high-profile event worth going to—from the annual White House Correspondents Association Dinner to the final Space Shuttle liftoff at Cape Canaveral—though only through the wheedling of her desperate and bedraggled staffers. Her windy declamations during Democratic caucuses were numbing affairs. One leadership staffer memorialized in his notes a caucus in which Sheila Jackson Lee strode to the microphone and, within a minute, shrunk her audience from approximately one hundred down to twenty.

And then there were the floor statements—and the jar.

The tradition of the jar dated back to the mid-1990s, during Sheila Jackson Lee's early days in the House. Its precise origins were long forgotten, but it began with a congressional aide who brought a jar to work and put a quarter in it once Jackson Lee made a speech on the House floor that day. The jar would then rotate the following day to an adjacent desk. If Jackson Lee spoke, the staffer was obliged to drop a quarter in the jar and move it to another staffer's desk. On the rare day that the Houston congresswoman did not speak, the staffer who had the jar that day was rewarded with all its contents. The Jackson Lee jar concept began to spread, with multiple jars springing up in numerous offices on the Hill, both Republican and Democrat—a rare unifying ritual in a time of divided government.

The jar-passing carried over into the next decade. In John Dingell's office, a fanciful staffer ornamented their Jackson Lee jar with felt embroidery. In Tennessee Congressman Joe Knollenberg's office at some point in 2006, the jar's contents became so heavy and the aides so sick of lugging it from desk to desk that they finally broke down and used all the money to pay for lunch for the entire staff. Rumors, most likely apocryphal, began to spread of hundred-dollar payouts.

It was not that her speeches were nonsensical or poorly conceived. Sheila Jackson Lee was a progressive in the mold of her iconic predecessor Jordan (and Jordan's successor, the famed liberal Mickey Leland, who was killed in a plane crash), and she often spoke with convincing passion on behalf of her otherwise voiceless constituents. The problem was one of ubiquity. Whatever that day's legislative consideration was—health care, energy, the wars, job creation, every single one of the bills being drafted by the twelve Appropriations subcommittees—Jackson Lee could be counted on to speak about it. If there was no legislation on the floor, she would find something else to talk about. Such as: Michael Jackson's funeral. A Super Bowl ad she deemed racist. The ground-breaking of a new stadium for Houston's soccer team. A tape loop of white-noise musings interrupted only by her final sentence—

"I yield back"—which implied that she still had time remaining on the clock when, invariably, she did not.

Early in her career, some of her Democratic friends spoke to the congresswoman about her excessive volubility. *You're diluting your effectiveness. You're smart as hell, but if you want to succeed here in the House, you need to pick one thing and focus on it.* Her friends reported back to the Democratic leadership that Jackson Lee thought the advice was sound. They did not know that Barbara Jordan had given her the same advice two decades prior, and that she had similarly responded with appreciation and then proceeded to ignore it.

On one very meaningful level, the criticism was unfair. Justice was her (primary) "one thing," and the metrics for defending the defenseless were not as cut-and-dried as the acquisition of highway funds or tax loopholes or regulatory exemptions or agricultural subsidies. Whether the subject was racial profiling in a small Texas town, Arizona's harsh immigration bill, or the spread of AIDS in Africa—a grim phenomenon she began speaking about after touring the continent with President Clinton in 1999—Jackson Lee's energies came early and insistently, if seldom with immediate outcome. And on occasions her orating worked to satisfying effect. In the wake of 9/11, when the Transportation Security Administration had to fill 1,200 new security-screening jobs for Houston's two major airports, Jackson Lee browbeat the agency into holding a job fair in the 17th District, which led to the employment of two hundred constituents. And in the early summer days of 2011, when the budget-strapped city of Houston moved to close fifteen of its pools and community centers, the congresswoman hit up two of the big oil firms in her district for $350,000 in donations. The venues stayed open throughout the summer's record-breaking heat wave.

And as for her other "one thing's": The veterans at Houston's Riverside General Hospital being treated for post-traumatic stress disorder, thanks to a $1 million Defense Department grant secured by Jackson Lee, were probably not complaining. The workers at the Houston Ship Channel—a beneficiary of a $99 million federal stimulus grant she helped acquire—were probably not complaining.

At other times, however, the counterproductive nature of her compulsions was painfully apparent. In early May 2011, the congresswoman offered up an amendment to a Republican bill that repealed the school-based health care clinics provided under the Obama health care law. Jackson Lee's amendment would require that the unobligated funds accrued from the repeal be posted on the Department of Health and Human Services website so that the public could see how much money had been saved. Her Republican counterpart on the floor that day, fellow Texan Michael Burgess, applauded the amendment as "an opportunity to increase transparency" and concluded by saying, "I urge an 'aye' vote on the amendment." A voice vote was called for. The ayes had it. Jackson Lee's amendment had won.

Then, as if seized by a demon spirit, Sheila Jackson Lee said, "Mr. Chair, I demand a recorded vote."

The vote was postponed to the next day, during which time whatever momentum of goodwill there was toward the congresswoman and her amendment evaporated. It was defeated, 207–218, with nine apparently annoyed Blue Dog Democrats casting the decisive votes against her. The Democratic whip team stood by their table on the House floor in a Rembrandt-like tableau of stupefaction. Jackson Lee, for her part, fixed her eyes on the board with the losing tally, her oblong face as implacable as the eternal glowers in Statuary Hall.

Though Sheila Jackson Lee had become an inviting target to right-wingers (including outright sexists and racists) and, in any event, did no particular harm to the Democratic brand, there was little sympathy for her among her colleagues. She was a tireless worker who could always be counted on when partnering on legislation or to assist at fundraisers, but her imperious style tended to grate on others. Jackson Lee's abusiveness toward subordinates had been reported on since her earliest days as a congresswoman; the annual poll of Capitol Hill staffers in *Washingtonian* consistently ranked her alongside David Obey and Bill Thomas as "meanest" boss. When she flew home to her district at the end of each workweek, a staffer would await her at the gate with a motorized cart so as to ferry her to her car, though the congresswoman suffered no infirmities—unlike her predecessor Jordan, who nonetheless walked on her own power throughout her days in office. And on a congressional delegation (or CODEL) trip overseas, the other members traveled from one stop to another in a military bus . . . while alongside them, in a black Mercedes provided by the host country, rode Sheila Jackson Lee.

Small wonder, then, that after the midterms of 2010, Jackson Lee failed in her bid to be elected chairwoman of the Congressional Black Caucus. She would later claim that she had "stepped aside" and permitted Emanuel Cleaver to take the post. In fact, the CBC put the matter to a vote. Midway through the balloting, when it was clear that Jackson Lee was headed toward overwhelming defeat, the congresswoman suddenly stood and proclaimed, "I move that we unanimously elect Emanuel Cleaver as our next chairman."

Cleaver was thereby elected. Several members, however, privately voiced their dismay. They wanted the voting to continue. They wanted Sheila Jackson Lee to see the final tally.

CHAPTER FOURTEEN

"You Hard Head"

It was March 2011, and Jeff Duncan wasn't feeling so agreeable anymore.

He and other House conservatives had gone along with Speaker Boehner, Kevin McCarthy, and the Appropriators in agreeing to pare down their Pledge to America from $100 billion in spending cuts to $61 billion. After the four-day marathon of amendments that led to passage of H.R.1 on February 19, the Democrat-controlled Senate defeated it with contemptuous swiftness. The House was back to square one.

Boehner was unworried. "We'll just keep hitting 'em with short-term CRs," he told his Republican colleagues. The Speaker's strategy was to get to $61 billion in increments. With a government shutdown date of March 4 looming, Boehner got President Obama and Senate Majority Leader Reid to agree to a short-term plan that would fund the government through March 18 while cutting another $4 billion from Obama's proposed budget. Duncan and all but six Republicans had gone along with that interim deal.

Still, the drip-drip incrementalism was maddening to Jeff Duncan. At this rate, he wondered how they would ever make a meaningful dent in Washington's monstrous spending apparatus. One voice of dissent was particularly influential to the four South Carolina freshmen—that of Senator Jim DeMint, the state's uberconservative, a patron saint of the Tea Party movement and political godfather to Duncan and the other Four Horsemen. DeMint had announced after the first short-term Continuing Resolution that "this is the last time" he would support such a measure.

On the evening of Friday, March 11, when the House Republicans met for a conference in HC-5 and Boehner announced *another* short-term CR deal—this time, funding the government through April 8 and targeting another $6 billion in cuts—Duncan decided that he'd had enough of the nickel-and-diming. After the meeting broke up, the four South Carolina freshmen huddled with Joe Wilson, the delegation's one senior member. All of them were inclined to vote no on Boehner's deal with the Democrats. The only wavering South Carolinian was Tim Scott, Duncan's roommate. Scott was one of the two freshmen (along with Kristi Noem of South Dakota) who served on the GOP leadership team. Voting against the Speaker's wishes would put him in an uncomfortable spot.

As the South Carolinians were discussing the matter, fellow freshman conservative Steve Southerland walked up. He, too, was nervous about siding against leadership. "Guys, I've got to find a quiet place to meditate and pray on this," Southerland muttered.

"Why not right here?" suggested Scott.

And so the five South Carolinians and the Florida freshman sat down together in a semicircle in the Capitol basement conference room. They bowed their heads. One after the next, each Republican murmured a prayer for their country and their vote. When it came Jeff Duncan's turn, he recited from memory a scripture from the book of Nehemiah: *He gives power to the faint, and to him who has no might he increases strength . . . they shall mount up with wings like eagles . . .*

"You know what?" Tim Scott said when they were done. "God has spoken through my heart. I'm a 'no.'"

The following day, Jeff Duncan was summoned to the whip's office.

Kevin McCarthy regarded the member of his freshman whip team with mild disappointment. "I just need to get a sense of where you are, and why you're a 'no,'" he said.

"The simple answer," replied Duncan, "is there's a guy across the building named Jim DeMint, and he's the barometer by which I'm judged in South Carolina."

He added, "The 'no' is a reflection of how my district feels."

In walked another South Carolinian, Trey Gowdy. He sat next to Duncan. McCarthy asked Gowdy the same question.

"Well, because Jim DeMint is a constituent of mine," Gowdy replied.

McCarthy laughed. "You guys rehearsing your answers together?" he asked.

It was another "continuing education" moment for the whip. The South Carolina freshmen were carving out a niche as the most radical deficit hawks in the House. Good to know—except that McCarthy needed votes.

The previous night during the conference, he had given his most impassioned speech since becoming majority whip. "Look at the headlines from this week," he told his fellow Republicans. He rattled off a few that applauded Boehner's negotiating strategy and that indicated political troubles for various Democrats. "Now, if we don't stay together on this vote," he warned them, "what will the headlines be the next day?

"In baseball, you don't just have guys who swing for the fences," he went on. "Sometimes you bunt. You do what you can to get on base. That's how you get more runs. That's what we're doing here. That's how we win."

McCarthy was addressing all 242 Republicans, but his message was an appeal to Duncan and the eighty-six other freshmen. Instilling in them a sense of loyalty as well as patience in the political process required frequent trips to the whip's vault of metaphors and homilies:

"Reagan made that famous speech, 'Mr. Gorbachev, tear down this wall.' But it didn't happen right then. It happened later, because of that speech. That was Reagan's approach: 'I didn't give up yardage. I always gained yardage.'"

"Political clout, it's like a block of ice. If you just sit on it, all it does is melt. But if you chop it up and put it in different glasses, you reach a lot more people."

"When you're coming around a corner, and you see your friend in a fight, what do you do? First, you jump in and you help beat up the other guy. And then when it's all over you can ask, 'Hey, what was that fight about?'"

When all else failed, McCarthy would squeeze every drop of significance he could manage from the movie *Braveheart*.

He wanted to come off as approachable to the freshmen. He wanted them to hang out in the whip's office, where the walls were covered with black-and-white photographs of the freshmen alongside more senior members, joining them all in a legislative Valhalla. McCarthy himself was in none of those photographs. His ambitions, whatever they were, would remain sublimated.

McCarthy loved the freshmen. Among their largely monochromatic ranks he could discern, if not exactly a Rainbow Coalition, then at least a varied bunch of conservatives full of little surprises. He loved the forthrightness of Jeff Duncan and the other South Carolinians, even if their intransigence on deficit-cutting was becoming a pain in the ass. He loved Blake Farenthold, who had met his wife while standing in line for tickets to a Jimmy Buffett concert. He loved Sean Duffy's relentlessly bright-eyed fighting spirit even as the Democrats were bombarding his district with attack ads in hopes of taking back Dave Obey's seat. He loved how Duffy and Trey Gowdy, a fellow ex-prosecutor, had formed a bromance and were practically inseparable.

He loved the class act that was silver-haired former U.S. attorney Pat Meehan of Pennsylvania—definite Senate material, McCarthy predicted. He loved Diane Black of Tennessee: at sixty older than the other freshman women, and as the wife of a major Aegis Sciences stakeholder, one of the wealthiest members in the House; but Black still drove a well-worn Oldsmobile and had no interest in media attention, only in getting work done. Michael Grimm of New York, on the other hand, clearly enjoyed the spotlight, with his *GQ* wardrobe and his at times intemperate comments to the press; but McCarthy loved the former Marine and FBI undercover agent's Staten Island scrappiness, not to mention Grimm's reverence for his late dad's old roofer buddies, even if it meant that the whip couldn't count on his vote for union-busting bills. He loved the rancher's-daughter backstory of Kristi Noem, and he appreciated the attractive South Dakotan's determination to avoid comparisons to Sarah Palin by focusing on the needs of her district. He loved the pure businessman's vantage point of Mike Kelly, a former Hyundai car dealer, and the jarring soft-spokenness of mammoth former offensive lineman Jon Runyan. He loved the wiliness of physician and Army reservist Joe Heck, who worked all the other docs and veterans in the freshman class and thereby secured enough of their votes to become one of three freshmen on the Steering Committee.

One of McCarthy's two family Labradors had recently died, and when the whip bought his two kids a new puppy, he noticed how the remaining older dog became perky around the rambunctious new household member. McCarthy saw the freshmen having the same effect on many of the senior Republicans. They were emboldened now—they had numbers behind them, but the effect was greater than simply becoming the majority: it was as if they had rediscovered why they themselves had run for Congress, however many years ago.

Of course, their newly acquired feistiness was shaping up to be a big problem for the whip. But the compulsively sunny McCarthy chose to view this reality as a virtue. The foremost regrets in his life were the risks he hadn't taken. When the Berlin Wall collapsed, or when the brave young protesters confronted the Chinese Red Army's tanks on Tiananmen Square, why hadn't young Kevin McCarthy bought an airplane ticket and flown to those countries to teach democracy? And how different would his life have been if he had chosen to serve in the military?

Kevin McCarthy loved how so many of the freshmen were risk-takers. He wasn't going to quash their spirit, even if he had the power to do so.

In McCarthy's view, there were two types of leaders. One was a thermometer, who could accurately discern the temperature in the room. The other type of leader was a thermostat, who could actually *change* the environment. Obama was a thermometer, a reader rather than a shaper of moods—except, of course, when he, Pelosi, and Reid were aggressively ramming a liberal agenda down Americans' throats.

Or, to dispense with the temperature-taking metaphor: McCarthy believed that humans are all products of their experience. The whip viewed himself as an entrepreneur, a creator of wealth and jobs (though in fact he had spent nearly his entire adult life in politics). On the other hand, look at Obama's experiences. Community organizer. Lawyer. Taking money from those who have and giving it to those who have not. *He was a wealth redistributor.* The man had no experience in how America prospers. And, thought McCarthy: *He focuses too much on being liked. Not enough on solving problems.*

McCarthy himself invested considerable energy in being liked. He knew he had a problem with some of the senior members. Boehner's old friends didn't trust the upwardly mobile Californian—above all because of his alignment with the other two members of the Young Guns troika, Eric Cantor and Budget Committee chairman Paul Ryan. McCarthy worked hard to gain the Speaker's confidence. He met with him at least once a day—maintaining his grin while thinking, *How do I always end up sitting in the direction where he's blowing his cigarette smoke?*—and they texted even more frequently. "Touching gloves," Boehner called it. And in turn, McCarthy had arranged for the entire freshman class to meet weekly with the Speaker, so that he could get a sense of what they were thinking while the new arrivals could get a dose of the House CEO's gruff wisecracking:

"Arrghh, your tie's too short . . . What's up with the hair? . . . Argghh, quit kissing up."

McCarthy also organized getting-to-know-you dinners between freshman and senior members. To break the ice, the whip liked to throw out a question like "What's the first concert you attended?" (One elder responded: "The Beach Boys." A freshman gave the same reply—except that the Beach Boys he had seen contained almost none of the original members. McCarthy's first concert had been Johnny Cash at the Crystal Palace in Bakersfield.) Or, "What was the most embarrassing thing that happened to you in college?" (One congresswoman admitted that she was nearly arrested for taking a lion from a petting zoo that was going out of business.)

During another dinner, McCarthy asked everyone, "What was the first job you had?" Jim Gerlach, a five-term congressman from Chester County, Pennsylvania, said his had been at a steel mill. Then Gerlach added, "You know, this is something we should convey better. The Democrats are labeling us as defenders of big corporations. But they're wealthier than we are—we're small businessmen. What I think we ought to do is go back to our districts and spend a day doing the first job we ever did."

This is a project we've gotta do, the whip thought.

"I love chaos!" McCarthy was heard to exclaim on the House floor earlier in the session. The whip tended not to get riled up about things. And so he didn't lose his cool when, after delivering his let's-get-people-on-base-and-score-more-runs speech at the Republican conference, fully fifty-four Republicans voted "no" on the second short-term Continuing Resolution—which would therefore have resulted in an embarrassing defeat for Speaker Boehner had several dozen Democrats not bailed him out by voting for the CR. Instead, McCarthy organized another dinner.

His guests were the two dozen or so freshmen who served as assistant whips, and Texas congressman Sam Johnson, the eighty-year-old Vietnam veteran who had led the House in a moment of silence back in February. The venue was Ruth's Chris Steak House, Johnson's favorite.

For three hours, they listened to the elder congressman recount his days as a fighter pilot and his years of torment with fellow POWs in the Hanoi Hilton. One of the freshman whips, Adam Kinzinger, was himself an Air Force pilot whose interrogation-resistance training had largely been based on what Sam Johnson had actually withstood.

The subject of the CRs—or anything political—never once came up. Nonetheless, McCarthy had made his point. *It's about being part of something bigger than yourself. It's about looking after each other. It's about unity.*

But the unity concept wasn't entirely taking hold.

Boehner was getting frustrated. He had been through this government shutdown stalemate before—in 1995 and 1996, during the Newt Gingrich years. If the American public tended to fault Democrats for loving government a little too much, they weren't likely to blame Obama and Reid if it shut down. In the Speaker's view, he was coming back with billions in federal spending reductions every time he emerged from a White House meeting. Then on the House floor his fellow Republicans would dismiss it as pocket change.

"I've been sticking my neck out—I'm getting a little tired of being abandoned," Boehner complained about the GOP defections during a conference.

Raul Labrador, the Idaho Tea Party freshman, practically lunged at the microphone. "I don't think we're abandoning you at all," he said. "I feel like you're abandoning us."

From the back of the conference came a chorus of low boos. Still, Labrador's show of disrespect to the House leader reflected a disgruntlement over Boehner's seeming passivity that many conservative Republicans privately shared. Jeff Duncan wasn't among them. He blamed his colleagues, not the Speaker. They should have refused to budge on the original demand to cut $100 billion. Instead, they had given Boehner a weak hand to play.

On the House floor, chief deputy whip Peter Roskam buttonholed Duncan. "So do you just intend to blindly follow Jim DeMint?" he asked the freshman.

"Peter, that's not fair," said Duncan. "On this issue, DeMint's right."

Fissures were emerging throughout the Republican ranks. As frustration set in over the immovable Senate, on April Fool's Day Eric Cantor brought to the floor the Government Shutdown Prevention Act. Its intent, according to Cantor, was that "the Senate has to act prior to the expiration of the C.R. If it does not act, H.R.1 becomes the law of the land." In effect, the bill was proposing that the upper body be stripped of its legislative functions.

The bill was greeted with derision, and not just by liberals. Kevin McCarthy approached Blake Farenthold on the House floor to explain how the legislation was not as ridiculous as it was being portrayed.

The Texas freshman brushed him off. "I'm a lawyer, okay?" he snapped. "I studied this stuff. It's unconstitutional."

On April 8, Boehner proposed a short-term Continuing Resolution that would keep the government running for only another week and would entail another $10 billion in domestic cuts—but would also fund the Pentagon for an entire year. The gambit would force the Democrats either to accept the painful cuts or to vote against paying America's warriors.

Allen West was appalled by the cynicism. The former Army lieutenant colonel blasted Boehner in a press release. "I am disgusted at the perception that the leaders in my own party who did not move a defense bill earlier and are now using the men and women in uniform, the individuals who are defending our freedom, as a way to pass yet another continuing resolution," it said. Though West voted for the CR "for my brothers and sisters in uniform," he conveyed his "disappointment in my own leadership."

Boehner never said anything to West about his missive. The same day that Boehner's short-term CR was passed by the House (and, predictably, rejected by the Senate), West walked off the House floor and approached a reporter he knew. He looked uncharacteristically stricken.

"I thought I'd let you know—I had a death threat," he said. "About two hours ago."

He went on to explain that someone had sent a package of white powder to his Fort Lauderdale office. A letter inside the envelope made reference to anthrax. The FBI was already on the scene.

"Oh, I'm fine," he insisted. "But my girl who opened it . . ."

West did not appear fine—though he momentarily chuckled when recalling that a few minutes ago, Democratic Minority Whip Steny Hoyer had quoted on the House floor West's denunciation of Boehner for using the troops as pawns . . . and had referred to West as "the representative of South Carolina"—apparently confusing him with Tim Scott.

Smirking, he said, "I know all us colored boys look alike. If a Republican had said that, they would've killed him."

Then his thoughts returned to the package sent to his office. His eyes narrowed.

"I'm sick of these attacks," West said. "They're the ones talking about civility . . ."

Steny Hoyer received a call from his counterpart Kevin McCarthy on Wednesday the thirteenth of April. The Democrat had hosted a lunch in his office with McCarthy shortly after the latter had been elected majority whip. Hoyer suggested that the two try to find some areas they could work on together. McCarthy responded that he had often partnered with Democrats while serving in the California State Assembly. The lunch broke up, and the two men had done no business together since then—until now.

McCarthy wanted to talk to Hoyer about a final Continuing Resolution that Boehner, Obama, and Reid had agreed to and that would fund the government until September 15. The good news for conservatives was that the CR contained a proviso that would ban federal funding of abortions in the District of Columbia. The bad news was that the final figure agreed to was $38.5 billion in spending reductions. That sum was far closer to what the Cardinals on the House Appropriations Committee had originally proposed than the $100 billion prescribed by the Pledge to America. McCarthy knew that he wasn't going to have enough Republican votes to pass the measure. He told Hoyer that he might need as many as seventy Democrats.

"Are you guys gonna fight this thing?" McCarthy wanted to know.

"Your president agreed to this. Do you view it in that way, or in some other way? That's what I have to know."

Hoyer promised McCarthy that he would furnish the necessary votes. But McCarthy knew that Hoyer would make the Republicans put up all their votes first. Later that day, word leaked to the media that he had asked for help from the minority whip. McCarthy thought that was classless on Hoyer's part.

But he had other worries. That day, an Associated Press story analyzing the CR had concluded that the bill would only cut an anemic $351 *million* in 2011. The whip's "yes" count began to plummet. Several members, already exhausted from the two-month slog, demanded to know whether Speaker Boehner had been duped by the White House.

McCarthy hastily organized a conference in one of the Capitol offices. Republican budget expert Douglas Holtz-Eakin walked the Republicans through the proposed cuts. The $38.5 billion was a legit figure, he maintained.

"Look, we all want more," the whip told his colleagues. "But you should be proud of what you've done here. We're one-half of one-third of the federal government. And what's happened here no one thought was possible."

Enough Republicans agreed. On the afternoon of April 14, the final Continuing Resolution passed, with the help of thirty-five Democrats— and despite the opposition of fifty-nine Republicans.

John Boehner happened to be on the House floor and walking down the aisle when he bumped into one of the Republican defectors, Jeff Duncan.

"Mr. Speaker," the freshman said in greeting, and offered his hand.

Boehner accepted the handshake. Then he pulled Duncan toward him and looked him in the eye.

"You hard head," the Speaker said.

Duncan decided to take it as a compliment.

The entire Continuing Resolution experience, Republican chief deputy whip Peter Roskam would later say, "was a miserable experience, like pushing a wet noodle." The new majority would immediately reward itself, however, with a more gratifying prospect—one in which the House wouldn't be squabbling over billions in cuts, but rather, trillions.

The author of the House Republican budget was Paul Ryan. Until very recently, Ryan had been an energetic advocate for fiscal reform but hardly a partisan warrior. His congressional district in southern Wisconsin was strongly pro-union. Though an avowed social conservative, in 2007 Ryan parted company with most Republicans (including Boehner, Cantor, and McCarthy) by voting for a Democratic bill that banned employment discrimination based on sexual orientation. He often spoke about the widening income gap between rich and poor. Having endured racist comments from friends while dating an African-American woman in college, Ryan was mindful of struggles within the black community and regularly accompanied Congressman John Lewis on the latter's annual pilgrimages to Selma, Alabama, where in 1965 Lewis and other civil rights marchers had courageously endured beatings by state troopers on Edmund Pettus Bridge.

Ryan was an avid bow hunter who skinned his own prey and was a fan of the works of Ayn Rand—even toying with her Objectivist embrace of man's "reason as his only absolute," before settling on Catholicism. Offsetting his straight-arrow retro handsomeness and perky informality were his dolorous eyes, seemingly still haunted by having discovered, at the age of sixteen, the body of his father, who had died of a heart attack. He frequently referenced his Tipperary, Ireland, roots and his three young children, who lived back in Janesville with his wife, Janna, a former tax attorney whom he first asked out shortly after seeing her wearing camouflage at a congressional Sportsmen's Caucus dinner.

Most of all, however, Ryan was a numbers geek and a Washingtonian—and only in the latter city could the former confer rock stardom. Straight out of college he became the economic advisor to Senator Bob Kasten. Later he went to work for Empower America, a nonprofit group founded by prominent cultural conservative Bill Bennett and supply-side guru Congressman Jack Kemp. The earnest young Republican supplemented his income by working at the Washington Sports Club and tending bar at a Capitol Hill restaurant called Tortilla Coast. Elected to Congress in 1998 at the age of twenty-eight, Ryan wasted little time impressing fellow House Republicans as a serious, almost monastic young fellow who stayed up nights on a rollaway bed in his Longworth

Building office leering at actuarial tables like soft porn. Following liberal Democrat Barney Frank's advice to him to "pick two or three issues and really focus on them," the freshman staked a claim as the Hill's most vigorous conservative "budgeteer."

In 2000, Democratic presidential candidate Al Gore pilfered Ryan's proposal to preserve Social Security trust funds in a "lock box." In 2006, Ryan turned down the offer to be President Bush's new budget director. Later that year, when the Democrats retook the House, the disheartened new minority turned the page by allowing Ryan to leapfrog over a dozen more senior Republicans and become their Budget Committee ranking member.

Despite all the accolades, Paul Ryan had functioned as little more than policy arm candy for his party. His Social Security lock box proposal had gone nowhere in the Republican-controlled House. Instead of reducing the federal deficit, as Ryan had advocated, the Bush administration opted for sizable tax cuts. Ryan had been among the few GOP House members to enthusiastically promote Bush's Social Security semiprivatization scheme and was chagrined to see his colleagues "hit the brakes" on the president's proposal, while Ryan described himself as "obviously a gas-pedal guy."

As the new Budget Committee ranking member in 2007, Paul Ryan earned the right to produce the GOP's budgetary alternative to that of the Democratic majority. Strikingly, forty Republicans—20 percent of the entire conference—found his budget too austere and sided with the Democrats in defeating it. Undaunted, the Budget Committee ranking member went at it again in 2008—this time with a budget that featured what would become, for better or for worse, Ryan's signature planks: reconfiguring Medicare and Medicaid. Again, 20 percent of the Republicans voted against their own budget. A month later, Ryan refined and repackaged his budget, dubbing it a "Road Map for America's Future." By the time it went to the House floor on April 2, 2009, Ryan was calling his budget "The Path to American Prosperity." Notwithstanding the new label, precisely the same number of Republicans voted against it as they had the previous year. Among those who took a dim view of Ryan's entitlement-reforming budgets were Fred Upton and Joe Barton, the two top Republicans on the Energy and Commerce Committee, which held jurisdiction over most health care issues.

Even in the summer of 2010, as Tea Party bloggers and conservative columnists began to throw their support behind Ryan's Road Map, his party's top two leaders could muster only tepid praise. Boehner told reporters, when asked about Ryan's proposed budget, "There are parts of it that are well done. Other parts I have some doubts about, in terms of how good the policy is." When conservative talk show host Laura Ingraham asked Cantor if he would sign on to Ryan's Road Map, the second-ranking Republican refused to give a direct answer.

Oddly, the only public official in Washington who seemed willing to publicly give Ryan his props was Barack Obama. While visiting a Republican conference in January 2010, the president waved a copy of the Road Map over his head and said, "I think Paul, for example, head of the Budget Committee, has looked at the budget and has made a serious proposal. I've read it. I can tell you what's in it. And there are some ideas in there that I would agree with, but there are some ideas that we should have a healthy debate about, because I don't agree with them."

A month later, shortly before passage of the Affordable Health Care Act, Ryan showed his gratitude toward Obama during a health care summit by assailing the bill to the president's face as "full of gimmicks and smoke and mirrors," ticking off its quantitative errors and then characterizing it with the Frank Luntz–tested phrase "government takeover of health care." Obama stared icily at the Budgeteer throughout his harangue.

By that time, however, Ryan had found the only ally he needed in Kevin McCarthy.

They complemented each other perfectly. McCarthy knew that the Republicans couldn't take back the House if they remained "the party of no," bereft of ideas. Ryan, for his part, had ideas but little expertise in selling them. Out of deference to Boehner and other senior members, McCarthy kept the Road Map out of the 2010 Pledge to America. And that summer, when Ryan appeared on McCarthy's interactive website "America Speaks Out" to tell viewers about his plans to restore fiscal discipline in Washington, he did not utter a word about Medicare or Medicaid. Already GOP congressional candidates like Sean Duffy and Gabrielle Giffords's opponent Jesse Kelly were taking heat for their earlier endorsement of the Road Map, with its controversial Medicare reform provision, and were furiously backpedaling. There was an election to be won, and McCarthy's tastes for risk did not run to kamikaze missions.

Even after reclaiming the House majority, McCarthy knew to proceed with caution. Budgets were historically difficult things to pass. Ryan liked to call them "moral documents." But moral stances tended to give way to political reality. Denny Hastert had told Ryan that his heaviest lift as House Speaker had been the Deficit Reduction Act of 2005, which barely passed the House and the Senate even though Republicans dominated both. In 2010, Democratic Budget Committee chairman John Spratt had met with every Democratic caucus and articulated the selling points of Obama's hefty $1.4 trillion budget. But the younger members in particular resisted—arguing that they hadn't been around when some of the big-ticket items were voted on—and then–Majority Leader Steny Hoyer finally told Spratt, "It's fruitless. We can't win if we take it to the floor." The Democrats elected instead to offer no budget at all that year. The Budget chairman was thereafter mocked on the campaign trail for failing to do his job and on November 2 was crushed by Jeff Duncan's South Carolina compatriot Mick Mulvaney.

McCarthy was optimistic, however. He had seen enough of the hot-blooded class of 2010 to believe that they could be brought on board with Ryan's budget, so long as it wasn't rammed down their throats. And he had also witnessed the Budgeteer's adroitness with PowerPoint presentations during freshman orientation and the Republican retreat—no one knew this stuff better than Paul Ryan. If McCarthy could create a forum where his GOP colleagues could interact with Ryan, much as he had done with his America Speaks Out project, then they would become invested in the Path to Prosperity and ultimately support it. He suggested to Ryan that they host a series of small-scale "listening sessions" in the whip's office.

Throughout February, March, and early April, upwards of twenty listening sessions took place in H-107, the Office of the Majority Whip, in groups no larger than fifteen Republicans. Ryan would lead off by producing his dire charts and graphs. *Our nation is $14 trillion in debt . . . Since Obama took office, nondefense discretionary spending has jumped 24 percent—84 percent if you include the stimulus . . . The EPA's budget has gone up 36 percent in that time frame . . . Social Security, Medicare, and Medicaid consume over 40 percent of the budget and will* *soon crowd out everything else . . . If it stays on its current fiscal path, the United States will be unable to afford its role as an economic and military superpower . . .*

Ryan's Path to Prosperity, he told those gathered, would "save Medicare" by providing those under the age of fifty-four with a subsidy known as "premium support"—he assiduously avoided the politically toxic term *voucher*—to help purchase a coverage option from a private insurer. It would also "repair a broken Medicaid system" by shifting the federal burden over to the states and compensating them with block grants.

The freshmen showed up to the listening sessions eager to slash spending. To Ryan's delight, they pushed for additional austerity measures: reducing farm subsidies, creating an attrition policy to downsize the federal workforce, squeezing corporate welfare. But most important, they required very little persuasion when the topic turned to Medicare and Medicaid. Ryan and McCarthy found themselves whispering to each other during the sessions, "Wow. We can go further on entitlements. If we don't, these guys probably won't even support the bill."

McCarthy knew that it wasn't enough to sell the Republican conference on what Ryan was up to. He had seen how conservative think tanks like Heritage Action for America had given low grades to a number of the freshmen for not siding with every single cost-cutting amendment during the H.R.1 debate. So as to foreclose another gruesome public spectacle of conservatives eating their own, the whip office conducted sidebar listening sessions with every right-of-center opinion-maker of significance.

The result was a Greek chorus of affirmation. From Grover Norquist's Americans for Tax Reform came the proclamation, "Paul Ryan's Budget Is What a REAL Conservative Budget Looks Like!" The Cato Institute labeled the budget "a huge opportunity to improve health care." And Ryan's seventy-three-page budget plan concluded with a seal of approval from the Heritage Foundation: the Path to Prosperity, the think tank decreed, "would significantly strengthen economic performance throughout the economy and dramatically improve federal fiscal results."

There was one disquieting contrarian: Charles Krauthammer, the highly influential *Washington Post* columnist and preeminent conservative thinker. Krauthammer termed Ryan's budget "recklessly bold" and tantamount to a "suicide note." The columnist clearly viewed the Budget Committee chairman as naïve for believing that Obama would actually engage in an honest, high-minded debate about America's fiscal future rather than launch a scare campaign about how Ryan and the GOP were seeking to end Medicare. His view was shared by many of the House Republicans' more senior members. When one of them learned that Ryan's budget would overhaul Medicare, he told chief deputy whip Roskam, "It's been great serving with you—I'm about to become a former member of Congress."

At least one senior member's major concern was addressed. Said NRCC chairman Pete Sessions during a conference, "Please—take on Medicare or take on Social Security. But not both." And so despite Paul Ryan's urgent cry in 2005 that by 2017 America would "no longer have enough money coming in to pay off all the benefits" for Social Security, the Path to Prosperity left the latter matter largely unaddressed.

The dramatic overhauls of Medicare and Medicaid remained unsettling to many. Boehner's friend and fellow Ohioan Steve LaTourette vigorously argued in conferences that the risks Ryan was taking were entirely unnecessary. "You could write a budget on a single piece of paper," LaTourette said. Since almost any Republican budget would almost certainly be defeated in the Senate, why put details out there that the opposition could demagogue?

LaTourette was a member of the minority-within-the-majority Tuesday Group, like Jo Ann Emerson and about forty other Republican moderates. Emerson had approached both Ryan and McCarthy with an idea. "Look, I know you've got groups like Heritage that say the budget is wonderful, but everyone's going to say they're biased," Emerson said. "Before you introduce it, why don't you take it to someone like [the accounting firm] DeLoitte so that they can verify that your budget does what you say it does?"

Both the whip and the Budget Committee chairman responded enthusiastically to Jo Ann Emerson's suggestion. But if any such independent vetting ever took place, the results of it were never announced to McCarthy and Ryan's fellow Republicans.

• • •

McCarthy and Ryan often worked out together in the House gym in the basement of the Rayburn Building. The Budgeteer conducted a morning exercise regimen with a few of his Republican colleagues called P90X, which involved outsmarting one's muscles by varying the workouts so that one's body would not adapt to a routine—seemingly an exercise that only a brainiac could love, except that McCarthy had lost twenty-eight pounds participating in P90X.

After a workout on the morning of Wednesday, April 13, Ryan told McCarthy that he had been invited, along with House GOP conference chairman Jeb Hensarling and Ways and Means chairman Dave Camp—all of them members of the so-called Bowles-Simpson Commission, appointed by Obama to address fiscal reform—to attend an address on the budget by the president at George Washington University.

"You want my advice?" the whip asked. "Why go down there? We invited him to the conference last year, and he just attacked you!"

McCarthy's view of what had taken place at the GOP conference was more than a little bit exaggerated. But he felt protective toward Ryan, whom he regarded as almost above reproach. "If there's ever been a person put at the right place at the right time, it's Paul," he would later say. His colleague was all about policy: a thinker, an economist who burned the midnight oil digesting data, an honest seeker of solutions, not a crass politician like Obama (or himself). Every time Ryan opened his mouth, the whip learned a new fact. In Kevin McCarthy parlance, it was a continuing education to hang out with the guy.

Ryan shrugged. "If the president invites you and you can go, you go." It was about the institution, not the man occupying it, in the view of the Budget Committee chairman. Besides, the White House staff and other Democrats had told Ryan, *You're going to really like what he has to say about Social Security*. Ryan assumed that, after the tax cuts during the December 2010 lame-duck session and the Continuing Resolution agreement a few days ago, the president's speech would amount to a third installment of engagement with Republicans. He was led to believe that Obama really wanted him to be there.

A senior White House official would later claim that the president and his speechwriters had been unaware that Ryan had been invited to the event. Obama's speech that afternoon amounted to a stern rebuke of the Path to Prosperity. "It's a vision that says America can't afford to keep the promise we've made to care for our seniors . . . Put simply, it ends Medicare as we know it . . . Many are someone's grand-parents who wouldn't be able to afford nursing home care without Medicaid . . . Some are middle-class families who have children with autism or Down's syndrome . . . These are the Americans we'd be telling to fend for themselves . . ."

Ryan sat and tried not to explode. The attack felt both gratuitous and personal to him. As he would later say, " 'Autism,' 'kids with Down's syndrome,' 'maybe your grandparents'—that's demagoguery. That's rank demagoguery, and it's beneath the office."

McCarthy didn't want to say "I told you so . . ." He wasn't the least bit surprised that the president had smacked down Ryan. It seemed to the whip that Obama was incapable of showing leadership. *He sits back and lets everything come to him—and then he decides on what political posture to take.*

Obama had made a strategic mistake, McCarthy thought, picking a fight with Paul Ryan. "I think Ryan's in his head," he would say. "Think about it. Ryan's a young guy. Ryan's risen fast. Ryan's got a great family. Ryan's got a lot of comparisons to the rise of where the president is. It's not so smart to raise him up by picking him as an enemy."

Predicted the whip: "If he picks a budget fight with Paul, Paul will beat him."

McCarthy was starting to feel sorry for Chris Van Hollen. Good guy, smart guy, wrong party.

"You're never going to be in play to win the majority as long as you keep your old leadership," the whip told the Maryland Democrat on the floor one day. "I'm not worried about you guys till the day I see one of you start a Young Guns program. Whoever does that is gonna be the next leader of your party. But someone has to hold the flag and charge the hill. And he'll need someone behind him so in case he gets shot, the other guy can grab the flag."

Van Hollen smiled and said nothing. McCarthy wondered if the nonresponse meant that in addition to being a good and smart guy, Van Hollen viewed himself as more of a Senate guy.

Chris Van Hollen had a number of options available. After he had served only two terms, a new leadership post, Assistant to the Speaker, was created for him in 2006. He had been chairman of the House Democrats' political arm, the Democratic Congressional Campaign Committee (DCCC), in 2008, and at Pelosi's insistence he remained at that post so as to minimize the damage during the disastrous 2010 cycle. The Democratic leader loved Van Hollen. He was progressive in his politics but moderate in tone—a gentlemanly and unflappable though tenacious debater. It was widely assumed that the fifty-two-year-old Marylander could write his own ticket: senator, governor, or perhaps one day Speaker. Or perhaps something even bigger.

At the moment, however, Van Hollen was the Democrats' ranking member on the Budget Committee—Paul Ryan's sparring partner. The Democrats saw the Ryan budget, with its "voucherization" of Medicare, as a breathtaking overreach by the Republicans and a glorious political opportunity for the minority. Many in the Democratic caucus argued that when Majority Leader Cantor brought the budget to the floor, their energy should be devoted entirely to condemning it. Van Hollen could sympathize with that viewpoint. He, too, found it galling that so many editorial writers lauded Ryan's "courage" in producing a budget that cut Medicaid for the most powerless people in society by $700 billion while reducing the corporate income tax and refusing to ask the wealthiest Americans to pay additional taxes to help bring down the deficit. And he was amazed by the disingenuousness of Ryan claiming that his Medicare "premium support" plan mirrored Congress's own health care plan. In fact, the way the Ryan budget saved money was in part *because* the government's contribution would remain flat for seniors, unlike the 28 cents on every dollar of coverage that congressmen were guaranteed. In other words, the Ryan budget got its money by *not* supporting the premiums as they got higher.

Still, Van Hollen argued in caucuses, the Democrats needed to show that they, too, were serious about deficit reduction—that they, too, had a plan. And not just Obama's plan, which was really only, to put it charitably, a "framework" that the Congressional Budget Office couldn't score because it lacked any meaningful details. No, the House Democrats needed to do the same thing that Paul Ryan's Republicans did when they were in the minority. They needed to put out an alternative budget.

Many in the caucus thought that the strategy was too risky—inviting attacks from the opposition when all the focus should be on the Ryan plan's shortcomings. But Chris Van Hollen's argument prevailed with Nancy Pelosi. For the first time in two years, the Democrats would be bringing a budget to the House floor.

Friday afternoon, April 15, 2011—the one hundredth day of the 112th Congress—found the People's House at its most pungent. For once, the visitors' gallery contained nearly a hundred onlookers. Kevin McCarthy strolled into the chamber, waving and slapping backs as if entering a favorite watering hole. McCarthy in fact drank very little—his grandfather had been an alcoholic and he believed himself to have an addictive personality—and so the House floor was the closest thing to his neighborhood bar, where he could quench his thirst for human contact.

The whip stood beside his committee on the floor and surveyed the House's tacit seating chart. Near the back of the right side sat the Texas delegation—and close to them, Raul Labrador, Justin Amash, Steve Southerland, and other hard-right freshmen. He could find at a glance the Tuesday Group moderates, or a clutch of freshmen women like Renee Ellmers and Ann Marie Buerkle, or the South Carolinians, or (as if there were even a point in reaching out to them) the twin contrarians Ron Paul and Walter Jones. And off to the far right, often by himself, sat Allen West, content to be alone. Just on the other side of the aisle in the back, the remaining tatters of the Blue Dogs—now, with the absence of Gabby Giffords and the resignation of Jane Harman, an all-male coalition except for Loretta Sanchez. Near the very front, the two ancient Michiganders, John Dingell and Dale Kildee, saying nothing and wearing identically neutral countenances.

McCarthy's almost hypnotically untroubled expression betrayed no hint of the morning's difficulties. Unbeknownst to him, one of his staffers in the whip's office had sent out an email to other Republican aides the previous morning, before the final vote on the Continuing Resolution. The email instructed the staffers to tell their bosses not to be "traitors" to the party when casting their vote. A photograph of actress Jane Fonda in her war-protesting "Hanoi Jane" mode was attached to the email. Some of the recipients were amused. Many were not.

At that morning's conference, McCarthy apologized for the email.

"That came out of my office, and I take responsibility for it," the whip said. (Later he fired the offending staffer.)

Feelings among the Republicans had been raw for weeks leading up to the conference. Many who had dutifully supported leadership by voting for the CRs were angry at Michele Bachmann, Steve King, Louie Gohmert, and Indiana conservative Mike Pence for leaving conferences midway and immediately giving interviews to reporters about the lousy deals Boehner was getting from the White House. At this morning's conference, Arkansas freshman Tim Griffin stood up and said, "Just because a colleague votes the other way doesn't mean he has to then go stick a thumb in my eye." Griffin spoke admiringly of the South Carolinians. "They vote their way, but you don't ever see them criticizing the rest of us."

The normally taciturn ex-offensive lineman Jon Runyan hulked over the microphone. Without referring specifically to any of his colleagues, the New Jersey freshman pointedly said, "You know, when I was playing for the Philadelphia Eagles, we didn't start losing till Terrell Owens joined the team. It only takes one guy to bring down a locker room."

Steve LaTourette whispered to a colleague, "Most of the ones who need to be hearing this aren't here."

Bachmann, however, was. She went to the microphone and, to the bewilderment of several present, applauded Runyan's remarks.

McCarthy was also glad to hear the freshman speak up, though for a different reason. He'd been hosting a dinner at the Capitol Hill restaurant Luigi's the night before. Runyan had been one of the invitees and had shared the Terrell Owens anecdote. "You've got to tell that story to the conference tomorrow morning," the whip had urged him.

It was in fact McCarthy's idea to stage the conference that morning. "We've got a problem with our members," he had warned Boehner. "We shouldn't let it fester."

Listening to Runyan, Griffin, and others vent their frustrations, McCarthy was secretly delighted. He thought, *This is how any family does it. You air it out. Everybody respects it, and you grow stronger.*

Three hours later, the House was gaveled to order, and debate on the budgets proceeded.

As a kind of undercard to the main event, Raul Grijalva, the chairman of the minority's Progressive Caucus, presented its own budget for floor debate. A freshman, Mo Brooks of Alabama, responded by say-ing, "We are at risk of insolvency and bankruptcy because the socialist members of this body choose to spend money that we do not have!"

From the other side, a livid Keith Ellison jumped up and raised a point of order. "I would like the gentleman's words taken down for the reference to certain members of this body as socialists," he declared.

Begrudgingly, Brooks stood up and moved "to strike the particular use of one word that the folks on the other side of the aisle have ob-jected to."

Debate then moved to the Republican Study Committee's alterna-tive budget, far leaner than the Ryan plan, as it proposed to freeze all nondefense discretionary spending to 2008 levels. A great number of House Republicans found the RSC budget to be austere in the extreme. Jeff Duncan was given a minute to articulate his support for it.

Holding up a prop, the South Carolinian said, "Mr. Chairman, folks, no prepared remarks, no fancy speeches. I brought with me a financial calculator. And regardless of how you calculate the numbers, America is spending too much money."

He rattled along in his auctioneer's cadence—concluding with, "Let's stop the spending insanity here in Washington, D.C., and let's do what we tell the folks back home we are going to do, and let's get our fiscal house in order."

The two budgets were then put to a roll call vote. First, the Progres-sive Caucus budget was defeated, with only its seventy-seven members voting for it. Then came the RSC budget. For this vote, Steny Hoyer had hatched a plan.

The Democratic minority whip knew that the Republicans would be throwing their weight behind the Ryan budget plan. But Hoyer also suspected that the RSC's 170 or so conservative members would want to show Tea Party groups and other right wing advocates that after the whole CR saga, they would never again vote down any plan that dra-matically reduced federal spending. Before the vote on the Ryan bud-get, they would all cast a symbolic vote for the RSC budget—expecting, of course, that the remaining Republicans would join with the Demo-crats in defeating it. Unless . . .

"Let's get everybody to vote 'present' on the RSC amendment," Hoyer instructed his whip team two hours before the vote. His deputies then fanned out and hovered by each door to the chamber. As a Democrat prepared to walk in, members of the minority whip team would whisper the plan to them.

McCarthy squinted at the tally board as dozens of the seldom-used letter *P* instantly popped up next to the names of dozens of Democrats. A number of Republicans began to murmur in confusion. Meanwhile, Jesse Jackson Jr. and other Democrats began to scurry up and down the aisles, no longer bothering to whisper anymore: "Change your vote to 'present'!"

Dingell's face turned sour when a whip gave him the instructions. "That's a pussy vote!" he snarled. But he did as told.

The Democrats had 172 members voting "present" instead of "no." That left the RSC budget with having more votes for it than against it—which, if that remained the case, would become the House's ipso facto budget, with the Ryan budget not even given an opportunity to pass.

Clever—keeps us on our toes, thought McCarthy. His whip team began to plead with several RSC members to change their "yes" to "no" so that their budget would not pass and they could then proceed to the Ryan budget. The Democrats hooted and cheered as Republicans like Louie Gohmert and Tim Scott abandoned their original positions. The RSC budget was defeated, 119 to 13.

Van Hollen then presented the Democratic minority's alternative budget—one that reduced discretionary spending while also raising taxes on the wealthy. Ryan began his response by complimenting his opponent. "It's not always that the minority offers an alternative budget," he said. "In fact, I know there are a lot of pressures not to do that. So I think Mr. Van Hollen is to be commended, and his very capable staff, for actually proposing an alternative. That's important." Van Hollen nodded his appreciation, and Ryan then proceeded with his criticisms that the cuts were far too shallow and the tax burden far too deep. All 236 Republicans present, plus twenty-three Democrats (most of them Blue Dogs), voted against it.

The main event was now at hand. Before speaking on behalf of his budget, Paul Ryan said, "I yield two minutes to the gentleman from California, the distinguished majority whip."

McCarthy rose and spoke into the microphone at the committee table. "What we are taking up today is the point of where this country goes," he said. After a few words about the debt and how the Path to Prosperity would address it, he then repeated one of his favorite binary characterizations: "Today could be the day that we create the great American comeback, or it could be the day that America goes into the long fade into history. The floor is made up of a microcosm of America— and all of America knows that we have to control the situation we are in.

"So today, a 'yes' vote is for jobs, for energy independence, and a new Path to Prosperity."

Suddenly, from the visitors' gallery, a loud youthful male voice semi-melodically bellowed out: *"Oh why can't you see . . . when you sell out the earth . . ."*

Rapping his gavel, the Speaker pro tempore, Republican Phil Gingrey, declared, "The Chair notes a disturbance in the gallery which is in contravention of the laws and rules of the House!"

"Oh say can't you see it's my country you're destroying . . ."

"The sergeant at arms will remove the person responsible for the disturbance and restore order to the gallery!"

The young man was pulled out of the audience and hustled out of the chamber by Capitol security.

Gingrey rapped the gavel several times more. It was Van Hollen's turn. "Mr. Chairman, we are turning back the clock," he said. "We're turning back the clock on progress and we're turning back the clock on—"

"If you look through my eyes . . ."

Another young man wearing a T-shirt was hoisted out of the gallery.

Van Hollen gazed pleasantly ahead and waited for order to be restored. "We see different paths and make different choices to—"

"Oh say can you see that the earth is in pain . . ." This time a young woman's singsong.

"Clear the gallery!" several Republicans hollered out as she was hauled off.

Van Hollen then said, "Mr. Chairman, if I—"

"Oh say can you see . . ." Another young woman.

"Clear the gallery!"

"Enough!" said Paul Ryan. "Enough!"

Gingrey threatened to clear the gallery. The chamber slowly simmered down.

"Mr. Chairman," continued Van Hollen, "we now all agree we have to act now to put in place a plan to reduce our—"

"You're supposed to represent this country, so why don't you . . ."

It was a third young woman. The others in the visitors' gallery began to look anxiously among their ranks to see if anyone else resembled the previous disrupters. Most of them did.

"Mr. Chairman," said Van Hollen, "I ask unanimous consent to begin my remarks from the beginning and reset the clock."

There was no objection. "As I said, nobody doubts that every person in this chamber loves this country and wants to do the right thing—"

"Oh when will you listen to our generation . . ."

Ryan walked over to Van Hollen and offered sympathetic words as another female protester was dragged off singing. Beside the Speaker's table, the clerks anxiously thumbed through what appeared to be antique registers as if trying to locate a precedent for such a ruckus.

"We shall overcome . . ."

At last, they overcame. The Ryan budget passed, 235–193. Only four Republicans—Walter Jones, Ron Paul, Denny Rehberg (who would soon be running for the Senate), and a West Virginia freshman named David McKinley (whose state had the highest rate of Medicare beneficiaries in the country)—voted against it. No Democrat voted for it.

Paul Ryan found Kevin McCarthy on the floor and shook his hand. "It's your listening sessions that made this happen," the Budget Committee chairman said.

Later that afternoon, McCarthy rode to Dulles Airport. Seated in the back of the black SUV was Jeff Denham, a freshman who had previously served in the California State Senate while McCarthy was in the State Assembly. That was five years ago. Now Denham was hitching a ride with the third-ranking House Republican's security detail.

The whip was chewing on a brownie while checking his BlackBerry. "Heck of a week," he exclaimed. "But it's good! I'd rather be in chaos than not!"

Said McCarthy, "We stayed on offense the whole time. When you look at it from afar, as an aerial chess game, here's one group, the Democrats, that outnumbered us. But *we* led. *They* reacted to *us*. As long as we keep leaning in, all they can do is react. I don't think they can come together."

That very afternoon, an obscure Democrat county clerk in western New York named Kathy Hochul sent out a press release. In it, she asked a question of her heavily favored Republican opponent in the special election to fill the vacated office of the 26th Congressional District of New York. The question related to the just-passed Ryan budget, and it read: "If Jane Corwin was currently a member of the House of Representatives, would she vote to slash benefits, increase costs, and hold America's elderly population responsible for fighting with insurance companies?"

A couple of hours later, Hochul's demand had goaded Corwin into issuing her own press release—saying that yes, she would have voted for the Ryan budget with its controversial provision to end the Medicare guarantee.

McCarthy was wrong. There was in fact a way for the Democrats to come together. The Republicans had just handed it to them.

PART THREE

✧

"YOU DON'T KNOW WHERE I'M COMING FROM!"

CHAPTER FIFTEEN

Draft Horse

Jeff Duncan's America was the 3rd Congressional District of South Carolina, which occupies the state's western flank, abutting Georgia and North Carolina. The upstate portion of the district was for nearly three hundred years the dominion of Cherokees, while farther south the territory was settled by French Huguenots in the mid-18th century. Though today its principal cities, Anderson and Greenwood, are the home to auto parts industries and other manufacturers, until a few decades ago the area was a haven for textiles—the business that brought John Duncan, a mill turnaround specialist and the father of the district's future congressman, to Ware Shoals to begin with.

The 3rd District's first U.S. representative, a wealthy planter named Daniel Huger, was ill throughout the drafting of the Bill of Rights but would become the patriarch of one of the state's early political dynasties. A half-century later, the 3rd District elected Laurence M. Keitt, a twenty-nine-year-old, heavily bearded ladies' man described by one contemporary as "the most irascible of all the Southern members." Keitt was a Fire-Eater, or ardent secessionist, who argued that "African slavery is the cornerstone of the industrial, social and political fabric of the South . . ."

He achieved lasting notoriety, however, for his violent antics on the House floor. In 1856, Keitt accompanied fellow South Carolina Congressman Preston Brooks into the Senate chamber and held off onlookers with his pistol while Brooks thrashed Massachusetts Senator Charles Sumner with his cane for blaspheming their state. Keitt was censured on the House floor and then resigned, only to win (according to one report) "unanimous reelection" a month later. He instigated at least two physical encounters in the House chamber—one in which

Keitt was knocked to the ground after calling another congressman a "damned black Republican puppy"—and beat his washerwoman at the Willard Hotel. After South Carolina seceded, the Fire-Eater commanded a Confederate regiment and was killed in the last year of the Civil War. Throughout Reconstruction, his former office would be occupied by a succession of Republican carpetbaggers, one of them an African-American.

The 3rd District returned to Democratic hands in 1877 and stayed that way for more than a century. The mills in the district had begun to close in the early 1980s. After Congressman Butler Derrick announced his retirement in 1994, the first Republican since Reconstruction, a state legislator and bartender's son named Lindsey Graham, rode the Gingrich wave to victory. Graham and his Republican successor, Gresham Barrett, were well attuned to two realities. First, the district was deeply conservative. Second, it was economically hurting. Both congressmen maintained unmarred pro-life and pro-gun voting records while making liberal use of earmarks to build new bridges and fund vocational education centers. They also championed in every way possible the district's largest employer in the post-textile era: the U.S. Department of Energy's Savannah River Site, a sprawling nuclear reservation.

When Barrett decided to run for governor in 2010, thus handing Jeff Duncan the opportunity to take his place, he brought to South Carolina voters one of the most conservative voting records in Congress—with one exception: Barrett had, at the height of the financial crisis of 2008, voted for President Bush's bank bailout, the Troubled Assets Relief Program (TARP). As a result of Barrett's dereliction, he was beaten in the primary by Tea Party star and Sarah Palin endorsee Nikki Haley.

And in the meantime, Jeff Duncan—who had condemned TARP as "disgraceful and un-American," and who campaigned pledging never to aid his district with earmark requests—was on his way to representing the land of Cherokees and Huguenots, secessionists and mill workers, Tea Partiers and recipients of federal largesse.

Three days after casting his vote for Paul Ryan's Path to Prosperity budget, Duncan was in his district office in Anderson, chatting with a Korean War veteran and his daughter, an Air Force officer who had recently returned from Kandahar. Duncan mentioned that he had not yet been to Afghanistan, or Iraq for that matter. He had, however, taken a day trip to the U.S. prison at Guantanamo Bay, Cuba, just last week, between votes.

"They're treated very well there," the freshman said of the detainees. "We went into a medium-security area with communal pods. It was interesting—we were in the hall, and there are windows with shades, and guards who observed them 24/7. And it was dark where we were, and very lit up in the area where they were. And I felt in the presence of evil in there."

He went on to say that he had only experienced that sensation once before. "My wife Melody and I were in Charleston in the market one day," Duncan continued. "We were walking up the sidewalk where there are shops. We went into one and were just looking around. And a few minutes later, Melody said, 'Let's get out of here. It doesn't feel right.' And I felt the same way. It turned out it was a black magic shop. I felt true evil there."

The father and daughter nodded and stared at the table where they and their congressman sat.

"Anyway—it was a great educational trip," said Duncan. He presented the soldier with a flag and plaque and thanked both visitors for their service.

Duncan's schedule in the district was full that week. He visited the Bosch manufacturing plant in Anderson, one of his district's bigger employers. The German-owned company employed 4,500 of Duncan's constituents to produce oxygen sensors, fuel management components, and other high-tech auto parts—by-products, in other words, of federal regulation.

"Of course, you can't be from South Carolina and be *supportive* of heavy regulations," one of the Bosch officials acknowledged with a knowing smile to the freshman. "But when you get data-driven information on safety issues, that does nothing but support our business. Because that's our niche. It's created job opportunities here."

Duncan listened quietly as the job creators spoke hopefully to him about a "collaborative effort with industry and the federal government." In other words, Bosch wanted money. Its labor costs here in South Carolina far exceeded the costs of their plants in Mexico. Any "public-private partnership" would help. The company urged Duncan to support the Advanced Vehicle Technology Act, a bill that would channel Department of Energy research funds into cutting-edge auto manufacturing, authored by Democrat Gary Peters and cosponsored by his fellow Michigander John Dingell.

Duncan's expression remained noncommittal—though he did nod his head solemnly when the Bosch managers discussed the need to reform the voluminous federal tax code.

"Four companies here have made the decision to move their plants out of Anderson," a manager said. "Three to other states and one overseas."

"It's a nationwide effect of the recession and job losses and layoffs and whatnot," Duncan said. "Other states are experiencing the same thing."

"Except that states like Georgia and Virginia have found alternative solutions," the manager said pointedly.

The antispending freshman dug in his heels. "The biggest question," he said, "is what we as a nation can *afford* to do."

He drove from one event to the next in his red Chevy Silverado pickup. Back when he was a heavy underdog in an eight-candidate Republican primary to succeed Congressman Barrett, Duncan had stood for hours in the bed of this same vehicle with his wife, Melody, holding hands and waving, during maybe twenty Christmas parades throughout his district. He had outworked the competition. As a result, his pickup now carried the license plate 3 SC.

As he drove, the news reached Duncan that President and Mrs. Obama had filed their 2010 income tax return and paid $450,000 in federal taxes on their income of $1.7 million. Duncan considered his own financial situation—which, as a politician and former real estate auctioneer, was certainly comfortable. He owned fourteen rental properties throughout the district. One of them, an old mill house in Laurens he had bought for $20,000 back in 1991, had recently been trashed and vacated by a young female tenant. A door had been ripped off its hinges. The damages would have to come out of his pocket.

"I'm an absentee landlord," he sighed. "It's one of those sacrifices you make when you come to Washington."

Duncan had an hour to kill between meetings. He decided to spend it at his alma mater, Clemson. Someone recognized him on the streets and told him that Duncan's old football teammate, Keith Jennings, was now running a hot dog stand on College Avenue.

Duncan's face lit up. He'd been a walk-on wide receiver and seldom got on the playing field. Jennings, on the other hand, had been a star. The former Clemson Tiger later played two seasons as tight end for the Dallas Cowboys and seven for the Chicago Bears.

Duncan walked into Jugheads Hot Dogs, carrying with him a Clemson-orange striped tie he had just purchased. The round-faced African-American man with the apron put down his skillet and appraised the customer with wide-eyed delight.

"Jeff Duncan—*congressman*? I can't believe it! Dawg, that's good stuff!" Jennings held out a gargantuan fist, which Duncan bumped with his own.

The two alumni descended into football gossip—what Coach Danny Ford was up to, whatever happened to Rodney Quick—before the subject turned to Jennings's hot dog enterprise.

"It's all good," he shrugged. "I can't afford to pay anyone, so that's why I'm back here. But anytime I want, I can flip that sign on the door—'Be back in thirty minutes'—and go down the street and have a beer."

Leaning over the counter, Jennings said to his former teammate, "Now when you get back to Washington, will you slap around some people and help out the small businessman?"

"We only control one-half of one-third of government," Duncan wearily reminded him.

That evening Duncan attended a Tea Party event by an outfit called Conservatives Taking America Back. The audience of two hundred or so was largely middle-aged, all white, and one of them wore a Revolutionary War costume complete with powdered wig. The freshman and his political godfather, Senator Jim DeMint, both spoke—though the most memorable words came from the meeting's cohost, local conservative activist Debra Daum, who set the tone of the evening by warning the attendees, "If your agenda is to fundamentally transform the

United States of America, then guess what—you've got to take out the patriots first . . . Now, Mr. Obama may have millions of sheep and their little ACORNs can get them to vote, but guess what: eighty percent of America is Christian. We are the majority! . . . But the truth is: Islam is on the rise in this country. Christianity is on the decline . . . I, Debra Daum, will not stand by and watch my country die!"

DeMint by comparison was folksy and understated. "I'm not trying to scare anyone," the senator said in a lamenting tone. "But I don't believe we can take four more years of this."

He then observed with a sly grin, "I understand there are a few people here who want to take their country back." Over the loud applause, he declared, "Well, you made a good start by electing Jeff Duncan!"

Duncan kept his remarks short. "I've only been up there for a hundred days, so I don't have quotes of my own," he began, and thereafter quoted others: Reagan, the Constitution, the book of Nehemiah, Thomas Jefferson. He thanked those present for being patriots. "Where else in the world," he said, "can people gather peacefully to talk about our concerns about government?"

His message was the same as it was and would be: "Let's stop the spending insanity. Let's get our fiscal house in order."

He carried that same message to the state capital of Columbia for the annual Washington Night meeting of the entire South Carolina delegation—hosted by the state Chamber of Commerce and sponsored by Nutramax, maker of pet foods, creator of jobs in Lancaster, South Carolina, and proud supporter of Christian-based missions throughout America. Duncan sat at the head table in the middle, alongside the state's other elected federal officials: fellow freshmen Tim Scott, Trey Gowdy, and Mick Mulvaney; Republican Congressman Joe Wilson and Democratic Congressman James Clyburn; and Senators DeMint and Lindsey Graham.

The Q&A lasted for well over an hour, but it was nonetheless hard, from among those eight strong voices, for Jeff Duncan to make any kind of impression with the audience. There was DeMint, the purist of the right, speaking scornfully of the Continuing Resolution that had been signed into law that week: "The amount of cuts we saw last week was so nominal as to be embarrassing." There was Graham, far and away the most learned of them on foreign policy—and speaking, on the subject of the state's foremost economic challenge, how to obtain federal dollars to dredge the seaport at Charleston, with pragmatic determination: "I'd rather lose my job than lose this port." There was Clyburn, the lone Democrat, assailing the Ryan budget as "unconscionable" while at the same time reminding the audience that his support for the Savannah River Site was unwavering, and that he took "some credit for getting the Obama administration to where it is" on nuclear energy. There was Joe Wilson, a starkly sotto voce contrast to the dissenter who bellowed out "You lie!" during President Obama's health care speech before a joint session of Congress less than two years ago.

All three of the other freshmen were more erudite than Duncan. His roommate Tim Scott described the delegation's "awesome" efforts to aid the Charleston port in his district with breezy self-assurance. The lawyerly Gowdy quoted from the seventeenth-century English writer John Bunyan and spoke movingly, when the subject turned to immigration, of his son's high school classmate, a girl from Sierra Leone whose hands had been amputated for attempting to vote. Said the clever and cocky Mulvaney when the topic turned to education, "I don't know anything about the schools in Wisconsin. Drove through the state once, don't care to go back. Why does anyone think I in Washington can or should do anything to impact education in Wisconsin? I was hoping we'd have in the [Ryan] budget something on education similar to what you saw on Medicaid: give the money back to the states and say, 'Go at it.'"

Duncan uncorked one acidic line when a questioner asked about the EPA. "They want to treat spoiled milk like an oil spill," he scoffed. Otherwise, he did not stand out. It was an experience—the congressional experience—to which Jeff Duncan was growing accustomed. It was frustrating enough that, even leaving aside the maddening intransigence of the Senate, the lower body was failing to address the key issues of the day. On the fight to reduce government spending, he believed that old bulls like Appropriations chairman Hal Rogers were just as dug in as the Democrats—that when the Appropriators offered their first feeble package of cuts, "Rogers knew all along that those weren't real numbers." And on his near-and-dear subject of energy independence, Duncan had concluded that the discussion had become fatally inclusive. "We've got to take the environmentalists out of the equation and come to some common ground," he would say. "And that's increasing domestic supply."

But the more vexing revelation to his first hundred days was his inability to be heard within the body. None of his legislation—the Byrd Committee program-slashing bill, the D.C. gun permit bill, the anti–National Labor Relations Board bill—had even seen any committee activity, much less been put to the House floor for an up-or-down vote. Sitting on three committees, he strove to find a moment, any moment, in which he could distinguish himself. But as with the Muslim radicalization hearing, there was little of substance to be achieved in five minutes' time. Back in the South Carolina legislature, Duncan could speak on the floor for twenty minutes on a topic. He could see himself moving votes with his words—it had actually happened. On the House floor, his speeches were limited to a minute, or thirty seconds, or even fifteen seconds—and with that Duncan would blurt out what he could, red-faced, in his auctioneer's patter.

He figured that maybe down the line he might become a subcommittee chairman. In the state legislature, Duncan had come to be viewed as a dependable, reasonable guy—a leader in his own unspectacular way. His colleagues there had awarded him a chairmanship after six years. As it happened, six years was precisely the term limit he had campaigned on for House members last year. Duncan would have to revisit that logic at some point.

In the meantime, his near anonymity extended even into his place within the South Carolina delegation. The *New York Times* had published a story about the four freshmen. The reporter had interviewed each of them, including Duncan, but he was the only one without a quote.

Duncan made his peace with it. God's divine wisdom would be revealed in its own time. During his junior year in high school, his father was dispatched from Charlotte, North Carolina, where the Duncans were living, to turn around a struggling mill in South Carolina. Jeff Duncan had been a big football star on his team. Now he found himself in the no-stoplight town of Ware Shoals, playing for a 1A team, in a graduating class of ninety. He'd hated his dad because of it—until he met a small-town girl named Melody.

She became his bride. South Carolina's 3rd District became his home.

As for the Four Horsemen, Jeff Duncan saw himself as "the draft horse. The one who's gonna plod along and be steady. I'm very convicted in what I believe. That's how I want to be seen. I don't want them to look up at the board to see how I voted."

CHAPTER SIXTEEN

The Winning Message

On the morning of April 7, 1965, the chairman of the Democratic Study Group, Congressman Frank Thompson of New Jersey, sent out a memo to all members of that now-defunct coalition of liberal Democrats. It urged them to "be on the House floor during the debate on HR 6675 to prevent delaying tactics of opponents, time-consuming quorum calls, and other dilatory maneuvers so that this important part of our Democratic legislative program can be passed by an overwhelming margin."

Thompson was referring to the Mills bill, which would later be known as the Medicare bill. The American Medical Association had bitterly opposed any form of national health insurance since such a measure was first brought to the House floor by John Dingell Sr. in 1943. Back then, the elder Dingell scoffed at the claims made by the physicians' lobbying organization. "Socialized medicine, of course, is just a bugaboo," the Detroit congressman said on a radio program in 1945. "It is a coined phrase, it is just a lot of medical bunk peddled by the physicians' organization organized in Chicago and fighting the battle for the reactionaries within the medical profession."

But the AMA succeeded in defeating Dingell Sr.'s early efforts to enact a national health insurance program. Now, in 1965, it aimed for a similar outcome with this new initiative. Early in the year, the AMA launched a $3–4 million nationwide advertising campaign—with airtime on 346 TV and 722 radio stations—in an effort to squash a preliminary version of the legislation. AMA president Donovan F. Ward condemned the bill as "a cruel hoax—a lure, not a cure, for the problems of the aged."

The massive lobbying effort had the unintended effect of driving the process underground, into the lair of Ways and Means chairman Wilbur Mills, the wily Arkansas Democrat who in previous years had played a key role in sinking attempts to provide federally funded health care for the elderly. Following the enormous gains made by Democrats in the 1964 election, Mills now believed that President Lyndon Johnson had the votes and therefore elected to lead the parade rather than be trampled by it. With the help of future Ways and Means chairman Dan Rostenkowski, and behind closed doors, Mills tied House Resolution 6675 to that year's Social Security amendments. It used payroll taxes to finance hospital insurance for senior citizens. It also provided 50 percent federal coverage for their health insurance and assisted the elderly poor through federal and state matching funds. This so-called three-layer cake came to the House floor on April 7, 1965, under a closed rule with no opportunity to amend the bill—meaning, it would be a fully baked cake or no cake at all.

The Speaker pro tempore who banged the gavel when Medicare passed the House on April 8, 1965, was thirty-eight-year-old John Dingell. President Johnson signed it into law on July 30, declaring, "No longer will older Americans be denied the healing miracle of modern medicine." Three months later, the AMA announced that it would not boycott the new legislation.

Only thirteen Republicans supported the new entitlement in 1965. Then and later, Medicare was anathema to market-based conservative orthodoxy. But it would also prove to be immensely popular among senior citizens—who, more than any other demographic, reliably express their sentiments at the ballot box.

Unsurprisingly, then, the most predictable subplot of any electoral drama would soon involve Democrats using any and all weaponry to push Republicans off of their Medicare tightrope: in 1980 against candidate Reagan, in 1996 against Speaker Gingrich, in 2000 against candidate Bush, and in 2008 by Obama against candidate John McCain. It was a strategy of artful demagoguery that the Republican House candidates would themselves employ in 2010 against Obama's health care bill by suggesting, repeatedly and inaccurately, that the legislation had cut Medicare benefits by $500 billion. The 2010 GOP nationwide

Medicare ad blitz was undoubtedly fruitful. In the 2006 midterms, the two parties split the elderly vote right down the middle. In 2010, seniors went for Republicans by a 21-point margin.

It became a Washington axiom: to tamper with Medicare, if only rhetorically, was to invite a politically lethal wave of "Mediscare." And until the passage of Paul Ryan's budget on April 15, 2011, Republicans had not only avoided revisiting Medicare reform but, in one notorious instance, had trampled on both conservative orthodoxy and House floor traditions, all in one fevered all-night melodrama.

That night in question was Saturday, November 22, 2003, when House Speaker Denny Hastert held the vote open from 3 A.M. until nearly 6 A.M.—longer than any vote in the recorded history of the House—in an attempt to secure sufficient votes to pass the Medicare Prescription Drug, Improvement, and Modernization Act of 2003. Since subsidizing prescription drugs for senior citizens amounted to a brand-new entitlement, Republicans were loath to support President Bush's bill. Only after Arizona freshman Trent Franks was ushered into a Capitol conference room and handed a cell phone with Bush on the other end of the line, and named his price—to have a one-on-one conversation with the president about who the next Supreme Court justice would be—did Franks switch his vote to "yes" and Majority Leader Tom DeLay announce that the Republicans had prevailed. Immediately following the unprecedented marathon vote, Minority Leader Pelosi remarked bitterly to the press, "We won it fair and square. So they stole it by hook and crook."

She would remember all of this.

The 26th District of western New York, which included the city of Erie, had been represented for the previous two years by Christopher Lee—a Republican who occasionally strayed from the party line. As a freshman, Lee had been one of the eight House Republicans whom Speaker Pelosi had convinced to vote for the Democrats' energy bill in 2009, and at the end of his first term he also voted for John Dingell's bipartisan food safety bill. But Lee's infamy was to come on February 9, 2011, when the news blog Gawker published a photograph Lee had taken of himself, shirtless, and posted on Craigslist as a means of soliciting contact with a transsexual. Following the disclosure, Lee's resignation from the House was instantaneous, and a special election was scheduled for May 24, 2011.

Nobody gave the Democratic candidate, Erie County Clerk Kathy Hochul, the slightest chance to win. The district was perhaps the state's most Republican, she did not even live within the district's boundaries, and polls a month before the election had her down by 15 points. But when her Republican opponent, Jane Corwin, acknowledged that she would have voted for Paul Ryan's budget with its controversial Medicare provision, the numbers began to change. The DCCC barraged the district with attack ads saying that Corwin "supports a budget that essentially ends Medicare." Nearly every sentence Kathy Hochul uttered during the last month of the campaign began and ended with the word *Medicare*.

The Democrat crushed Corwin by 10 points. Within the Republican conference, blame quickly focused on Corwin's lackluster campaign and the meager support shown by the NRCC. *They always bungle special elections*, Republican members and staffers repeated incessantly.

The Democrats weren't buying it. Here was the first test case of how voters reacted to the House Republican agenda. DCCC chairman Steve Israel knew that most of the GOP freshmen had won on an anti-Obama/Pelosi sentiment but were largely blank slates to their own constituents. Now Israel knew how to define them. In a caucus, he showed his fellow Democrats the very ads that the NRCC and conservative outside groups had run in 2010, accusing Israel's colleagues of having voted to slash Medicare benefits.

"If I could, without violating copyright laws, I'd run the same damn ads against them!" he told them.

Nancy Pelosi and Steve Israel were in a mind-meld. Shortly after Kathy Hochul's upset victory, the minority leader brazenly announced her party's three top issues for the 2012 election:

"Medicare, Medicare, and Medicare!"

"I hope you get cancer!" a woman hollered at Renee Ellmers at the conclusion of her town hall, as the North Carolina freshman was being escorted out by local sheriffs' deputies.

"You want to kill Grandma!" another woman yelled at New York freshman Michael Grimm during a town hall in Staten Island.

At Cavalry Chapel in Fort Lauderdale, Allen West stood onstage wearing a suit and yellow tie. Three minutes into his town hall presentation, the heckling began.

"I want to tell you this," he said in a calm voice. "You're not going to intimidate me."

The pro-West attendees who made up almost the entire audience leaped to their feet and applauded. But when the cheering died down, a bald white man stood up and began to yell in protest and was promptly escorted out by security staff.

"There are people that don't want to face the truth," West observed. "We all"—referring to military veterans such as himself—"sacrifice, so that you can have the freedoms of liberty."

More applause. Another heckler stood and began to shout. He, too, was escorted out of the building.

"Run someone against me," said West, "and let me beat them, too."

Another standing ovation.

A middle-aged woman was seated just behind West's wife, Angela, near the front, and was videotaping the proceedings while periodically muttering "Lies!" Angela West turned around and glared.

"Oh, so I'm not allowed to speak?" she hooted.

A security official appeared and leaned over to the woman with the video camera. "Do you want to be escorted out?" he said.

"No, I'm not doing anything!" she replied.

"Do you want to be escorted out?" he repeated.

"No," she said, and he left.

The freshman worked through his PowerPoint presentation about the national debt, America's insufficient sea power ("If we continue on this path, the world's greatest naval fleet will be flying under a Chinese flag"), and the unsustainable economic path that Congress now had to address. He then took questions. But unlike his previous town halls and unlike town halls being held by the other Republican freshmen, there was no open microphone for questioners. Instead, all questions had to be submitted in advance, in writing, with no opportunity for a follow-up. West figured that he could go through more questions this way, without long-winded pontification from the audience members. He also knew that as a military strategy, it had the effect of disarming the enemy.

"There's a huge stack of Medicare questions," the moderator observed. "The first is from Angel: 'Please explain who will be affected by the Ryan budget plan.'"

West ticked off his answers: "If you're fifty-five, no changes. If you're fifty-four or younger, you'll see a different kind of system ... We have to move away from fee-for-service in Medicare, which lends itself to a lot of waste and fraud ... We need to put American citizens in charge of their health care decisions ..."

The woman behind West's wife began to holler, "That's a lie!" West stopped talking; the woman kept shouting. A cascade of booing ensued. West stared at the woman with an expression that looked almost pitying. His staffer, built like a linebacker, strode from the side of the stage to its very edge—standing there with legs spread as if to protect the congressman from an assault. A security guard grabbed the woman by her arm and pulled her out of her seat. A second woman, pro-West, stood up and clapped. "Stupid bitch!" screamed the woman with the video camera as she was dragged out of the town hall.

"I've kinda been shot at, almost blown up, used to jump out of airplanes at the middle of the night," Allen West told the crowd at the conclusion of the night. "Takes a whole heckuva lot to scare me."

Even as Nancy Pelosi and the Democrats had settled on a narrative by which to define the Republicans—as a party that refused to ask sacrifices of billionaires and big oil companies while robbing the old and the poor of their Medicare and Medicaid—they had decided to ask for help in defining themselves. So in May Pelosi called Roy Spence, the Texan whose fiery "making-a-difference" presentation at the Democratic retreat in January had led Anthony Weiner to stalk out but had entranced everyone else.

"We need to get clarity in our message," the minority leader told Spence. "We've got to find a way to get people in my caucus to know what it is we're saying."

He agreed with her. Reagan had boiled the Republican worldview down to a phrase fit for a bumper sticker: "Morning in America." The Democrats ... well, they liked to govern. They enjoyed getting in the weeds. But what was the unifying theme between a Sheila Jackson Lee and a Heath Shuler?

Spence saw the Democrats' diversity as a strong point, given that America's original motto was *E pluribus unum* ("out of many, one"). But ultimately, to move the republic forward, commonality had to trump diversity. "My deal is, forget what the American people think," Spence told Pelosi. "What do *you* believe in?"

Pelosi loved his higher-ground approach. She told her caucus, "This is going to be between you all and Roy. I'm not going to give any introductory this-is-what-I-want-to-see. It's about what you cook up together."

Spence put his associate, Haley Rushing, on the project. Rushing was a cultural anthropologist. She knew almost nothing about any of the congressmen. Spence viewed that as an asset. Rushing would interview every one of them by phone for nearly two hours. She would hear what they had to say about what drove them, what they believed their purpose here in the House was. And then she and Spence would go over all the answers and come back to the Democratic leadership with a distillation of their findings: *Here is what you are about.* And then the Democrats would presumably use that bumper-sticker version of themselves as their slogan for 2012.

Spence told Pelosi that though he happened to be a lifelong Democrat, this wasn't about winning to him—it was about helping out his country. "To be honest, Nancy," he told her, "if the Republicans asked me to do this, I'd do this for them, too."

The minority leader knew not to worry about this. For better or for worse, Republicans were unlikely to ask Roy Spence—or anyone else, for that matter—to help them explain what they stood for. It was a Nancy Pelosi kind of thing, not a John Boehner kind of thing.

CHAPTER SEVENTEEN

Side Pockets on a Cow

"We're celebrating a great day—the American auto industry is coming back!"

John Dingell stood outside in the middle of a makeshift car lot in suburban Detroit, surrounded by hybrid vehicles and a small bank of TV cameras. He leaned on his cane, but through his lenses the old man's eyes glowed with unquenchable zeal.

"These are *American* cars," he continued lustily. "I come down with an acute rash when I go by a foreign-made car. Our workmen, our engineers, and our union members are still the best in the world. The United States is coming back!"

A local reporter asked the congressman if American consumers would be receptive to green-technology vehicles. "You betcha!" Dingell declared. "I'm no advocate for rising oil prices. But I have to say, they've shifted the buying tastes of the American public and probably in the long run will be necessary to break our dependence on foreign oil, which poses such a risk to the United States."

"Is there anything else you'd like to add?" said the reporter.

Dingell faced the cameras squarely and offered a wide grin. "Tell our American people that, by golly, we still make the best right here in southeast Michigan!" he said. "Come on by and see and buy these great cars, put Americans to work, and get the best for your money!"

With that, the eighty-four-year-old congressman climbed into the backseat of his American-made SUV and sped off to his home in Dearborn.

Earlier that morning, Congress's foremost pitchman for the domestic auto industry was celebrated at a "Green Leaders" event in downtown Detroit for his contributions to local conservation efforts. The drive from Dearborn ferried him through the semi-evacuated rusted shell of a once-muscular city, and though Dingell was not an excessively sentimental man, he became somewhat younger as he stared out the car window and conjured up the ghosts of his childhood. He had grown up on Detroit's West Grand Boulevard in the bottom floor of a flat where his dad brewed beer in a back bedroom. He remembered John Dziegle-wicz as a brilliant philosopher of a man with an eighth-grade educa-tion whose Polish last name had already been bastardized by the time the meat salesman decided to run for the newly created 15th District in 1932. He remembered how the Polack old-timers stood agape with tears running down their ruddy cheeks during the candidate's victory speech, when John Dingell Sr. officially became one of ninety-three Democratic freshmen to join FDR in forging a New Deal. He remem-bered traveling from Detroit to Washington for his father's swearing-in, and at the age of seven standing agog on the floor of the House chamber, the biggest room he had ever seen.

He remembered Detroit as a company town where for a time the men wore their union buttons under the brims of their hats or behind their coat lapels in the manner of a secret society. During pheasant sea-son, young John Dingell would balance his .22 rifle on the handlebars of his bicycle and pedal out to the woods, along what would later be known as 8 Mile Road, the de facto line of racial demarcation, and he would shoot fowl all day. The city population was nearly a million back then; its inhabitants were Polish and Czech and Irish. No one locked their doors back then. Nowadays, no one would think not to. But John Dingell still loved this city, though it had long been carved away from the 15th District that he represented.

The Green Leaders breakfast was attended by the city's new mov-ers and shakers—many of them young, many of them Arab-American or African-American. Implicit throughout the morning's award-bestowing was the broadly shared hope that the Motor City was at last emerging from the wreckage of economic malaise and beginning to turn a corner. The sixteen awards to Green Leaders were decided by the event's sponsor, the *Detroit Free Press*—which, while saluting Dingell, noted that "the longest-serving member ever in the U.S. House has angered some by battling for Detroit automakers against tough fuel efficiency standards."

Dingell made no mention of this in his acceptance remarks. But after the event, the dean of the House climbed back into his American-made car and vented his annoyance. The storyline that the obstinate old protector of auto industrialists and foe of environmentalists had finally come around was one he found tiresome and, frankly, bullshit. "If you look," he said gruffly, "you'll find that what I did was make these laws tolerant for industry. And I would tell the industry folks, 'You've got to go along. I will get you a bill that you will hate, but it will be a bill that you can live with.'"

His efforts in other environmental matters constituted a long list that put him in the forefront of American conservationists. In 1963, Dingell drew industry's ire by authoring a bill that would allow the federal government to establish water quality standards, and by sponsoring another bill that empowered the government to sue businesses for destroying fish and waterfowl. Three years later, Dingell demanded national standards for air quality as well. In 1969, he led a successful effort to quadruple President Nixon's cash-strapped water pollution budget. He coauthored the National Environmental Policy Act of 1969, wrote the Endangered Species Act of 1973, cosponsored an amendment in 1976 that banned PCBs, and was a driving force behind scores of other conservation initiatives.

And he played a leading hand in the shaping and passage of the Clean Air Act, both in 1970 and in its reauthorization two decades later. But that hand was not the same unflinching hand that struck fear in the hearts of water polluters. It was instead a hand that held the hand of the beleaguered American auto industry, a hand that pushed back hard against environmental activists demanding reductions in carbon monoxide that befouled whole cities and caused thousands of fatal respiratory illnesses and heart attacks each year. And it was the hand that held the levers of power at the House Energy and Commerce Committee.

Most of FDR's New Deal legislation ran through what was then called the Interstate and Foreign Commerce Committee, chaired by Sam Rayburn. But when Mr. Sam assumed the Speakership, power in the House became centralized and Commerce ceded some of its jurisdiction. That changed when Dingell became its chairman in 1981. He recruited aggressive legislators to join the committee and encouraged them to develop bills that would maintain, and often broaden, its jurisdiction. At the same time, Dingell instructed his committee staffers to review every single bill that was dropped in the House clerk's hopper to ascertain whether any involved an Energy and Commerce matter. Turf disputes frequently erupted between him and the Judiciary and Natural Resources chairmen. Dingell invariably won. His committee now included the word *Energy*, having beaten back an attempt to create a committee solely focused on that subject. Dingell kept an aerial photograph of planet earth on the wall above his chairman's perch. When people asked him to describe his committee's jurisdictional territory, he turned around and pointed to the photograph.

Dingell also chaired its oversight subcommittee, from which he interrogated government officials and corporate executives with bullying efficiency. If outnumbered on a committee matter, Chairman Dingell was known to say, "You may have the votes, but I have the gavel," and then with a bang adjourn the proceedings before a vote could be taken. A year into his new assignment, a poll of House members concluded that John Dingell was viewed by his peers as the institution's best chairman—but also arrogant and domineering, a man who used his six-foot-three frame and his caustic verbiage to get whatever he wanted. It was likewise true that Dingell was a superb builder of coalitions, worked well with the other side of the aisle (including Gingrich and DeLay), and was universally regarded as a man of his word. But his reputation as a hard-ass, and as a congressman who fiercely protected the interests of his automaking constituency, did not bother Dingell in the slightest.

It did, however, bother him (though he would never say so) to be called Dirty Dingell and Tailpipe Johnny by the left, to have his office picketed by the Sierra Club, and to be viewed by fellow liberals as a toady for the Big Three automakers. From a smog-choked California district that included Beverly Hills came a short but no less brash congressman named Henry Waxman, who managed to get on Dingell's committee. In Waxman's slice of America, children and senior citizens were dying of lung and heart diseases as a result of the polluters in Dingell's America. A decade's worth of legislative mano a mano between the two Democrats ultimately led to the bipartisan and much-heralded Clean Air Act of 1990. But a mutual dislike now ran deep—all the more so as an alliance developed between Waxman and another Californian, Nancy Pelosi.

Dingell had supported Pelosi's opponent, Steny Hoyer, in the 2001 whip race. She in turn campaigned on behalf of Lynn Rivers in 2002 when redistricting threw Dingell into a primary challenge with Rivers. After the Democrats regained the majority in November 2006 and the Energy and Commerce gavel fell back into John Dingell's hand, he reverted to the methods he had used to such great effect as chairman from 1981 to 1994. He held all of the committee members to a blood oath to protect the committee's vast jurisdiction. He worked with both sides of the aisle and the full gamut of outside advocacy groups. He developed his committee's legislation, as he would say, "from the center"—bringing everyone to the table, hashing out differences together, and forging strong consensus.

What he had failed to recognize was that the House—and perhaps Washington politics writ large—had, between his two tenures as chairman, ceased to function in this fashion. His own leader, Nancy Pelosi, had no intention of working this way. Her Speakership would instead be in the mold of her immediate Republican predecessors, Newt Gingrich and Denny Hastert. Power would be centralized. The legislative agenda would emanate from the top. Member fealty would be to her, not to chairmen like Dingell—and she would monitor their loyalty, rewarding it and punishing breaches of it. Those were the new rules, and they were clear to seemingly everyone except John Dingell.

Among Speaker Pelosi's first acts in 2007 was to create a House Select Committee on Global Warming—which clearly poached on the Energy and Commerce chairman's turf, and which Dingell thus proclaimed "as useful as feathers on a fish." Henry Waxman opposed the select committee as well. As it turned out, the ongoing robustness of Energy and Commerce was something in which the Beverly Hills congressman had a vested interest.

Dingell's friends and subordinates could smell a Waxman challenge coming. They knew as well that he had made himself vulnerable by antagonizing Speaker Pelosi. Dingell seemed thoroughly unaware of the spot he was in. During the summer of 2008, he had a conversation with

Pelosi on the House floor. The subject was his continued desire to be chairman in 2009 and beyond. The Speaker had said words to the effect of "You're doing a good job." Dingell told others that he took her remark to be an endorsement.

His wife, Deborah Dingell, was not so sanguine. The former General Motors executive had wide contacts in Washington and was hearing rumblings. One late summer afternoon in his Capitol hideaway office reserved for the lower body's dean, Dingell's wife convened a meeting with the congressman, a couple of current and former staffers, and longtime friend and Democratic operative Anita Dunn. Together they warned Dingell that his chairmanship could be in jeopardy. Dunn reminded him that since his 2008 general election campaign would be a cakewalk, his energies were better spent shoring up support among his colleagues. Dingell assured them that he had the backing of both the Democratic caucus and the Speaker.

Dingell was due to undergo reconstructive knee surgery in October. His staff had urged him to have the procedure done in August, which might make it difficult for him to campaign for reelection in the fall but would ensure that he would be at full strength by late November, when the Democratic caucus and its new members met to vote on committee chairmanships. Dingell did not take their advice. He elected to put off the surgery until early October. He then suffered a minor cut on his knee—and so as to avoid infection, the doctors put off the procedure until the very end of October.

On November 5, 2008, the day after Barack Obama's victory, Henry Waxman announced that he would challenge John Dingell's chairmanship of the Energy and Commerce Committee. The first call Dingell made when he got the news was to Nancy Pelosi. "You told me you had my back," he said.

"That's not what I said," she reminded him.

Steny Hoyer wanted to avoid a bloodbath. The incoming majority leader attempted to broker a deal in which Dingell could keep his chairmanship for two more years. Waxman was not amenable. The matter would therefore be put to a vote.

On November 20, the Democrats convened in the caucus room on the third floor of the Cannon Office Building. The thirty-two Democratic freshmen got their first look at the incumbent chairman. Three weeks after his surgery, Dingell was pale, cadaverously thin, and wheelchair-bound. Waxman had already dined with nearly all of the freshmen and had cut ten-thousand-dollar checks to their campaigns. His staff had also helpfully placed on each caucus chair a copy of a recent op-ed by *New York Times* columnist Thomas Friedman about the Detroit auto executives who had flown to Washington in their private jets to testify as to their industry's need for a bailout. Friedman had assailed Dingell as being "more responsible for protecting Detroit to death than any single legislator."

Dingell's side lost the coin toss and therefore gave their speeches first. Dingell had wanted to be the closing speaker on his behalf. But his staff and his chairman campaign whips, Bart Stupak and Mike Doyle, had prevailed on him to deliver first. They knew that he did not look good and wanted him out of the way.

Stupak wheeled Dingell up to the front of the caucus room. The chairman spoke only briefly about his past accomplishments. He instead emphasized his desire to work with President-elect Obama on finally getting a health care bill passed. It was not Dingell's best speech, but under the circumstances he had done adequately.

The last to speak was John Lewis. The civil rights hero spoke generally about the value of maintaining the seniority system, which in recent years had been the means by which black members had at last been elevated to power. Then Lewis said, "Think about what you're doing to this man, after all he's done for this institution. After all he's done for *you*."

None of the speakers had said a negative word about Henry Waxman. When Waxman's turn came, his fourth speaker, an Iowa first-term congressman and former trial lawyer named Bruce Braley, took off the gloves. Dingell, said Braley, had obstructed the work of environmentalists. He had failed to get a health care bill passed out of the committee in 1994. He had been weak on consumer protection. Weak on climate change. It was a devastatingly effective and, thought Dingell's supporters in the room, profoundly disrespectful speech.

Waxman went last. When he was finished, Nancy Pelosi—officially neutral throughout the race—was the first one out of her chair clapping. The signal was not altogether subliminal.

Dingell was standing outside the Cannon caucus room, leaning on his cane, during the fifteen-minute tallying of the votes. He remained convinced that victory was his—until a Democratic staffer stepped outside and gave a sad nod to Dingell's chief of staff, Michael Robbins. Dingell turned away, even as Pelosi on the other side of the door was asking unanimous consent that John Dingell be named the committee's "chairman emeritus," a request that was greeted with hearty applause. He began walking down the hall with his cane. A staffer brought him his wheelchair. Dingell sat down in it and told the staffer that he had something he would like to do now.

The ex-chairman wanted to get his new member ID photo taken for the 111th Congress. And so off they went.

The image captured was that of a man in his eighties wearing a big, defiantly beatific smile.

"Consuela? Madam Overseer?" John Dingell used to beckon Consuela Washington, his longtime securities advisor. "Come in and tell me how we're going to hurt the white people today."

Dingell's epic pugnacity did not dissolve into embitterment following his defeat at the hands of Henry Waxman. Having garnered a half century's worth of triumphs and disappointments, the dean of the House chose to view his dethronement as another page in an episodic career that, God and the voters willing, was not yet over. He moved on.

Like before, Dingell would begin the morning with a call from home to his Rayburn office—unfailingly greeting the answerer with "Hello there! This is John Dingell." Later that morning, he would enter with his cane, offering up an arid spray of "How ya be?" and "Blessings on you" before settling in and inquiring, "What to tell me? . . . What else? . . . What else?" A staffer who had screwed up would be condemned with the greeting: "Dear friend . . ." Or, if he or she had screwed up royally: "Beloved friend . . ."

He would insist on directness: "Do not be difficult to agree with." And on practicality: "Kill the closest snake first." But also on satisfaction: "Be comfortable. Are you comfortable?" He would remind them of his seniority ("I've been doing this since you were an itch in your daddy's crotch"), counsel patience ("You have to shoot the bear before you can skin it"), express his distaste for the Senate ("that no-good congregation of shit-hooks"), and invoke the hard realities of Beltway politics

("There is no substitute for a public hanging"). When nature called, he would excuse himself so that he could "salute the president."

The list of Dingellisms was long and faithfully remembered by his staffers, who tended to stay in his employ from one to three decades at a stretch and periodically threw reunions so that they could luxuriate together in memories of blackguards and lickspittles and the time the boss was madder than a boiled owl or uncomfortable as a frog in a skillet or doubled up like a monkey fucking a jug. Sometimes Dingell himself showed up to share a glass—staying and pretending not to bask in their love of him until "the lovely creature," aka "the sawed-off-blonde," aka "the blonde whirlwind," aka the Lovely Deborah came to whisk him away in their American-made automobile.

Soon after losing to Waxman, Dingell called the latter and told the new Energy and Commerce chairman that he wished success for him and would assist however he could. Waxman in turn let the chairman emeritus retain two Energy and Commerce staffers. Dingell threw his energies into the health care bill. During an Energy and Commerce meeting, one of the progressives on the committee complained loudly that the Blue Dogs had made the legislation far too middle-of-the-road for him to support.

"No one here is more progressive on health care reform than I am," Dingell interjected sternly. "I've always supported a single-payer system. My father introduced the first universal health care bill. Long before you were here, I was doing the same. You can support this." That was the end of the subject.

In the spring of 2010, Chris Van Hollen introduced legislation in the wake of the Supreme Court's *Citizens United* ruling, which permitted unlimited campaign advertising and contributing by outside political groups. Van Hollen's bill would ban campaign participation by foreign-owned corporations and require that outside groups disclose the extent of their financial participation. Almost immediately, Heath Shuler protested that the DISCLOSE Act would land himself and other Blue Dogs in hot water with the NRA, which had been accustomed to spreading around its vast resources with impunity.

Van Hollen knew whom to call. John Dingell brought the NRA to the table, garnered their support for a carve-out exemption tailor-made for the gun group (exempting any organization with five hundred thousand members or more), and the DISCLOSE Act narrowly passed the House with substantial Blue Dog support. (In the Senate, however, its newest member, Republican Scott Brown, cast the deciding vote against the DISCLOSE Act. The bill failed to become law.)

After Dingell beat back his Tea Party opponent in the 2010 general election, he relished the Democrats' final legislative triumph before power changed hands: the FDA Food Safety Modernization Act, a monumental overhaul of FDA inspections aimed at preventing food contamination, of which John Dingell was architect. After it had spent fully eighteen months in "the cave of winds"—a Dingellism for the Senate—President Obama signed the legislation on January 4, 2011. Sixteen days after that, Dingell announced that he intended to stick around for another term.

The new Energy and Commerce chairman after Dingell and Waxman was Republican Fred Upton. Dingell was quite fond of Upton and watched with philosophical bemusement as his fellow Michigander underwent a radical transformation so as to secure the chair. Dingell knew Upton as an old-school moderate. His coauthorship of a 2007 bill with Democrat Jane Harman to phase out incandescent lightbulbs incited Tea Party outrage and the denunciation by Rush Limbaugh of "nannyism, stateism." (In the 112th Congress, Michele Bachmann would introduce a bill repealing the Upton-Harman initiative, luminously titled the Light Bulb Freedom of Choice Act.) In 2010, Upton prevailed in a fierce primary contest against a Tea Party candidate, but his troubles were far from over. The conservative activist group FreedomWorks had put up a website, www.DownWithUpton.com, and was showing up to Republican Study Committee meetings urging members to reject his bid for the chairmanship.

Upton's staffers deluged RSC officials with memos, briefs, and assorted assurances that in fact their boss had always been a true conservative—and that in any event, Upton got the message and would do better. Upton himself sent out an email to fellow Republican members: "The voters have spoken. The failed job-killing policies of Nancy Pelosi and Barack Obama have been soundly rejected . . . My Pledge to

You: I will protect the sanctity of human life . . . I will reveal, repeal and replace ObamaCare . . . I will exert tireless oversight of the EPA . . ."

It was the kind of naked belly-crawl that Dingell had refused to do for Nancy Pelosi, and it had cost him his chairmanship. Regardless, Dingell believed he could work with Upton—though on what, in this Congress, remained unclear.

Still, he had a couple of small but dear projects of his own. The trick was getting the money for them. Fortunately, there were some kinds of tricks that only an old man would know.

✦ ✦ ✦

Jeff Duncan and the other three South Carolina freshmen were in a fix.

There was nothing more important to their state's economy than the port at Charleston harbor. That fact was true even in Duncan's upland district. The BMW plant was there because of the port. Michelin received its rubber and shipped out its tires through the port. The economic value of the port was obvious to the freshman. But he was also its booster because the port made sense. It was America's closest port to an open ocean. The Charleston port's history was, for better and for worse, bound up in the very formation of the great state Jeff Duncan now represented. He, Tim Scott, Trey Gowdy, Mick Mulvaney, Joe Wilson, Jim Clyburn, and Senators Jim DeMint and Lindsey Graham were in lockstep on this one issue: funding for the port to be deepened, so that supermax tankers and other big boats could dock there, was essential to South Carolina's economic vitality.

And the matter would have been resolved in 2010, via a $400,000 earmark request by Senator Graham. The problem was that Senator DeMint opposed it and all other earmarks. As a result, the Senate Appropriations Committee did not include the Charleston port in its funding request. And now the Four Horsemen, all of whom had run for office supporting the ban on earmarks that was now in effect, had their work cut out for them.

Duncan and his other three colleagues sat down with Transportation and Infrastructure Committee chairman John Mica at least a half-dozen times. They did what they could to educate him about the Charleston port's value to South Carolina—that without it, companies like Boeing wouldn't be there. As Trey Gowdy would later say, "We went to Chairman Mica on bended knee, saying, 'Please. Do not punish South Carolina.'" But Mica offered them nothing.

They went as well to Chairman Hal Rogers of the House Appropriations Committee and pressed for him to insert it into a funding bill. With a straight face—but, it was believed, with barely disguised glee—the wily lawmaker once known as the Prince of Pork lamented that, alas, their request appeared to be an earmark, and alas, earmarks were banned.

On the House floor, Gowdy said to Rogers, "I don't know who you're trying to punish—if you want my seat, I'll go back to being a DA!"

It seemed abundantly clear that the old bulls were making the young turks pay for the beliefs they shared with their political godfather De-Mint. Meanwhile, Lindsey Graham was staging press conferences, drafting legislation, and threatening to hold up all White House appointments. All to no avail—until he reached across the aisle to the lone South Carolina Democrat, seventy-year-old, nine-term congressman Jim Clyburn.

Clyburn called the White House Office of Management and Budget. An OMB official contacted the Harbor Maintenance Trust Fund. The money was procured. It was not an earmark. Rather, the telephone request was direct and paperless, a so-called phone-mark—the way most such funding requests historically took place, so long as you knew someone to call, and as long as that someone would take your calls, perhaps because they owed you a favor or knew that they could count on you for a favor down the line.

It was how business got done in Washington. The freshmen stood on the sidelines—compliant but, as another Dingellism would have it, "as useless as side pockets on a cow."

Dingell, of course, knew how to do such things.

In October 2010, America's 393rd and newest national park, the River Raisin Battlefield, was officially inaugurated. It was the site of the bloodiest battle during the War of 1812, where nearly a thousand U.S. soldiers were slaughtered by British troops and Native Americans. Its location was Monroe, Michigan, which happened to be in John Dingell's district.

Like many Michiganders, Dingell had regarded the battlefield as a sacred site. But it had for many years been the property of a paper mill, which went out of business in the late 1990s. Dingell convened a meeting with Monroe County authorities in 2005. He proposed turning the battlefield into a national park. Dingell saw that the authorizing legislation would move slowly in the House and therefore persuaded his friend, Michigan Senator Carl Levin, to sponsor the bill in the upper body. Still, to accomplish what he had in mind required money. Dingell knew where to find it.

For years he had been sitting on about $5 million that he had once obtained to move railroad tracks out of Monroe County. The railroad companies had been slow to negotiate, and it appeared that the rail consolidation project was going nowhere. Dingell told his people, "I want to transfer that money. Figure out how to do it." The opportunity arose in 2008, when a transportation "technical corrections bill"—an interim measure between five-year transportation authorization bills—was sent over to the Senate from the House. Dingell's staffers inserted an earmark that split up the $5 million into various projects—among which $1.2 million would go to purchasing the River Raisin Battlefield.

Dingell had already figured out how to use some of the rest of the money. As a boy, he and his father used to go hunting for waterfowl along the Detroit River. Its shorelines were now despoiled with abandoned industrial brownfields, including a former forty-acre Nike plant—and yet bald eagles, osprey, lake sturgeon, and other wildlife had begun to thrive as the economy declined. In 2000, he solicited the advice of conservationists on both the Michigan and Ontario sides of the river. From those discussions, Dingell decided to establish the first international wildlife refuge in North America.

The dream was realized slowly, parcel by parcel. In 2003 he procured an Appropriations earmark for $3.1 million. The next year, he secured $1 million from the Charles Stewart Mott Foundation. From the leftover railroad fund Dingell took $1.8 million for the refuge. From the Migratory Bird Commission—an obscure group of which Dingell was one of six members, and which spent money to acquire land from the proceeds of duck-hunting stamps—Dingell acquired another million dollars. The former bankruptcy lawyer swooped down on every financially troubled landowner he could find. He also kissed a lot of ass.

Half of the land came from wealthy donors like the Ford Motor Company. Some of it was previously owned by the Army Corps of Engineers and became Dingell's through a Department of Defense authorization, with an additional $150,000 stipulated for the department to clean up its site—to which Senator John McCain objected, seeing it (not unreasonably) as an improper earmark . . . but Dingell himself headed over to the Pentagon and said to the proper authorities, "Come on, fellas. I could really use your help here." The decision was made not to say no to John Dingell. As the coup de grâce, one of Dingell's people managed to convince the Seabees to do the cleanup as part of their diving training exercise.

Dingell had one unfinished piece of business, however. He wanted fully funded visitor centers for both the River Raisin Battlefield National Park and the Detroit River International Wildlife Refuge. And so in June 2011, he brought Secretary of the Interior Ken Salazar to see Michigan's two new crown jewels of nature.

Salazar had a gift basket from Dingell's staff waiting for him at his hotel on the night of his arrival. Unfortunately, late that same night, the House Appropriations Committee posted its new proposed budget for the Interior Department. Wetlands conservation had been cut by more than half. The Land and Water Conservation Fund had been slashed by 90 percent. Interior had been gutted. It was the worst time imaginable to be asking Ken Salazar for money.

But it was not just anybody asking. As the secretary would say later that day at a lunch reception overlooking the Detroit River, "I cannot think of a greater conservation hero than John Dingell." Dingell was a friend to the cause—an originator of the cause, even. It was Dingell's father, in fact, who crafted one of the first direct appropriations to the Interior Department, via the Dingell-Johnson Act of 1950, which taxed fishing gear to pay for federal land acquisition.

And so on a sunny day in June 2011, the secretary toured the River Raisin Battlefield with the congressman to celebrate an acquisition of property that very day (thanks to Dingell's connivances) that would quadruple the size of the national park. That afternoon, they visited the Humbug Marsh tract that had just been added to the refuge (again due to Dingell's efforts). Both men gave speeches and interviews and saluted the two splendid additions to America's conservationist heritage.

At the end of the day, as the secretary was saying his goodbyes, John Dingell saw the moment and seized it. He asked Salazar to sit inside his American-made SUV for a moment.

They talked for only three or four minutes. Then the interior secretary stepped out of the SUV, was swept up into his security detail, and whizzed off to the airport.

Dingell did the same. He had made his case. He had shot the bear before skinning it. He had made himself not difficult to agree with. And now he was comfortable.

CHAPTER EIGHTEEN

"Here Is Your Shield"

One late evening at the end of June 2011, Allen West walked into Ben's Chili Bowl wearing a navy suit and red tie and carrying his helmet bag festooned with labels from his various tours of duty. He squinted at the sign behind the counter of the famed U Street institution that had been spared from arson and looting during the 1968 riots: *People who eat for free at Ben's: Bill Cosby. Barack Obama. No one else.*

The freshman smirked. Something else for him to aspire to. He ordered a smoker and sat down.

A few people recognized him and shook his hand. This was not surprising, since by now West was a regular on Fox and continually named in Tea Party circles as a desired presidential candidate for 2012. Not all the attention was flattering. The left could not resist mocking the Florida freshman. A couple of weeks earlier, he and a few combat veterans had decided to go scuba diving and were renting equipment when the shop owner suggested that West take an American flag down to the bottom and be photographed with it. West thought it was a great idea. But of course the photo found its way onto the Internet, along with the suggestion that the congressman was guilty of violating Title 4, Chapter 1, Section 8, subsection B of the United States Code, in which allowing the flag to touch water is forbidden by law.

Sitting at a table at Ben's with his sandwich in both hands, West dismissed the left-wing accusers as "loons" and "crackheads" and wondered aloud, "Maybe I should've just burned the flag—y'all would've been happy then." It just made them look like idiots, questioning Allen West's patriotism. But fair or not, the more lasting element of the whole saga was the actual image—somewhat extraterrestrial, more than a little ridiculous—of a wide-eyed, begoggled public official encased in a wet suit, planting a flag on the ocean floor of Deerfield Beach.

West had also drawn snickers from liberal bloggers for remarks he had made in April at a Boca Raton gathering of Christian conservative women called Women Impacting the Nation. After fretting that today's liberal women were "neutering men," West reminded his audience that the Spartan warriors had learned toughness from the women of Sparta: "And when the Spartan mother gave that young Spartan warrior a shield, she gave him this basic commandment: 'Spartan, here is your shield. Come back bearing this shield or being borne upon it!'"

Critics from the left observed that Spartan women had no political rights, and thus that West's comments were further proof of his misogyny. West found this assertion every bit as foolish as the slight on his patriotism. He had two daughters and a wife with a PhD!

And anyway, he made no apologies for his admiration of the Spartans. West was reminded of the movie *Patton,* and of the great American war commander's belief that he was meant for another time. A student of history himself, West wondered aloud: "A guy like Alexander, twenty-six years of age, could you have done what he did? Never had odds better than one to three. And he still was so brilliant. Like a Julius Caesar, I don't want to have the same demise, but . . . a Hannibal. 'We will invade Rome from the north.' It's just magnificent."

Though, he added with a laugh, "I'd have to have been a white guy. Otherwise it wouldn't have worked out so good."

Whatever else tea partiers, liberals, the media, and his fellow House Republicans saw when they beheld the 112th Congress's most famous freshman, Allen West continued to regard himself as a warrior. And from the warrior's perspective, America was imperiled. Though most attention thus far in the 112th Congress had properly been focused on the nation's predominant concern—the sagging economy—events overseas also commanded attention. In the early months of 2011, dictators in Tunisia and Egypt were overthrown, with Yemen's despot soon to follow. In late March, NATO troops with U.S. backing enforced a no-fly zone over Libya to protect rebels seeking to depose the tyrant Muammar Gadhafi. On May 1, President Obama announced that after nearly a decade on the lam, Al Qaeda's ringleader Osama bin Laden had been located in a Pakistan compound and killed by a squadron of Navy SEALs.

The other twelve freshmen on the Armed Services Committee looked up to West. It amazed him how some of his fellow Republicans remained clueless when it came to the basics of foreign policy—including Afghanistan, where America had spent the past decade at war. He had winced when he heard presidential candidate Mitt Romney referring to "the Afghanis." Afghanis were the country's currency! "Hugely embarrassing," West said. (Months later, when GOP presidential contender Herman Cain dismissed his own ignorance of the country he referred to as "Uz-beki-beki-beki-stan-stan," a disgusted West muttered, "Not funny at all.")

Of course, West took a far dimmer view of the Democrats. Some of the ones on Armed Services seemed bent on turning the U.S. military into a social experiment. Allowing gays to openly serve in the military—demanding that the military change its behavior, rather than gays changing theirs—was only the beginning, he feared. "I'm just waiting on the next big-hurdle thing," he said, shaking his head. "Women in combat units. I can see it coming."

Earlier that month, West had visited Afghanistan. Everybody in uniform seemed to know him there. His first commander was now General David Petraeus's liaison to the State Department and a two-star. The deputy commander for Afghanistan's tumultuous Regional Command East had served with West as captains. Several of the Marine staff down in Helmand Province he'd known back at Camp Lejeune.

"You guys tell me the real truth," he exhorted them. What they told him in return was: *We want to win and we're making progress. But it can all slide back in a hurry.* They showed him the ammonium nitrate coming over from Pakistan to fashion deadly new improvised explosive devices, or IEDs. A young female captain asked him about Obama's recent nationally televised address announcing the beginning of a troop drawdown in Afghanistan. "Why did the president give that speech the other night?" she wanted to know. "What was he trying to say?"

"It's all political," West told her. The president was appeasing his antiwar base. It was hard for West to understand how a substantive individual could be drawn to Obama.

His fear was that as Obama began pulling troops out of Afghanistan, the ones left there would become increasingly vulnerable to attacks by the Taliban. As West said on Sean Hannity's Fox show just before his CODEL, "You still have a vicious, very determined enemy that is still on the battlefield . . . Having spent two and a half years in that part of the world, they only understand strength and they only respect strength."

One of West's two colleagues on the trip was a Democrat, Jim McGovern of Massachusetts. McGovern, West believed, "went over with a preconceived notion, and nothing was really going to change it—that we just need to quit, and go home. He doesn't care about success." West did. He believed that the United States needed at minimum to maintain its troop strength in Afghanistan. He also believed that victory in that country was impossible unless America also dealt with Pakistan. He believed that the United States should cut off aid to the Pakistani government, and then see if it responded more as a true ally should.

It had flabbergasted West that, in the immediate aftermath of the killing of Osama bin Laden in Abbottabad, Pakistan, the Republicans had brought a bill to the floor defunding school-based health centers. "Why aren't we talking about defunding Pakistan right now?" he asked Kevin McCarthy and chief deputy whip Peter Roskam. "That's $3 billion right now, instead of $100 million over ten years! I mean, nobody's been speaking out against Obamacare more than I have—but why *this* provision? We're just setting ourselves up for the other side to beat us down. It doesn't seem like you're really in tune with what's happening."

The whip and his deputy couldn't explain their logic to West's satisfaction. "This great thing has happened, and all these second- and third-order effects . . . and you're talking about school-based health care," he recalled with disgust. "Show that you have the ability to adjust fire! Shift your target!"

As West had first told the RSC and would later say at a thoroughly candid Heritage Foundation speech on May 31, he believed the United States needed to develop a national security road map, just as Paul Ryan had crafted his Road Map to Prosperity. West, of course, had a few ideas as to what some of the road map's highlights should be.

He would "absolutely" build up America's naval forces, which had seen a decline in war vessels from 546 in 1990 to 243 today. "All the great civilizations have had them, going back to the Phoenicians, the Athenians, the Romans." And he would use those vessels to go after the Somali pirates—"hunting their ships on the open seas, not allowing their freedom to maneuver." This would require a continued naval presence along the Horn of Africa. West was for it.

And he was for "beefing up our southern border"—which, as West told a questioner at his April 26 Fort Lauderdale town hall, he regarded as "a war zone." He asserted that "Iran is in South America. Hezbollah is in South America . . . This is a Chamberlain-or-Churchill moment."

He was for peace between Israel and Palestine. But, as he told the Heritage audience, he believed no peace was possible "until you eradicate or eliminate Hamas. And that's my story and I'm sticking to it."

West, then, was for a continued troop presence in Afghanistan, a greatly augmented sea presence, a robust military presence on America's southern border, and an all-out Hamas eradication program. Nation-building, however, was another matter. West viewed the so-called "Arab spring"—the forced departure of dictators in Tunisia, Egypt, and Yemen—with suspicion and even derision, mentioning it in the same breath as the bathroom soap Irish Spring. He had no reason to believe that the new leaders would be in any way better than the ones who had been thrown out. The most organized political force in Egypt was the Muslim Brotherhood. Yemen was Al Qaeda's greatest stronghold. As for Libya, just who were these rebel groups?

"My concern is, we're being co-opted into something in North Africa and the Middle East," he said. "Egypt, now Libya—and in my mind this is not coincidental. We've contracted out the U.S. Air Force and Navy for a bunch of people we don't even understand."

He had spoken up in a Republican House conference for the very first time, in early June, when Speaker Boehner tried to dissuade his members from voting to cut off funds for America's military role in forcing the ousting of Libyan dictator Gadhafi. Antiwar Democrats and many Republicans believed that Obama had violated the War Powers Act by engaging in hostilities without Congress's authorization.

West didn't buy Boehner's sentiment that "we can't let NATO down." The freshman told the conference, "The oath we took—it's not an oath to NATO. If we're not going to stand up for the Constitution and our laws, then what do we say to the men and women in the combat zone? This is a no-brainer."

But as to what actually should be done in Libya, West himself seemed to be at war with his own conflicting instincts. He disagreed with Obama's decision to send in aircraft to enforce a no-fly zone. Instead, West said, "I would have dropped a drone on the guy even before" Gadhafi's troops began to kill dissenters—"because he *is* a bad guy. I wouldn't have allowed it to get to this point."

But would his policy be to kill every bad state actor—even if, as in Gadhafi's case, he had done nothing to harm U.S. interests?

"No. I can't go around and try to protect innocent civilians. I'd be all over the place."

But he would nonetheless drop a drone on Gadhafi?

"Well, I don't like the guy. Period."

But weren't there lots of guys not to like, such as Assad in Syria and Ahmadinejad in Iran?

"Well, I think the resolve you show makes a lot of these guys go to ground."

Then what sort of resolve should the United States show?

"I think we should've come out with a very strong condemnation. I think we should've told him, 'If you continue in twenty-four hours with this type of action, there'll be a response from the United States of America of a kinetic nature. And I think you have to be serious. But see, once again, you have to establish a precedent, so that they know you're serious."

But if Gadhafi's behavior rose to the level that required such a response, then was that also true in the case of the behavior shown by Assad and Ahmadinejad?

"If that's the new litmus test."

But what was *his* litmus test?

"Mine is one that threatens the interests of the U.S., the open sealanes of commerce, threatens our allies. Those are my litmus tests."

And so the situation with Libya did *not* in fact rise to that level?

"It hasn't risen to that level."

Even in Allen West's indecision, he showed certitude. Grinning, he said, "I heard you say that I'm kinda all over the place. I think that's a strength. You can't nail me down and say, 'This guy is gonna go this way—he's absolutely predictable.' When you go into a football game and you've got the quarterback who can pass or run—absolutely. You don't know where I'm coming from."

CHAPTER NINETEEN

"Dropping Out of Things Is What I Do"

On the afternoon of Wednesday, June 1, 2011, the newest member of the New York delegation was sworn into office. Just a few hours beforehand, Kathy Hochul had gotten her first glimpse of the workplace on the seventh floor of the Longworth Building that Christopher Lee had vacated months ago. "Is this it?" Hochul asked no one in particular, grinning nervously as she stepped inside, as if crossing into some wondrous new dimension.

Now she stood in the well of the House floor, surrounded by her fellow New York congresspersons, who engulfed her with greetings the moment Speaker Boehner executed the swearing-in. One of those New Yorkers who shook her hand was Anthony Weiner. He had no way of knowing this at the time, but in fifteen days he would be resigning from the very body into which Kathy Hochul had just been sworn.

Weiner had walked into the chamber a few minutes beforehand, carrying on an animated discussion with one of his friends, fellow New Yorker Joe Crowley. He then sat on the front row with Steny Hoyer. For several minutes Weiner gave a rundown of what was fresh on his mind, having just now completed a succession of interviews in his office with several TV reporters about an incident last Friday in which a college student claimed she had been sent a photograph of a male's underwear-clad crotch via the congressman's Twitter account. Over and over he had told the reporters that he did not know this young woman and that the transmission of the photo must have been someone's idea of a prank. But when asked whether the photo was of Weiner's crotch, he refused to say "definitively" or "with certitude" that it was not.

Hoyer listened, his face knotted with concern. When Weiner was finished talking, the minority whip said, "You need to put everything on the table and get all the facts out there and do it as fast as you possibly can. That's the most important thing."

Weiner agreed with Hoyer—or rather, he said that he agreed with him. Then, for the next five days, Anthony Weiner continued to lie about what had happened.

The possibility that Anthony Weiner might be tweeting photographs of himself to women across America seemed unfathomable to his staff. Not because he was happily married to Huma Abedin, which he was; but rather, because he was so insanely driven, to the point of making life miserable for everyone who worked for him, that it was impossible to believe he would risk throwing it all away over some random Internet hookup.

If anything, Weiner was overly cautious when it came to women. If he and a female staffer were the last two remaining in his office at night, Weiner would invariably leave. Rather than flirt with his female employees, he treated them with precisely the same level of disdain that he did the men.

Weiner wanted a lean, efficient office. He wanted a breaking-news statement issued daily. He wanted his legislative staff to be focused on creating events and messages rather than on bills that were coming out of committees. He wanted a visual aid from the House graphics department to accompany his floor statements. And at the same time, he did not want to know a thing about his staffers' personal lives. He did not want to mentor them or retain them forever as outside counsel. He did not want to think about them, ever.

He wanted only one thing, really: to be the mayor of New York City. He obsessed over creating a Rockaway-Brooklyn-Manhattan ferry service, imagined applying the Defense Department's performance management model to city government, and lunged at every legislative opportunity to ingratiate himself with the Big Apple's law enforcement community. Though he had lost the mayoral race in 2005, Weiner evidenced something almost resembling serenity during that run. He could be himself, not imprisoned by an institution of 435. He could be the Park Slope middle-class son of lawyer Mort and schoolteacher

Fran; he could be the guy who once sold bagels at an outer-borough shopping strip; he could sit on stoops and shoot the bull at diners.

But he could not beat Michael Bloomberg, not with the latter's bottomless resources. And so Weiner sat out the 2009 mayoral race, instead setting his sights on 2013.

In the meantime, nothing that did not contribute to that end seemed to animate him. Though he shared living space with Mike Capuano of Massachusetts and occasionally caroused with a few other male colleagues, Weiner remained a lone wolf in the Democratic caucus. He invited only three House members—fellow New Yorkers Crowley, Steve Israel, and Nita Lowey—to his wedding in 2010. He showed no interest in paying his annual DCCC dues or raising campaign money for his colleagues—since, after all, a day on the road at some fund-raiser was a day not spent in his district. He showed up for Energy and Commerce oversight subcommittee votes only when he absolutely had to. Once, after stepping into a subcommittee hearing just long enough to give a rather grandstanding speech, a fellow member thanked him for his contribution and was shocked by the flip arrogance of Weiner's reply: "Anytime you need me to help save you guys, just let me know—I'm right down the hall."

Hoyer had been sufficiently impressed with Weiner's floor acumen that he convinced Pelosi to give the New Yorker a seat at the messaging table. Even then, Weiner expressed no appreciation for being bestowed such an honor and participated only when it was convenient for him; and when Hoyer suggested a title along the lines of Parliamentary Whip, Weiner balked, because something like that would be offputting to his constituents in the outer boroughs.

It was striking to contrast his behavior with that of the other floor strategist deployed by Hoyer and Pelosi, Rob Andrews of New Jersey. Earlier in his twenty-year congressional career, Andrews had shared Weiner's knack for rubbing his colleagues the wrong way. Though never as caustic as Weiner, the former lawyer struck other members as being deeply impressed with his own intelligence. In 1994, he cosponsored with Republican Bill Zeliff the "A to Z Spending Cut Plan," infuriating his party leaders by calling for a special session devoted solely to cutting discretionary spending through his and Zeliff's bill rather than through the Appropriations process. Andrews was fixated on the New Jersey governorship during the first half of his career, but after losing in 1997 and briefly mulling over running again in 2005, his ambitions turned to the Senate. He became an overnight pariah in the New Jersey delegation in 2008 when he decided to run against Democratic Senator Frank Lautenberg—and he further annoyed his colleagues by having his wife, Camille, simultaneously run for his House seat, only to move her aside when Lautenberg beat him in the Senate primary.

What resuscitated Rob Andrews's political career was the health care bill. In 2009 he happened to be chairing the Health, Employment, Labor, and Pensions subcommittee of the House Education and Labor Committee and thereby became one of the authors of the sprawling legislation. Along the way, he came to understand its intricacies better than anyone else in the caucus—and more importantly, he knew how to articulate it in a way that made sense to nonexperts. "Here's how I explained it in my town hall," he would tell the Democrats, and then proceed with a substantive but concise distillation.

"I'd really like to talk to you," said then–Majority Whip Jim Clyburn after hearing one of Andrews's health care elucidations. The New Jersey congressman thereafter became Clyburn's advisor on a wide range of issues. All of a sudden, Andrews was more valuable than annoying to his colleagues. And at the same time, he ceased looking for exit strategies from the House. He began having periodic get-togethers in the House dining room with John Dingell. Andrews would ask questions about the institution—its history, but also procedural matters, how to run a subcommittee hearing, how to build relationships—and then he would let the dean of the House do the talking. Andrews had not listened when Dingell advised him not to run for the Senate. He was listening now.

Meanwhile, Andrews began dropping by the Rules Committee office and seeing if the Democratic staffers had any suggestion for a floor tactic he could employ on the floor for the party's benefit. He volunteered parliamentary maneuvers so frequently that Pelosi and Hoyer decided that they might as well include him in their message meetings as well. By the start of the 112th Congress, Rob Andrews had not only rehabilitated his image within the caucus but was now a favorite among the Democratic leadership. He had become the anti-Weiner.

Andrews was unfailingly courteous to his employees, which also set him apart from Weiner—who was not content simply to tell his subordinates that they were wrong, but to describe, at very high volume, the many ways in which they were *fucking idiots*. One day Huma showed up at the office and, while standing in the reception area, heard the congressman viciously chewing out a subordinate. She stepped into his office and with a horrified look exclaimed, "What is going on here?"

It became clear to his staffers that there were some things about Anthony Weiner that his wife did not know.

"Friday dump Scotus style? I'm hearing disclosures released today. #ConflictsAbound"

"Lets review: for more than a decade #ConflictedClarenceThomas forgot nearly $800K on his filings."

"Tonight Me and Rachel on MSNBC. #The PerfectFridayDate UhKindaSorta"

Anthony Weiner's postmodern public disclosures of his semiprivate life on the afternoon and evening of Friday, May 27, 2011, were interrupted briefly by his appearance at 30 Rock in midtown Manhattan for Rachel Maddow's MSNBC show. There he criticized Supreme Court Justice Clarence Thomas for only just now offering financial details of his wife's involvement in opposing Obama's health care legislation—which, he argued, should compel Thomas to recuse himself from any cases on the subject. Weiner concluded his five-minute segment by laughing about Maddow's segues and saying, "These Friday night visits are turning out to be very interesting to me."

Later that evening he tweeted a baleful *"My tivo ate the hockey game! #WhoCanISue?"*—personifying the banal agony of a home-alone-on-Memorial-Day-weekend jock-sniffing sofa spud to his forty-three thousand followers. But to one twenty-one-year-old female follower in Washington state, he shared a different sort of message.

On Saturday afternoon, conservative blogger Andrew Breitbart posted a photograph of a man's genitals encased in gray briefs, claiming that it had been sent from Weiner's Twitter account. Though Weiner immediately told *Politico* that his account had been hacked, he didn't sound particularly concerned or outraged. Breitbart, in the meantime, declared, "I have much more."

Weiner's former chief of staff, Marie Ternes, now an outside advisor, implored the congressman to set up a conference call with his kitchen cabinet, which included consultants Tom Freedman and Jim Margolis and pollster Joel Benenson.

"I don't see why that's necessary," Weiner said.

"Then let's go through what we know," Ternes persisted. "Let's go through the facts so that we can push back on what's being said to prove our case."

When Weiner continued to be evasive, Ternes suggested that he bring the Capitol police into the situation.

"Well, *you* didn't," Weiner responded, referring to Ternes's personal email account having previously been hacked into.

"I'm a civilian, not an elected official," his former chief of staff retorted. But Weiner ignored all of her advice. Blithely he endeavored to return to the life of the legislator who just the previous Monday had passed a bill to establish a memorial in Arlington National Cemetery honoring the thirteen Jewish chaplains who had lost their lives in armed conflict; whose www.ConflictedClarenceThomas.com project had established himself as the Supreme Court justice's chief tormentor in Congress; whose rapier counterthrusts against the Republican agenda had made him a liberal darling; who, up until this very moment, remained the prohibitive front-runner to replace Bloomberg as Hizzoner of New York City.

Huma believed that her husband's account had been hacked. In that Clintonesque manner of plowing one's way through crisis, she told Weiner that he should proceed with plans to speak at the Wisconsin State Democratic Convention on Friday, June 3. But as the date approached and Weiner's responses to media questions became increasingly hedged with qualifiers, Margolis and other advisors persuaded him to cancel.

"My wife saw that photo and said, 'Yeah, you *wish!*'" he snickered to colleagues on Wednesday, June 1, the day he acknowledged to MSNBC's Luke Russert a lack of "certitude" as to whether the photo was of her husband's genitals. That same day, Weiner Tweeted, *"Ok, howz about I get back in the game over here. #ScrappyHasBlownPastCrazy."*

A friendly colleague confronted him. "Anthony," the colleague said,

"I don't think you were hacked. I think there's more to this. You need to tell me what's going on here."

"Nothing, nothing," Weiner insisted. "The execution of my explanation leaves a little to be desired, and I'm gonna clean it up by the end of the day."

But later that week, as new photos and new women began to come forward, Anthony Weiner did something that he had never done before. On the House floor, he sat down on the far left side of the chamber, among the members of the Congressional Black Caucus, and engaged in prolonged, lighthearted chatter with them.

As one of the CBC members would later say, "We knew it right then, when he came to the group that is seen as the most forgiving and compassionate—we knew then he was guilty of what was being reported."

He confessed to his wife at their home in Queens on the morning of Monday the sixth of June. He then began calling and emailing others. Nancy Pelosi was one of them. She was furious and instructed him to come completely clean.

When he told the truth to his former boss and mentor, Senator Chuck Schumer, both men began to cry.

At about one that afternoon, Weiner and several of his associates met in the midtown Manhattan office of his longtime counsel, John Siegal. Huma was there as well. She seemed extraordinarily composed and had brought her husband a suit to wear to his press conference. Weiner had decided to take any and all questions—and his staff, exhausted and largely in the dark as to what the facts actually were, figured there was no alternative.

For the next few hours, his advisors—Siegal, Benenson, Margolis, Freedman, Ternes, Anson Kaye, Glen Caplin, Jeff Pollack, and Risa Heller—fired likely questions at the embattled congressman. Sometimes his answers contained truths they had not known. Sometimes the answers were untrue, but they had no way of knowing this, either. More than once, Weiner broke down in tears.

At 4:25 P.M., Weiner walked into the ballroom of the Sheraton hotel, making eye contact with no one. No one had bothered to check press credentials. The immense throng included his chief accuser Breitbart, as well as crew members from shock-jock Howard Stern's radio program.

"Thank you very much for being here and good afternoon," Weiner began in a voice that was both formal and strained. "I'd like to take this time to clear up some of the questions that have been raised over the past ten days or so, and take full responsibility for my actions.

"At the outset, I'd like to make it clear that I've made terrible mistakes that have hurt the people that I care about the most, and I'm deeply sorry. I have not been honest with myself, my family, my constituents, my friends, and supporters and the media. Last Friday night I tweeted a photograph of myself that I intended to send as part of a direct message as a joke to a woman in Seattle . . . In addition, in the past few years I've engaged in several inappropriate conversations that were conducted on Twitter, Facebook, email, and occasionally over the phone with women I have met online. I've exchanged messages and photos of an explicit nature with about six women over the last three years. For the most part, these communications took place before my marriage, though some sadly took place after . . ."

Swallowing back tears, the congressman's statement concluded with "I'd be glad to take any questions that you might have."

He responded to the cacophony in a weak voice, moist-eyed, without any of the usual flashes of petulance or bemusement:

"I am not resigning . . ."

"I don't know why I did it . . ."

"My home computer is where I usually did these things . . . I don't believe I used any government resources . . ."

"I was trying to protect myself from shame . . ."

"We have no intention of splitting up over this . . ."

After twenty-seven minutes, Risa Heller handed him a slip of paper urging him to wrap things up. As the Howard Stern associate hollered repeatedly, "Were you fully erect?" Weiner left the podium.

Weiner and his advisors agreed that it had gone as well as could be expected. They discussed putting some town halls and Congress on Your Corner events on the schedule.

Two days later, however, Weiner remained in his home, which was surrounded by reporters. A photograph, supposedly of the congressman's erect penis, was now on the Internet. Pennsylvania Congresswoman Allyson Schwartz, the DCCC's recruiting director, became his first colleague to call publicly for Weiner's resignation.

"Do you think I should resign?" he asked an associate that day.

The associate responded that Weiner had broken no laws and had done nothing that would prevent his continuing to be an effective representative to his constituents. It was the affirmation Weiner wanted to hear.

On Friday, June 10, it developed that one of Weiner's contacts had been a female minor in Delaware. The police rushed to her parents' home to gather information. White House political director Patrick Gaspard told Weiner's advisors, "We were willing to stand by him before, but I don't see how we can do it any longer."

"Guys, I don't know what to do," Weiner told his inner circle on Saturday. "I just can't figure out what I should do."

Earlier that day, Leader Pelosi, DCCC chairman Israel, and Democratic National Committee chairwoman Debbie Wasserman Schultz had each released statements calling on Weiner to resign. Now he sounded almost lifeless. His wife was traveling overseas; Weiner wanted to forestall any decision until he could speak to her in person. Huma had gone out on a limb by marrying a Jew, which was not an easy pill to swallow for her conservative Muslim mother living in London. By now word had leaked out that Huma was pregnant. It was no doubt her preference that their child not be burdened by the stigma of a father who had resigned in disgrace from political office.

He left that day for inpatient therapy somewhere out of state, going to great lengths to conceal his trail and his future whereabouts. Huma flew back to the States and met him at the clinic on Wednesday the fifteenth. That evening, he called Steve Israel, who was at the White House attending the annual congressional picnic. Israel handed the phone to Nancy Pelosi. Weiner told her what he had just finished telling Israel: he was resigning the next day.

He did so, at a perfunctory news conference where he took no questions. Complimented by a friend for his composure, he emailed back: "Thanks. Dropping out of things is what I do."

Then he and his wife retreated to his brother's place on Long Island for the weekend.

On Sunday, June 19, Anthony Weiner returned to Washington. He submitted a two-sentence letter of resignation the next day to Speaker Boehner, Leader Pelosi, and New York's governor and secretary of state. Then the clown prince of Capitol Hill somehow entered his office in the Rayburn Building without being detected, cleaned out his desk, and disappeared from Congress for good.

His name did not come up in the next Democratic caucus. His colleagues did not offer public expressions of mourning. Instead, they returned to their mantra of jobs/Medicare/oil subsidies, which for the previous three weeks had been drowned out by scandal. The media scrum disappeared from outside Rayburn 2104—and inside, the same staffers as before now simply answered the phone, "Ninth Congressional District of New York," as if to expunge all memory of the forty-six-year-old man who had spent the last eleven and a half years as that district's representative.

It was as if a brutally efficient celestial correction had taken place. A master of multimedia had been undone, caught in the act of high-tech overindulgence. An employer who had shown so little consideration for others had become fatally ensnared in the sort of Internet dalliances that were attractive precisely because they required no emotional interaction. The ultimate independent agent had been severed from the congressional corpus without a drop of blood to show for it. Having never demonstrated much in the way of fidelity to the other 434, Anthony Weiner in the end became, for all his flair and promise, a mortally wounded liability that was culled from the herd and consigned to the political wilderness.

And indeed a couple of months later, he was just another guy at a Brooklyn barbecue, listening to his wife tell the others how she had not been displaying the usual signs of pregnancy—no morning sickness, no hunger pangs.

"Yeah," Weiner could not resist interjecting. "But she's been *really angry* at her husband the last two months."

Everyone laughed. That, too, was part of the correction.

CHAPTER TWENTY

"You Are *Wrong!*"

On June 1, 2011, Majority Whip Kevin McCarthy threw a dinner for the House Republican women at Ruth's Chris Steak House. The event was primarily for the benefit of the nine GOP female freshmen—and for McCarthy, who hoped to cultivate a reliable voting bloc. It began with a cocktail reception featuring a handful of prominent Republican women—among them former Bush White House press secretary Dana Perino, former Senator Elizabeth Dole, and former labor secretaries Ann McLaughlin Korologos and Elaine Chao—so as to welcome the new arrivals into the larger Washington sorority. McCarthy was well aware that the presence of women in the GOP conference (24 of 240, as opposed to 48 of 194 in the Democratic caucus) could stand improvement. He also knew that the class of 2010 contained a fairly high-testosterone component. Tonight the women would only have to suffer the company of McCarthy and his wingman, chief deputy whip Peter Roskam.

Jo Ann Emerson was among the dozen or so senior members in attendance. It was generally her inclination to avoid the whole Republican-women-solidarity thing. In early April, when GOP conference vice chair Cathy McMorris Rodgers and Mary Bono Mack were rounding up women to stage a press conference rebutting Democratic National Committee chairwoman Debbie Wasserman Schultz's claim that the Republicans were pushing "an extreme anti-woman agenda," the Missouri congresswoman begged off. She was also a no-show in June, when McMorris Rodgers floor-managed a "special order" during which a succession of her female colleagues each contributed a few minutes' worth of personal history so as to, in the vice chairwoman's words, "tell you the story of the Republican woman." Emerson also did not appear in the NRCC's "Republican Women" Web montages aimed at recruiting more female candidates for the GOP cause.

There was no confusion at work here: she was a proud Republican and a proud woman. Nor was she, by nature, antisocial. It was Emerson and another colleague who conceived and organized the annual Congressional Women's Softball Game, despite the fact that she was not the world's best athlete. But the concept of that event was—in keeping with Jo Ann Emerson's governing philosophy—nonpartisan. Her co-organizer happened to be Wasserman Schultz. The two had bonded in 2009, while enduring a ten-day CODEL in Southeast Asia, during which they both marveled at how consistently perfect Guam Representative Madeleine Bordallo looked throughout the trip while everyone else looked like crap. The House men's softball game was approaching, and when Wasserman Schultz mentioned that she had been a fairly scrappy ballplayer in high school, the two women hatched the idea of an alternative game. So it came to pass in 2009, and in the years that followed, that Republican and Democrat women played on the same team against a team of women from the Washington media. The game was highly competitive and great fun, raising a nice purse of money for the Young Survival Coalition, a nonprofit breast cancer organization, along the way, and thereafter it became understood that the DNC chairwoman would never launch an attack against any of her Republican teammates.

Emerson did not regard party affiliation as a passcode into her personal life (a good thing, considering that in 2000 she married attorney Rod Gladney, a registered Democrat). And though she tended to be a mostly reliable vote for the Republican whip team, it was telling that on September 15, 2009, Jo Ann Emerson was one of only seven GOP members voting for a House resolution disapproving of Joe Wilson's "You lie!" outburst during President Obama's joint session health care speech. For her, party loyalty ended where partisan disrespect began.

Her aversion to I-am-Republican-woman-hear-me-roar pep rallies notwithstanding, Emerson decided to make an exception of tonight's dinner. Until now, there hadn't been an opportunity for her to get to know her new female colleagues. They tended not to speak up in conference in the manner of Raul Labrador or Steve Southerland, or to cast dissenting votes on important matters like the South Carolinians, or to gravitate toward the TV cameras as in the case of Illinois congressman Joe Walsh—who had told some of his Republican colleagues, with a straight face, that he had "a cult following."

As something of an accidental congresswoman, Emerson had trouble identifying with women who were lifelong office seekers. For the most part, these nine freshmen were not of that ilk. Ann Marie Buerkle, for example, had been a lawyer and right-to-life activist in Syracuse, New York, before bumping off a one-term Democrat with very little support from the NRCC. Bedford, New York–based Nan Hayworth, an ophthalmologist with no political experience, had defeated Democrat incumbent John Hall, a musician best known for the song "Still the One," which Hall had to ask both Bush in 2004 and McCain in 2008 to refrain from using as a campaign jingle. Vicky Hartzler had grown up on a farm in Archie, Missouri, and briefly served in the Missouri legislature a decade ago but since then had devoted her energies to the anti-gay-marriage movement and to authoring a faith-based campaign book, *Running God's Way.* Sandy Adams of Florida had served in the state legislature for eight years but as a deputy sheriff for nearly two decades before that.

The thirty-nine-year-old woman seated next to Emerson, Kristi Noem of South Dakota, had attained Republican celebrity status before her arrival in Washington. A striking brunette with glacier-blue eyes, Noem had defeated Stephanie Herseth Sandlin, the Blue Dog leader whose political pedigree—her father had been a longtime state legislator; his father was South Dakota's governor and his mother its secretary of state—had made her appear invulnerable the previous three election cycles. Noem's looks and rancher's-daughter rugged backstory enabled comparisons to Sarah Palin that Noem herself took pains not to encourage, but which enthralled McCarthy. He promoted her and Tim Scott (the other African-American Republican, besides Allen West) as the nominees for the two seats at the House GOP leadership table allotted to the freshman class. As no other nominees were on the ballot, Noem and Scott were duly elected. The whip subsequently brought Noem and Sean Duffy back to his district for a local Republican dinner, introducing the telegenic ex-lumberjack and the woman who saved the family ranch after her father's death as the quintessence of a camera-ready Republican youth movement.

Kristi Noem struck Emerson as clearly intelligent and focused on proving herself legislatively—but was also, for an anointed leader, pronouncedly reserved. Emerson engaged in a far lengthier conversation with Martha Roby, a former city councilwoman from Montgomery, Alabama. Roby was a personal favorite of McCarthy, and Emerson could see why. She spoke with an unvarnished southern-girl frankness and had told a funny story that evening about the day she informed her mother she was getting married and subsequently peeled out in a big-rig truck. Her dream had been to work in the music industry.

Roby was also thirty-four, just a year older than Emerson's oldest daughter, Victoria. The freshman herself had two young kids, aged two and six, who lived back in Montgomery with her husband, Riley. Three weeks earlier, Roby had spent Mother's Day on a CODEL in Afghanistan. Like most of the class of 2010, she had run on an anti-Washington message. But, she asked Jo Ann Emerson, "What do you think about living here?"

Emerson advised Roby to seriously consider bringing the family up to Washington. During Bill Emerson's first term in 1981, Jo Ann was thirty-one and had stayed back in the district with their two young children. They rarely saw Bill, and she came to resent him for not being an active parent. After three years, they decided to relocate the family to Washington, where Jo Ann Emerson had lived ever since.

"That's how we did it," she concluded. "I can't speak for anyone else, obviously." But she could see the relief on Martha Roby's face. Emerson imagined that she might be having another regular dining companion in the not-too-distant future.

One freshman Emerson didn't get much of a chance to visit with that evening was Renee Ellmers, though she had already seen quite a bit of the North Carolinian on television and on the House floor. Ellmers was blond, wore eye-catching outfits, and possessed an open-faced Dixie charm. Unlike Emerson, whose path to Washington had been paved by her husband's colleagues, Ellmers had been shunned by the Republican establishment. Now, in six months' time, she had become a favorite of the House Republican leadership team.

How Renee Ellmers climbed her way up from the bottom rung would stand as an object lesson in political entrepreneurship. Neither the ex-nurse nor anyone on her staff possessed Washington experience, and she relied on a blogger back in her district to fulfill press secretary responsibilities. In late January, Ellmers missed an opportunity to speak at a well-attended pro-life function on the Hill because her aides took a circuitous twenty-minute drive to the event, which was a five-minute walk from the Capitol.

Her early forays into the public eye were unsteady. When she attended Cathy McMorris Rodgers's press conference in April to push back against Debbie Wasserman Schultz's criticism of the GOP's "extreme anti-woman agenda," Ellmers delivered her brief remarks with the jittery intonation of a hostage victim: "The Senate needs to pass H.R.1. It needs to do it today. The issue is the spending. And we need to come to an agreement—we need to put that certainty back into Americans' lives . . ."

Ellmers powered through her misadventures with the kind of aplomb that Newt Gingrich liked to call "cheerful persistence." When a tornado struck her district on April 16, she chose to attend to some of the victims rather than fly to Washington to appear on the Sunday TV show *This Week with Christiane Amanpour.* Kevin McCarthy could not stomach the sight of blood and admired the trauma nurse's casual toughness. He helped arrange for the ABC show to film her at a nearby studio. Ellmers had not been shy about reminding the whip of how completely he had overlooked her during the 2010 cycle. The two came to develop a brother-sister fondness—the whip giving the freshman staffing advice that usually went unheeded, the sassy North Carolinian clapping her hands in the Californian's startled face when she felt she wasn't getting through to him.

In late April, she finally got around to hiring a Washington-based press secretary. Tom Doheny had no previous experience on Capitol Hill, but the twenty-six-year-old press aide's résumé—which included stints working for Vice President Dick Cheney, the billionaire Koch brothers' conservative advocacy group Americans for Prosperity, and the Delaware and Pennsylvania state Republican parties—was that of a consummate go-getter.

Immediately after Ellmers hired him, Doheny contacted nearly every reporter on the Hill and invited each of them for coffee. He believed that Republicans tended to have an aversion to the media, to their detriment. Doheny's strategy was to be forward leaning: *Congresswoman*

Ellmers is one of the very few Republican freshman women. She's young, she's energetic, she's got a great story, she's never been in politics before this . . . Doheny created new email lists. He established a standard format for press releases. He taught the office assistants how to put a snippet up on YouTube. He began having coffee sessions with the communications directors for each committee, seeking to convince them that the diamond-in-the-rough North Carolinian was fast acquiring polish and ready to be a face of the Republican majority.

In the meantime, Doheny began to work one-on-one with his new boss. He learned quickly that Ellmers functioned poorly when inundated with briefing books. She did far better with face-to-face dialogue. The freshman often spoke in long, tangled sentences. But when she slowed down, Ellmers came across as sensible and empathetic. Together they would sit and watch Chris Matthews mutilate fellow freshman Joe Walsh on *Hardball*. "See, this is exactly why (a) we don't do *Hardball*, (b) we vet all the requests we get, and (c) we're prepared," the young aide would tell her.

Ellmers was a quick and self-aware study. She knew what she didn't know. The congresswoman was not about to go on the air to expound on Libya or North Korea in the pontificating manner of Sheila Jackson Lee. She would focus on jobs and health care, and her approach would be pitched in the reasonable cadence of the small-town nurse and Wal-Mart habitué that Ellmers was. By early June, she was logging multiple appearances on Fox every week, the message as unwavering as her plaintive gaze into the camera: "removing that uncertainty" caused by "burdensome regulators" so as to motivate "our job creators." The Speaker's office began to take notice. When Doheny released a statement from his boss praising the soldiers at Fort Bragg, North Carolina, following the killing of bin Laden, Boehner's press secretary Mike Steel sent over his assessment: *Smart*. The day after Obama visited her state for a jobs summit, Boehner's people asked that Ellmers join a House GOP leadership team press conference to say a few words about the jobs roundtable *she* had conducted a month ago. A few days after that, Boehner senior advisor Johnny DeStefano asked the freshman if she would deliver the Republicans' weekly address. She did so on June 25, repeating yet again the somber song of the American Job Creator: "Uncertainty, burdensome regulations, and the fear of higher taxes are making it harder to create jobs and stay afloat . . . They don't want a bailout. They just ask that we get government out of the way."

But Ellmers was more than just Kevin McCarthy and Tom Doheny's apt pupil. As the Victory Mosque ad had demonstrated, she possessed her own flair for drama. On the eve of Treasury Secretary Tim Geithner's testimony before the House Small Business Committee, of which Ellmers was a member, she and her staff huddled to discuss how she should handle her five-minute questioning segment. The congresswoman was urged to forgo theatrics and instead stick to the subject of the hearing, which was small business job creation. Ellmers, however, had her own ideas.

At the hearing on June 23, she wore a casual off-white dress and beaded necklace—an unfussy everywoman squared off against the bloodless and stuffy Geithner, who for all the months and months of efforts by White House handlers still came off as condescending and galaxies removed from the plight of small business owners. Ellmers began her segment by asking why the Treasury secretary would raise taxes on people making more than $250,000 when "those are our business owners."

"They're three percent of your small business owners," Geithner could not resist correcting.

Countering with her own favorite data point, she replied, "Sixty-four percent of jobs created in this country are from small businesses."

The secretary agreed. But, he said, the high deficits necessitated an increase in revenue. Otherwise, Geithner said, "I'll have to go out and borrow another trillion dollars over the next ten years to finance those tax benefits for the top two percent. I don't think I can justify doing that. And if we were to cut spending by that magnitude to do it, you'd be putting a huge additional burden on the economy—probably a greater net economic impact than that modest change in revenue."

"What is the goal, then, in increasing taxes?" Ellmers asked.

The goal, Geithner reiterated, was to reduce the deficit.

Believing that she had scored a point, Ellmers pressed, "But if as you stated, only three percent of small businesses will be affected, then how can that increase in taxation be that significant to turn that around?"

"Well, you're making our case," Geithner said. He went on to explain that, as in the case of the Ryan budget plan, failure to increase taxes meant that deficit reduction would have to come from "exceptionally deep cuts in benefits for middle-class Americans."

"Okay, I'd like to reclaim my time," Ellmers eventually cut in. "We all agree: jobs are the answer. And yet, you are willing and more than capable of putting that excessive burden—which we already know from our small business owners is the issue—why would we do more? Why would we harm them more? Why would we create more uncertainty in the private sector?"

Geithner seemed a bit confused. "I'm not sure we disagree fundamentally," he managed. "Our economy needs to grow to create jobs. Our basic challenge . . ." And from there the Treasury secretary listed what he believed were the planks to such a foundation: increasing exports, expanding infrastructure and education, and "a balanced, growth-friendly approach to deficit reduction over time. Because if you don't fix that problem, you'll leave a broader cloud over the economy, longer-term. But we've got to be careful how we do it, so we don't hurt the economy."

"Well, Mr. Secretary," said Ellmers as she looked earnestly into Tim Geithner's eyes, "I would just like to close by saying that on behalf of the business owners in North Carolina, and across this country: you are wrong."

YOU ARE WRONG became the *Drudge Report*'s insta-headline. The Ellmers-Geithner YouTube video went viral. Though her declaration had been willfully unresponsive to Geithner's points—a kind of playground so's-your-face rejoinder—Ellmers was savvy enough to know what mattered. What mattered was the cinematic appeal of a spunky Republican freshman from a small North Carolina town uttering those words to the imperious Obama cabinet secretary and Wall Street titan. The next day, a reporter saw her and Ann Marie Buerkle emerging from the House chamber and called out, "Mr. Secretary, you are *wrong!*"

"I love it!" Renee Ellmers exclaimed, and held up her hand to offer a high-five.

Now she was an insider, aligned with Republican leadership on virtually every vote and being blasted by both sides back home for simultaneously cutting too much and too little. But now she was protected: the North Carolina Republican establishment had awarded her a newly redrawn district map. Ellmers's territory now stretched into the conservative Raleigh suburbs, while every nearby Democratic neighborhood had been shunted off into a thirty-mile appendage and attached to the Chapel Hill–based district long represented by Democrat and former professor David Price.

Ellmers still viewed herself as a nurse, housewife, and mother, all of which required that she be practical. In her view, too many of her fellow freshmen were feeling the heat of the Tea Party movement. Their impulse, she believed, was to "go storming the White House with pitchfork and torches," tearing down Big Government on a single rampage. A few of them could not resist thwarting the Republican message "with an alternate one, because they're the smartest guys in any room at any time. So what they do is divide us."

A reporter had recently asked the nine female freshmen if they thought of themselves as feminists. Among them, only Ellmers responded in the affirmative. As she saw it, the party of old white males had to change—and those who effected the change needed to be not simply women, but unabashedly ordinary women. On a Fox appearance with several other congresswomen (including, for once, Jo Ann Emerson), she and her colleagues lingered with the live female-only audience after the taping ended. They shared stories and hugs and one of the ladies exclaimed, "You guys are *congresswomen*? But you're so . . . regular!"

Ellmers thought, *It's because there are only two faces to the women's conservative movement: Bachmann and Palin.* Ellmers wished the audience could have attended the recent Republican conference in which two of her fellow North Carolinians, Virginia Foxx and Sue Myrick, stood at the two microphones and forcefully defended the Republican leadership against a few critics—who were, of course, male.

Ellmers just loved how those two tough birds shut up those loudmouths. *You are WRONG*—loved it!

PART FOUR

RASCALITY

CHAPTER TWENTY-ONE

Coffee with Your Congressman

At 7:30 on a spring morning in Ingleside, Texas, Blake Farenthold walked into the local youth community center and nodded appreciatively at the stock of Starbucks coffee and breakfast tacos that his staff had provided for whoever might show up. That had been the big question throughout the "constituent work week": was he ever going to meet the majority of registered voters in the 27th District, most of them Hispanic, who had not bothered to vote in the previous election but would likely do so in 2012?

He had not met them at his town hall two nights ago, on the border city of Brownsville. That audience had been almost entirely Tea Party libertarian, most of them Anglos. Nor had he met them at last night's town hall at a Corpus Christi elementary school. "I'm gonna be real honest with you—I'm a little disappointed with the turnout," the congressman had said to the hundred or so who had filed in. Several of them were local Democratic activists. One of them trained a video camera on Farenthold throughout and had criticized the Ryan budget plan's refusal to raise taxes on the wealthy while cutting programs to the poor and ending the Medicare guarantee. "Not all of us were born with a trust fund," the Democrat concluded pointedly.

Farenthold had not responded to the matter of his personal fortune—which *Roll Call* had estimated at $8.51 million, placing him at thirty-ninth in wealth among the 535 in Congress. But he did conclude that evening by telling the activists, "Can you and I find some time to sit down and talk about issues and see where we can find common ground? Because I want a better life for this district and I just think we differ on how to get there."

Of course, the "better life for this district" for Blake Farenthold, politically speaking, was to have a better district. The Republican-controlled Texas legislature was on the case at that very moment. Assuming that it withstood court challenges, Farenthold's new district would extend no farther south than Corpus and would instead be stretched northward along the Gulf Coast and then cut sharply westward into the Hill Country, like a bloodhound hot on the trail of conservative white constituents. He would no longer represent the border city of Brownsville, whose transit authority director had recently pled with him not to reduce federal funding for the city's bus lines. The previous congressman, Solomon Ortiz, had procured millions in grants for the Brownsville Transit Authority. Farenthold had nothing to offer the director.

Still, for now, this was his district, and he intended to represent everyone in it. He had visited some of the rural community health clinics and could see their value. If the Republicans succeeded in repealing Obamacare, such clinics were the only answer for thousands of his low-income constituents. The clinics, of course, were being slashed as well.

It did, nonetheless, irk Farenthold, this wholesale dependency on, as he put it, "what can the government do for me?" At the previous night's town hall in Corpus, the normally placid and good-humored congressman had suddenly become red-faced as he said in a rising voice, "As you listen to the budget debate and you listen to people saying don't cut this, don't cut that, the government's got to do this, the government's got to take care of that problem, I'm reminded of something John F. Kennedy said: 'Ask not what your country can do for *you*; ask what *you* can do for your country.' And it's not the government's job—*this is the greatest country on earth! People are risking their lives every day to sneak into this country illegally, just for the chance to have an opportunity! And we are sitting here bickering! This is still the land of opportunity! We get there through hard work, self-reliance, helping our family, and helping one another!*"

The JFK line "just popped into my head," Farenthold said as he waited for the Ingleside crowd to trickle in. "And again, I feel like that's what's wrong with America today. We were built on rugged individualism and that's the American dream: going out and becoming a millionaire as a result of the fruits of your labors and the brilliance of your idea, not by sitting home and watching *Jerry Springer* and getting your welfare check . . . If you talked to every successful person, they'll have failed at something. I was fired at my first job at the radio station by the guy who's now the Republican chairman of Nueces County and one of my biggest supporters."

Why, exactly, was he fired?

"I deserved to be fired," Farenthold grinned goofily. "It was, uh, a behavioral issue. I was sixteen, and indiscretions were committed."

Committed in the radio studio, perhaps?

"No comment," said the freshman, blushing somewhat.

The people from Blake Farenthold's sliver of America filing in to have coffee with their congressman had greater preoccupations than the sins of his youth. The unemployment rate remained at 9 percent, and job growth had ground to a halt. On April 18, Standard & Poor's downgraded its appraisal of the United States' debt from stable to negative for the first time in the nation's history. "We believe there is a material risk that U.S. policymakers might not reach an agreement on how to address medium- and long-term budgetary challenges by 2013," the financial services firm intoned.

The looming issue of the moment was the debt ceiling. In a GOP conference, Speaker Boehner had warned his colleagues that failing to raise the ceiling would amount to "Armageddon." That was not what Farenthold was hearing at the town hall in Brownsville the other night. The tea partiers in attendance maintained that such apocalyptic talk was baloney. Farenthold wondered if there was a way to leverage the issue into something that would please the conservative base. He wrote Boehner a letter about the debt ceiling matter just the other day.

"My fear," the letter said, "is that the debt ceiling is very possibly a hostage we're unwilling to shoot."

Boehner had not yet responded to the letter. "Politically, I would be better off voting 'no,'" he mused aloud. "But all the financial people tell me it's gonna be Armageddon. So at this point I'm officially undecided."

Gesturing to the people filing in, he continued, "The purpose of these town halls is to discuss this and get a feeling. Again"—he interrupted himself—"I'm a representative. And part of being a representative is listening to the people that elected you. But leadership is doing what you think is right. You're a leader *and* a representative. And not always do those coexist. But you have to do both."

He sounded more than a little miserable.

Nearby stood a white-haired man in a black T-shirt. He stepped away, shaking his head. "I was listening in, trying to figure out if he's left[-wing]," the man said of his congressman. With disgust, he added, "He's left. Undecided on the debt ceiling, to me, is left."

"I'm going to get started—feel free to get your coffee," Farenthold announced as he headed to the front of the gathering, which numbered no more than twenty-five. He asked one of his district office employees to lead them in prayer.

Farenthold then began as he always did, as pretty much all of the Republican freshmen did—with a monologue on the nation's debt, Washington's addiction to spending, and the oppressive state of government overregulation. "Texas is particularly hard hit—it seems that they don't particularly like us," he said of the EPA. "No one gets fired in Washington, D.C., for saying no. We need to change that culture to where you get fired *if* you say no."

The audience applauded warmly. Once again, Blake Farenthold found himself preaching to the Tea Party choir. The other voters of the 27th District had yet to surface.

His voice became sheepish as he turned to the nation's spiraling debt. "We all went up to Washington on a mission to change things," he said. "What I found is that the Founding Fathers set it up where it's a little more difficult to do. We've got the Senate and the president to deal with. So we're trying to put the brakes on the spending without creating too much of a situation where . . ."

Farenthold stared at the floor and said nothing for several seconds.

"I'm just gonna say it," he then continued. "There's a real concern about shutting down the government."

The reaction to those last words was instant, almost Pavlovian:

"Why? Why not shut it down?!"

"I lived through it before—we shut it down twice!"

"Didn't hurt a thing!"

"And that's what we need to talk about, and this is what I want to listen to you guys about," he said hurriedly, a calming hand up in the air as he toggled from "leader" to "representative" mode.

The questions he fielded were uniformly of the antigovernment sentiment: the dubiousness of the debt ceiling, the foolhardiness of taxing the wealthy, the illegal immigrants on Medicaid. Then Ingleside's city manager, a middle-aged man wearing a tie and lizard-skin boots, named Jim Gray, stood up. "You mentioned jobs," he said. "Ingleside right now is probably the largest job creation area in this region. But it's a small community, and about ninety percent of the people who work here live somewhere else. The infrastructure costs are borne by the city."

The city manager was referring to the fact that Ingleside had been the home of a naval base that was designated to be closed in 2005 as part of the Base Realignment and Closure (BRAC) program. The Ingleside port remained active, but the federal funds promised from the base closure program had not materialized. Gray continued, "We have a chance to put six thousand jobs in this area. We are a job creation area! And we've heard all the talk about what government *isn't* going to do— but I've got a $15 million sewer plant and a $15 million road I need, and that doesn't count the water tank we're already going to fund with our ratepayers . . . Do we put it all on the backs of our taxpayers? Or do we come to you for help, when you were elected *not* to spend money? I mean, I get the dichotomy . . ." His voice trailed off helplessly.

The freshman seemed paralyzed for a moment. "You've got a good answer, you tell me," he finally said. "But government runs up the cost of everything you do." Chuckling darkly, Farenthold added, "You want to build an overpass here—I guarantee you it's gonna take you six years to get it permitted, even forgetting about the cost for now—"

"We're trying to work a public-private partnership," the city manager cut in, his voice plaintive. "But the issue is, we can't throw up our hands and say, 'Well, the government's not going to help us'—when we keep hearing the government tell us, 'Create jobs!' We're doing that here! And we're hearing the government say, 'We can't help you.'"

Farenthold smiled, looked at his feet, shrugged. "Bring me a solution," he said.

The city manager said that he would endeavor to do so, smiled bravely, and sat down.

The radio talk show atmosphere quickly resumed as audience members decried the big spenders in Washington. "As much as I hate to say it," Blake Farenthold lamented, "what I'm coming to realize is that all we're really able to do is put the brakes on. Imagine going real fast in a Flintstones car, and my heel is out there. I went to Washington to change the world, and all I can do is put my heel out."

Pacing, the cherubic congressman awkwardly waved an arm and said, "You've got the Michele Bachmanns and that group out there saying, 'Cut, cut, cut.' And another group out there saying, 'We can't do that, or we'll never get elected.'"

"But you *will* get elected!" someone in the audience protested.

"That's the tension in the Republican Party right now," Farenthold said helplessly. "The government was built on compromising. And it's frustrating as hell."

"But you didn't get elected to compromise!"

"But you have to, if you want to get things done," Farenthold mumbled. He sighed. "It's a delicate tightrope."

"The only time anyone compromises is when the Democrats want something!"

Farenthold nodded vigorously. "I said this during the campaign, and I'll stand by it today," he declared. "One of the problems the Republican Party has had is that we're too fast to compromise. You can compromise on the little stuff, but you can't compromise on your core principles."

Almost to himself, he murmured, "I worry about it every hour of every day."

"We've got an idiot in the White House with no experience who creates czars," growled a man who introduced himself as Old Weird Pete and happened to be the city's mayor.

"What part of 'illegal' do they not understand?" demanded a retiree. "Illegal aliens are taking a lot out of our budget, and we can't afford it. They need to get 'em out of here!"

"If you want to get rid of some of the waste and fraud and abuse, get rid of foreign aid!" the mayor chipped in.

An elderly woman said in a slow, grave voice, "I hope y'all are keeping a list of what that man Obama does every day to harm our country and to take away our freedoms, so that when we *do* get control of our government, hopefully everything that this man has done will be undone."

Farenthold nodded compliantly and gestured to another questioner. But the woman was not finished. "Also, I'm concerned about our national security," she said, "and these rockets that are coming over. Someone is practicing."

She turned to the others for validation. "Now, we saw the one from

California. But there have been others—my pastor and some other gentlemen saw something heading real low over Rockport. And San Antonio and Austin—what if it wipes out that population? Can you please find out what's going on?"

Farenthold licked his lips. Choosing his words carefully, he replied, "I'm just gonna tell you the sense that I get. And this isn't the result of any classified briefing that I get. I think our enemies are sensing weakness at the highest level of our government and are flexing their muscles right now."

He speculated that with all the current unrest in the Middle East, "the Muslim Brotherhood or some other organization that doesn't like us sees this as an opportunity to do something when we're unwilling to respond."

Looking at his watch, Blake Farenthold added, "We've only got five minutes left"—referring to the Q&A, not America as a whole.

Jim Gray lingered for a few minutes after the event broke up and Farenthold departed to another "Coffee with Your Congressman" event elsewhere in the district. The Ingleside city manager acknowledged that he was a steadfast Republican, and that he and the town's eight thousand voters "may have swung Blake's election." At the same time, Gray admitted that the freshman's predecessor Ortiz—a fourteen-term incumbent with considerable seniority on both the Armed Services and Transportation and Infrastructure committees—had been quite helpful to Ingleside in securing millions of dollars in road construction and economic development grants.

"Ortiz was a ranking member of Congress," Gray observed. "If he goes to deal with a government agency, something happens."

Sighing, he added, "When Blake goes . . . well, I'm sorry, but . . ."

CHAPTER TWENTY-TWO

The Hostage

After a first legislative session more productive than any that would follow it, the spring 1790 session of the First Federal Congress became mired in the singular topic of how to secure the nation's financial credit. At the time, the national debt amounted to $54.1 million. In addition, the individual states owed a combined $25 million to their creditors. Treasury Secretary Alexander Hamilton brought to Congress a detailed plan for how to reorganize the debts. Some elements, such as paying back foreign creditors in full, attracted no controversy. More worrisome to several legislators was Hamilton's stipulation that America commit to paying interest on its debts. But the secretary's provision that the federal government would assume all of the debts incurred by the individual states immediately provoked outrage, particularly from southerners who rebelled against the very concepts of a national bank, indebtedness to a centralized government, and commingling of state and federal monies.

As the Hamilton report prepared to hit the House floor for debate on January 28, 1790, Fisher Ames of Massachusetts immediately moved for a postponement, so that members could have more time to absorb its contents. For Ames himself, the matter was simple. An assumption of state debts would buttress the young federal government—and, frankly, the 1st District of Massachusetts needed the bailout from its $5 million in debts incurred during the Revolutionary War. Many of his constituents did not side with him. They feared high land taxes, and investors doubted the favorability of the repayment terms. Others—and perhaps Ames was among them—were hopeful that after all accounts were set to balance, the state of Massachusetts might wind up in the position of creditor. Regardless, as Ames wrote a friend, "In any country, a public debt absolutely afloat will produce agitation. How necessary then for us to act firmly and justly!"

The devil was not just in the details, however. The thunderous Georgia congressman James Jackson predicted that a permanent national debt would "settle upon our posterity a burden which they can neither bear nor relieve themselves from." Jackson's sentiments had the effect of causing members to revisit the largeness of the debt itself. But Ames, a staunch advocate of property rights, argued that if such debts were not viewed and thereby honored as public contracts, then neither were the people's other social compacts guaranteed.

James Madison then weighed in with a proposal that would discriminate in financial terms favorable to America's original creditors. Ames and Madison, both Federalists, had now become foes, the former arguing that the latter's plan would "rob on the highway to exercise charity." Ames's side prevailed, but the greater debate would be over assumption of state debts. Ames pointed out that the ammunition used at the Battle of Bunker Hill had been paid for by the state of Massachusetts but was, by any reasonable standard, a federal expenditure. Madison countered that it was unwise for the United States to assume an additional $25 million in state debts that it might not have the means to repay. Madison also feared that under assumption, his state of Virginia would pay more than it received.

From January through May, the matter of the national debt consumed all legislative oxygen. (The exception involved brief consideration of a Quaker antislavery petition, which touched off new salvos from states' rights advocates and had the effect of further dividing the North and South on the debt issue.) Ames and Madison became opposing legislative gladiators. The former fell back on the patriotic call to pay off war debts. The latter took refuge in the Anti-Federalist suspicion that certain states were likely to be treated unjustly. The public grew restless and creditors even more so, yet the impasse carried on into June with no resolution in sight.

Then a new wrinkle developed. The Pennsylvania delegation, a swing bloc, declared their wishes that the federal government's temporary residence be placed in Philadelphia. In return, the Pennsylvanians would vote to defeat assumption of state debts. Secretary Hamilton caught wind of the gambit and offered the Pennsylvanians the *permanent* residence in exchange for assumption votes. When the New York delegation refused to accept Philadelphia as the new seat of government and threatened to pull *their* support for assumption, Alexander Hamilton then turned to Virginia to determine the delegation's price.

Their price was the permanent residence for the federal government, on the banks of the Potomac River.

The Pennsylvanians agreed to go along, in return for hosting the temporary residence in Philadelphia.

Ames relented, and the Massachusetts congressman got assumption of state debts out of the bargain. Still, he wrote to a friend after the deal was struck, "I despise politics, when I think of this office."

Kevin McCarthy began each week in the late spring and early summer of 2011 by leading a group of his Republican colleagues on a field trip.

They would pile into a Capitol police van and drive a couple of miles west of the Capitol, to an unmarked ten-story glass building next door to a Five Guys Burgers & Fries restaurant. Since 1999, the building had been under lease by the Department of the Treasury's U.S. Mint, though in 2002 an inspector general's report had concluded that the space was excessive for the mint's needs. At present the building housed the Bureau of the Public Debt—which is why McCarthy liked to tell people that the building was located in Chinatown, though technically the office was a few blocks north of that neighborhood.

The congressmen would pile out of the van, enter the lobby, and take an elevator up to a boardroom where they would sit through a Power-Point presentation explaining how the bureau manages the public debt. Then they would stand behind a window and observe the sterile, emotionless spectacle of federal traders auctioning off America's debt by selling Treasury bills and U.S. savings bonds to foreign countries. As the bidding began, the multidigit numbers would crawl across the monitors, marking billions of new debt. The congressmen would be rendered speechless, as if bearing witness to a state-sponsored execution.

"So which countries is America invested in?" McCarthy asked at one point.

"None," was the answer. "We don't invest anymore."

The whip could see the impression that these field trips had, particularly on the freshmen. The sensorial enhancement of actually seeing America sell itself to China, Japan, and other countries made the subject of the debt less of an abstraction to them. They could now go back to their town halls and declare, *I care so much about this issue that I actually went to the building where we sell off our debt to the Chinese—and get this, folks: it's in Chinatown* . . . And after these field trips, they began to ask more questions.

And this was a good and necessary thing, since Kevin McCarthy knew something that many of these freshmen apparently did not—which was that Congress would ultimately need to raise the debt ceiling by August 2, so that the country could pay its bills and maintain its AAA credit rating. By the late spring of 2011, most of the eighty-seven freshmen and many of the more senior conservative House members were not of a mind to raise the ceiling, regardless of the consequences. McCarthy was working to change this.

During orientation last November, pollster Frank Luntz was doing a presentation in front of an audience of nearly all the freshmen. "How many of you are going to vote to raise the debt ceiling?" Luntz asked.

Four hands went up. "How many of you are going to vote against it?" he asked.

All of the others raised their hands. Luntz, whose expertise lay in messaging rather than policy, replied, "Good for you, because your base is going to kill you if you vote to raise the debt ceiling."

When Luntz said this, he noticed McCarthy making an unpleasant face. Luntz didn't understand why at the time. The pollster knew how the game was played. It was the president's job to raise the debt ceiling, and the opposition party's job to condemn him for doing so.

Eric Cantor took Luntz aside after the presentation. "You've caused us a problem here," the new majority leader said.

Luntz was aghast. No one told him that the Republicans were going to *help* Obama raise the debt ceiling.

Boehner was strangely unworried. In his view, the debt ceiling presented what he viewed as a historic opportunity to extract dramatic concessions from the White House. Specifically, he saw it as a path to enact major entitlement reform *and* have the signature of a Democratic president on it. His office had in fact sent out a letter to all Republican members after the passage of the Ryan budget on April 15, asking them to list their preconditions for raising the ceiling. But it would largely fall to Kevin McCarthy to move the freshmen from a hard "no" to a "yes, if."

The whip began holding a new round of listening sessions in his conference room, which just that spring sported a new feature: a mammoth canvas covering the entire northern wall, painted by McCarthy's friend Steve Penley, an artist celebrated by Sean Hannity, Glenn Beck, and other conservatives for his patriotic themes. The canvas depicted an expressionistic take on Emanuel Leutze's classic rendering of George Washington crossing the Delaware River on Christmas Day, 1776, to begin the Battle of Trenton. McCarthy loved the image, for among Washington's fellow passengers there appeared to be a woman, a black male, and a Native American. *All of America in the same boat. Paddling together.* The ultimate team-building metaphor.

At the listening sessions, David Camp, the Ways and Means Committee chairman, led off with a brief presentation on the 220-year history of the debt ceiling and Treasury Secretary Tim Geithner's statement that it must be raised by August 2 in order to avoid a federal default. Though he did not volunteer this, Camp himself had voted to raise the debt ceiling in the past, as had the next two speakers, Paul Ryan and McCarthy. Ryan then discussed some basic options for the members to consider demanding of the White House, including mandatory spending caps as a percentage of gross domestic product.

Then McCarthy gave his presentation, which he entitled, *Lessons Learned from the CR.* One such lesson: "Let's not do numerous votes on this." They had done this from February to April with a series of short-term Continuing Resolutions, and all the experience had done was create divisions rather than promote unity within the conference. The whip advised them to settle on a package that could muster 218 votes. Two other lessons: they should avoid continually modifying the original proposal and thereby risk confusing the message; and they should develop their own numbers rather than allowing other numbers to be imposed on them.

The members then contributed their thoughts. Some said that they would vote to raise the debt ceiling only if serious spending caps were mandated. Some demanded that Obama agree to repeal his own health care legislation. Many insisted on a balanced budget constitutional amendment as a precondition. But during the early sessions, most of the questions and comments expressed doubts that the debt ceiling actually needed to be raised.

McCarthy wrote down all of their ideas on a notepad. He rejected none of them as impractical or wrongheaded. On the contrary, he encouraged them to think big. "We all ran for a reason," he reminded them. "What's most of concern to you? What is it that we think will change America?"

To the whip's delight, several of the freshmen began coming back for more listening sessions. They were drilling down deeper. Everyone was having their say. By McCarthy's informal count, by the end of May only a dozen or so freshmen were still a "no" under any circumstances. The rest would vote "aye," if the deal was right.

At 10 A.M. on June 1, 2011, President Obama met with the House Republican conference in the East Room of the White House. Though the meeting had no agenda, everyone present was aware of the looming August 2 deadline to raise the $14.3 trillion debt ceiling by $2.4 trillion in order to prevent a default on the nation's obligations.

The previous evening, Ways and Means chairman Dave Camp brought to the floor a "clean" debt ceiling bill—that is, one with no preconditions attached—and promptly urged his colleagues to vote against it. No Republican voted for it, and House Democrats derided the bill as an unserious ploy. But from the White House there was silence. Already Obama had tacitly accepted that a raising of the debt ceiling would have to come with some kind of deficit reduction package. Already the Republicans were winning the negotiations.

"I'm deadly serious about facing up to the debt and the deficit," the president began. "Time is of the essence—we can't wait until August 2."

To the Republicans' surprise, Obama then said, "We need to reform entitlements."

The president also surprised them by saying, "If you're truly interested in reducing health care costs, I'm ready to do something about tort reform."

But Obama also indicated his determination to see revenue increases as part of any deficit reduction package that would accompany a debt ceiling deal. And several members gasped when the president observed that negotiations would be eased if all sides toned down the "demagoguing."

Paul Ryan had something to say on the latter subject. The Budgeteer reminded the president who had recently claimed that the Ryan budget would end Medicare for autistic children. "You've mischaracterized my plan," Ryan said. He then proceeded to reexplain the "Medicare premium support" component to his Road Map to Prosperity. When he was finished, the Republicans awarded him a standing ovation.

Speaker Boehner urged the president, "This is the moment. Let's not kick the can down the road. We're waiting for a plan from you."

Obama responded that any plan he sent over to the House would likely "be dead on arrival."

Only if it wasn't a serious plan, countered Kevin McCarthy. "The budget you sent over wasn't a serious one—it didn't get one vote from any Democrat in the Senate."

After the Republican leaders and committee chairmen each spoke, there was time for a comment from a single freshman. McCarthy had seen to it that the designee be Reid Ribble of Wisconsin. Ribble was a plain-spoken owner of a highly successful roofing business. During one of McCarthy's dinners, Ribble spoke of a regulation that had once been on the books forbidding workers from carrying plastic water bottles up to a rooftop—thus necessitating frequent (and dangerous) trips up and down the ladder to drink. McCarthy wanted Ribble to share that story of egregious overregulation with the president.

In fact, Ribble had already received face time with the president when he, as a Wisconsin native, was invited to the White House on Super Bowl Sunday to eat sports bar food and drink Hinterland beer while watching the Green Bay Packers defeat the Pittsburgh Steelers. But in addition to being a personal favorite of McCarthy's and the quintessential small businessman, Ribble had also been a loyal team player, never once crossing the Republican leadership on a major vote.

Ribble reintroduced himself to the president and mentioned unfair regulations. But his main message was about the debt. During the American Revolution, the Civil War, and World War II, the freshman said, America took on debt for the sake of "a bigger cause than ourselves." But today, by asking for a higher debt ceiling, the president was asking "future generations of this country to pay a debt for ourselves."

The freshmen clapped for their colleague. But after seventy-five minutes, there had been only speeches and partisan applause and nothing close to agreement.

Just after the meeting broke up, Idaho Tea Party freshman Raul Labrador made his way up to the president. Not one to mince words, Labrador said to Obama, "I actually want to take issue with—well, with a lot of things. But specifically, I don't think this freshman class would treat anything you send to the House as dead on arrival. We're more interested in actually getting something done. If your issues and values are going to be close to our issues and values, we can actually work together."

Obama seemed to be listening intently. "I can't speak for the senior members who've been here and are more jaded by politics," Labrador went on. "But the freshmen really do want to fix the problems of the country."

"I'm glad to hear that," the president replied. He looked around and noticed that several other freshmen were standing by, nodding along with Labrador's sentiment. "I'd like to work with you, too." The new House liaison for the White House, Jonathan Samuels, stepped forward and handed Labrador his card.

The freshman never heard from the White House after that. Nor did the White House hear from Labrador.

On Wednesday, June 22, Democratic Congressman James Clyburn had lunch with fellow members of the Congressional Black Caucus. The previous day, Clyburn had met for the ninth time with a bipartisan group of representatives and senators led by Vice President Joe Biden to discuss a debt ceiling deal. His fellow CBC members were as skeptical of such backroom negotiations as the Republican Tea Party freshmen. They felt that the final Continuing Resolution agreement hammered out by Boehner and Obama unfairly targeted discretionary programs for the poor and minorities while leaving defense spending and tax giveaways for the rich largely intact. Now they feared that the so-called Biden talks would produce the same outcome.

Clyburn's presence at the table was intended to quell those concerns. He had repeatedly called for "compassion" during such talks. Clyburn's definition of compassion was in fact broader than simply looking after the less fortunate. He had in mind the biblical parable of the Samaritan who tended to a man that had been robbed and beaten—presumably a man of some means, perhaps even a job creator. As the sole Democrat in the South Carolina delegation (albeit one in a district protected by Voting Rights Act provisions to guarantee minority representation), Clyburn had learned how to make himself relevant in a conservative state. He was pronuclear and along with Senator Lindsey Graham had been instrumental in acquiring funding to deepen the Charleston port. Nonetheless, his role during the Biden talks was clearly that of the Democratic Party's conscience. At one point, Eric Cantor proposed block-granting food stamps—a popular conservative idea that Speaker Gingrich's House Republicans had pushed in 1995 and had also been included in the Ryan budget plan. Much as with what Ryan had in mind for Medicaid, the proposal would essentially do away with the food stamp program and instead send each state a lump sum of federal money to spend on feeding the poor however they saw fit.

"If you knew the history of my state," the South Carolina African-American told the Republicans, "you wouldn't be in favor of that."

Cantor backed down immediately, and the subject did not come up again.

At the CBC lunch, Clyburn had good news for his black colleagues. The talks were going very well, he assured them. "I'd be very surprised if we didn't get something very positive done that each one of you guys will be able to vote for."

After the lunch, Clyburn returned to the Capitol to meet for the tenth time with Biden, fellow Democratic Congressman Chris Van Hollen, Republican House Majority Leader Eric Cantor, Democratic Senators Max Baucus and Dan Inouye, and Republican Senator Jon Kyl. What Clyburn did not know was that it would be the group's final meeting.

Throughout the talks, four documents sat alongside the seven men: the Ryan budget proposal, President Obama's budget framework, the report by the White House debt commission known as Bowles-Simpson, and the bipartisan task force plan steered by former Republican Senator Pete Domenici and former Clinton White House budget director Alice Rivlin. Obama's framework proposed to reduce the deficit by $2.5 trillion over the next decade; Bowles-Simpson by $3.8 trillion; Rivlin-Domenici by $6 trillion; and Ryan's plan by $6.2 trillion. Three of the four proposals included revenue increases as part of the package. Only the Republican plan authored by Paul Ryan did not.

During the very first meeting, on May 5 at Blair House, across the street from the White House, the vice president made clear that President Obama would only sign on to a deal that included revenue increases. Cantor and Kyl did not object. After the fourth meeting, on May 24, Biden repeated publicly the stipulation that "revenues are gonna have to be in the deal," while Cantor publicly said the opposite: "Tax increases are not going to be something we're going to support in the House."

Chris Van Hollen was not picking up on the positive vibes that had compelled Clyburn to speak so hopefully to his Congressional Black Caucus colleagues. Over the course of several meetings, both sides had outlined potential areas of spending cuts. The Democrats had also offered a menu of possible cuts in the mandatory health programs—all with the understanding that nothing was agreed to unless everything was agreed to. The vice president wanted to pay out the rope, keep the process going, hoping that the Republicans would be sufficiently encouraged by the Democrats' willingness to show their hand that they might finally do the same. Cantor in particular had impressed the Democrats with his congeniality and depth of policy knowledge. For a time, they interpreted these qualities as evidence that the majority leader was eager to cut a deal.

The day just prior to the CBC lunch, the Biden group had convened with a single item on the agenda: revenue proposals. Two Treasury officials, including Secretary Tim Geithner, went through a menu of options. The Republicans listened politely but declined each revenue-raising possibility. The Democrats were plaintive: *You guys just tell us which one of these you hate the least. Can we start with corporate jets? Oil and gas subsidies? Just tell us.*

It was clear to Van Hollen that Cantor and Kyl's strategy was to elicit from the Democrats what they would be willing to give up on the entitlements side while offering no such list of revenue options in return. Later that afternoon on the House floor, Democratic caucus chairman John Larson of Connecticut inquired hopefully about the progress.

"We're screwed," Van Hollen told him.

At the Wednesday meeting immediately following Clyburn's lunch with the CBC, the Democrats decided to be more emphatic about where they stood. After acknowledging the concessions the Democrats might be willing to make on Medicare and Medicaid, Van Hollen then said, "We're not going to engage in this debate seriously unless you're going to engage seriously on the revenue piece."

Cantor replied that the Republicans had no intention of going there.

"What are you guys giving, then?" Biden asked.

"Well, we're giving you the vote on the debt ceiling," said Cantor. "You may not think that's a big deal. But you've got to understand, I've got a lot of guys who think that not raising the debt ceiling wouldn't be such a bad thing—that in fact it's just what we need."

The Democrats weren't sure what to say.

Cantor added, somewhat abashedly: "We're working hard to educate our guys."

The meeting broke up cordially. Biden said, "Guys, we're running out of time. We'd better schedule some more meetings." Everyone agreed to do so, including Eric Cantor.

The others in the room were not privy to the wheels turning inside the majority leader's head. Despite the attack-dog nature of his job, Cantor was an exceedingly cautious man. He did not want to get far ahead of his own conference and thus become 2011's version of Roy Blunt, who had played a critical role in negotiating with Democrats the details of the 2008 Troubled Assets Relief Program, which multitudes of Republicans ended up voting against and for which conservatives would never forgive Blunt. If Cantor's conference was not willing to consider revenue increases, there was no point in pretending otherwise. It did not help matters that, as Cantor learned after the fact, Boehner had met privately with Obama at the White House a few hours after the Biden meeting on Wednesday to discuss possible tax reform as part of a "grand bargain." Cantor and Biden had struck up a rapport along the way, and the VP had told him some things about ongoing dialogue between Boehner and Obama of which Cantor had not been aware. The majority leader didn't see how he could continue to negotiate one kind of deal with the vice president while the Speaker was negotiating a different—and, from a revenue standpoint, antithetical—deal with the president.

The next morning, Thursday, June 23, Cantor informed Boehner and McCarthy that he was pulling out of the Biden talks. The reason he gave surprised both men—and would have surprised the Democrats, too, since it had no basis in fact: according to Cantor, Nancy Pelosi and Harry Reid intended to call a press conference announcing that the Democrats were walking away from the talks. Better to blow things up before Pelosi and Reid had a chance, Cantor argued. He then informed *Wall Street Journal* reporter Janet Hook of his intentions. That evening, Jim Clyburn emerged from a White House meeting with the president, during which Clyburn had told Obama that he remained "very encouraged" by the talks.

Then Clyburn saw the Hook story pop up on his BlackBerry and realized he had clearly been missing some signals.

"I want to let you know," Nancy Pelosi said to her caucus on the evening of July 6, "that we stand for Medicare, and we stand for Social Security. And tomorrow I'm going down to the White House to represent you to the president. And so I would just like to know."

The minority leader offered a coy smile. "Do I have your permission," she continued in a rising voice, "to go over there and say, *We're not cutting Medicare, we're not cutting Social Security?!*"

Those attending the caucus applauded wildly. Word had leaked of a meeting that day between Obama and Boehner during which the president indicated a willingness to include major entitlement reform as part of a "grand bargain." And tomorrow the president was inviting all top congressional leaders—including Pelosi and Steny Hoyer—to the White House to continue the negotiations.

Pelosi was well aware that the central focus of DCCC chairman Steve Israel's "Drive to 25" campaign to take back the House by capturing an additional twenty-five seats involved attacking Republicans for siding with Paul Ryan's "Medicare voucherization" budget plan. She had no intention of letting Obama hand the Democrats' winning formula over to Boehner as a sacrificial offering.

Twice during her brief remarks that evening, Pelosi said to her fellow Democrats: *Even if we make defensible changes in Medicare, such as cost containment, it'll be interpreted as us doing the same thing the Ryan budget is doing. It'll be interpreted as us cutting Medicare. We saw what happened in 2010. So we're not going to go there again. No way. No cuts to Medicare of any kind!*

Medicare was off the table, and so were revenue increases. That was the state of the debt ceiling negotiations with less than a month to go before August 2.

On the late afternoon of Wednesday, July 13, a group of two dozen senior House Republicans, including Kevin McCarthy and conference chairman Jeb Hensarling, met in the whip's office with an economist in his late fifties named Jay Powell. A decade ago, Powell had served as undersecretary of the Treasury in charge of finance. Among his duties had been to manage the debt limit. In recent weeks, Powell had been making the rounds at the Capitol to advise members on the looming issue of the debt ceiling.

Now he showed the same PowerPoint presentation to McCarthy, Hensarling, and the others. Powell's material was very cut-and-dried, free of editorializing. His slides showed the projected inflows and outflows in August and how that would impact the funding for federal programs. The picture he painted was unbelievably stark.

"This is a big deal," Hensarling said to his colleagues in the room when Powell was finished. "No matter where you stand on the issue, I think the conference needs to see this as a neutral source of information." When McCarthy and the others did not object, he turned to Powell and said, "I want to get this to them as soon as possible. When are you available?"

Powell said that he would make the time.

Hensarling warned him that the freshmen and other conservatives in the conference would react poorly if it appeared that Powell was trying to lead them to a conclusion. Even if Powell presented his data with utmost impartiality, as he was now doing, Hensarling prepared Powell for the likelihood that he would still encounter some hostility.

Hensarling sent out word to the House Republicans that Jay Powell would be giving a presentation at a conference on Friday the fifteenth at eight in the morning in HC-5. Staff would not be allowed to attend.

The Capitol basement conference room was nonetheless packed with more than two hundred members that morning. "I don't give political or tactical advice," Powell told his audience. "But I do understand how this statute works and several years ago had the job of managing it." He then showed a series of slides depicting how actual cash flows would, by August 2, dissolve into actual shortage. Powell also addressed the two "silver bullet" options: for the Democrats, having President Obama invoke the Fourteenth Amendment ("The validity of the public debt of the United States . . . shall not be questioned") as his executive authority for raising the debt unilaterally; and for the Republicans, selling off American assets as a means of settling debts. Powell dismissed both options, saying, "There's no bag of tricks."

Then the economist turned to the most sobering part of the presentation—"going from the thirty-thousand-foot level of rhetoric to parachuting down into the jungle," as he put it. Powell showed what the month of August would look like. The Treasury would be taking in $172 billion. Its obligations that month would be $306 billion, a shortfall of $134 billion. After first paying the interest, enough money would be left over to pay approximately half the bills. It would be left to the Obama administration to determine winners and losers. As a factual matter, Powell pointed out, it would be impossible to pay the troops in the field and all Social Security, Medicare, and Medicaid benefits at the same time. Institutions such as federal prisons would simply have to be shut down. The average American's home mortgage rate would skyrocket.

The first person to the microphone at the conclusion of Powell's talk was freshman Steve Pearce of New Mexico. "This was completely biased," he barked. "I'm outraged that you would be doing a presentation without once mentioning our long-term fiscal problems!"

Hensarling hastened to the front microphone. "I asked Mr. Powell to just talk about the debt ceiling," the chairman explained. "Paul [Ryan] is going to talk about long-run fiscal issues later."

"That's not an answer!" the freshman persisted. "Why didn't you address this, sir?"

Right behind Steve Pearce was Georgia Congressman Phil Gingrey, who began by saying that until yesterday he had never heard of Powell's Bipartisan Policy Center. "You did a nice job with your presentation," he said. "But we heard from Karl Rove yesterday—and frankly," he grinned, "I like him better." (Rove had met with Gingrey and about thirty other conservatives for breakfast the morning before, as part of a weekly "Theme Team" gathering hosted by Congressman Jack Kingston. Rove's column "Obama Owns the Debt Ceiling Fiasco" had just been published that same morning in the *Wall Street Journal*.)

Then Gingrey proceeded to read an email off his BlackBerry, forwarded to him by a friend who was an investment broker, quoting various bankers and other sources casting doubts about the validity of the August 2 deadline. With evident satisfaction, Gingrey concluded, "I have made my point and I will take my seat."

Republican Policy Committee chairman Tom Price interjected, "This is not the period for member statements. Unless you have a question for the gentleman, please hold your comments until the end."

They did so, and although a number of attendees asked thoughtful questions, Louie Gohmert of Texas and Californian Tom McClintock took turns disparaging Powell near the end. Renee Ellmers was among those who were thoroughly embarrassed by her colleagues' rudeness. A number of the members approached Powell after the conference, thanking him for his insights and apologizing for the misbehavior of their fellow Republicans.

And yet Pearce, Gingrey, Gohmert, and McClintock were far from Republican outliers. They represented a point of view—embraced by many freshmen and senior conservatives, but also by millions of Americans—that the nation was on the brink of something every bit as perilous as default. As they saw it, and as they believed any rational person would see it, the country couldn't go on this way, spending unfathomable sums of money that it did not have, becoming ever deeper in debt to the Chinese and thereby consigning America's children and grandchildren to a second-rate future. As the senior members well knew, excuses could always be found in Washington to ignore reality. But to the freshmen, and the movement that had elected them, excuses were no longer acceptable.

Boehner himself had said it over and over: "This is the moment." But a number of freshmen continued to wonder: did the Speaker really believe that? And for Boehner, did "the moment" mean another backroom compromise with Obama?

After Cantor and Kyl had departed the Biden talks, Boehner had indeed resumed discussions with the president, along with other congressional leaders, to try to formulate a "grand bargain" that might encompass not only significant spending reductions but also entitlement and tax reform. At the first White House meeting, Cantor produced a chart of all the entitlement reform options the Democrats at the Biden talks had suggested they might consider—a violation of the nothing-is-agreed-to-until-everything-is-agreed-to pact that infuriated the Democrats.

Boehner, for his part, was upset that the White House continually leaked the framework of each discussion before it had actually taken place. That was not the Speaker's way, and definitely not the way of his secretive chief of staff, Barry Jackson—and in a way, their way was part of the problem.

At a conference in late July, Boehner had led off by describing how his talks with Obama indicated that the president was willing to make big concessions on spending and entitlement reform. Raul Labrador immediately went to the mike and said, "I have to tell you, I feel a whole lot better than I did thirty minutes ago. Thank you for sharing the information with us. And I urge you to keep doing that in the future so that we don't have to learn about it in the newspaper."

After the conference, a number of senior members thanked the frequently contrarian Idaho freshman for his show of appreciation. But they were missing the point—which was that Boehner's reticence was an ongoing matter of concern to the Tea Party mavericks like Labrador who had come to Washington innately distrusting both its customs and the leaders who practiced them. One monologue by Boehner had hardly quelled all suspicions.

Around the time of Labrador's remarks, four of Boehner's closest pals in the House—Mike Simpson of Idaho, Tom Latham of Iowa, and Steve LaTourette and Pat Tiberi from Boehner's state of Ohio, constituting the core of the "Friends of Boehner" group that convinced him to run for majority leader in 2006—contacted Barry Jackson and told the chief of staff that they needed to have a meeting with the Speaker right away. The four members first sat down with Jackson.

"John may not see what's going on, but we do," they told Jackson. "Cantor's staff is running around telling people that Boehner actually told Cantor to walk out of the Biden talks because Boehner was mad that Cantor was getting all the ink. Bullshit like that."

"That's what Cantor and Ryan want," Jackson smirked. "They see a world where it's Mitch McConnell [as Senate majority leader], Speaker Cantor, a Republican president, and then Paul Ryan can do whatever he wants to do. It's not about this year. It's about getting us to 2012, defeating the president, and Boehner being disgraced." That, said the chief of staff, was Cantor and Ryan's "Young Guns" vision of a better world.

Boehner's four friends repeated their concerns in their meeting with the Speaker. They were aware, as one of them would later say, that "when John was meeting with the president and put revenues on the table, some of the members had started to scream." They knew that Boehner was not by nature a worrier—but, they warned him, in this instance he needed to be. "You're more between a rock and a hard place than any Speaker I've ever seen," one of them said. It wasn't just the freshmen, either. Latham and LaTourette along with Boehner had been present for the overthrow of Speaker Newt Gingrich. It only took a small handful of disgruntled members to start the brushfire. And Cantor would leave no fingerprints.

"What you cannot do," they told Boehner, "is come back from the White House with some kind of deal that's only going to get fifty votes in our conference. It's going to be like Son of TARP—some of the freshmen don't have a grasp of what the facts are, and they're going to rebel. You'd be finished."

The Speaker became contemplative. "Okay," he finally said. "I've got to think about this. I appreciate you guys coming."

Boehner had never thought that a balanced budget amendment to the Constitution was particularly necessary. At a Club for Growth event during the spring, he told his Republican colleagues that such an initiative was little more than a "gimmick." A number of senior members did not share that opinion but had come to the conclusion over the years that passage of a constitutional amendment was simply too heavy a lift.

The freshmen, unsurprisingly, did not see things this way. During Kevin McCarthy's listening sessions, the concept grew in desirability until it emerged as the singular predominating solution—one that was structural and history-making. The whip advised Boehner, "You've got to have some tie to a balanced budget amendment to get the bill through."

Boehner relented. He often summed up his practical (and to some, passive) view of leadership by saying, "If you say, 'Follow me,' and no one does, you're not leading—you're just taking a walk." Having heard the warnings from his four Republican friends, Boehner had no interest in taking a lone walk, particularly if it amounted to walking the plank.

Instead, on July 14, he held a press conference with Cantor conspicuously by his side, and announced, "I can't think of anything that would do more to ensure such spending restraints are set in stone than implementing a balanced budget amendment to the Constitution ... Frankly, it's just common sense."

But the next day, Boehner yielded again to the advice of McCarthy and Cantor and scrapped the balanced budget amendment legislation drawn up by Virginia Congressman Bob Goodlatte. In its place was a bill conceived the previous month that would cut the deficit in half within a year's time; cap all future federal spending to an amount not exceeding 18 percent of the nation's gross domestic product; and raise the debt ceiling contingent on passage of Goodlatte's balanced budget amendment—which also stipulated that any revenues raised to help balance the budget would require "super-majority" approval of two-thirds of Congress.

On July 19, the House voted on a largely party-line vote, 234–190, to pass Cut, Cap, and Balance. Three days later, the bill went over to the Senate, where defeat was virtually assured.

A number of the more moderate Republicans were okay with the bill's futility. Though time was fast running out before the August 2 deadline, they understood that Boehner had to let the freshmen and the senior conservatives—and their Tea Party constituents—feel as if they had exhausted all options, had fought the good fight.

Still, the disconnect between what Boehner himself had termed fiscal "Armageddon" and the bullheadedness of the tea partiers unnerved members like Jo Ann Emerson. She sidled up to one of the freshmen one day and said, "I need you to explain why you don't think there's anything wrong with us defaulting on the debt. I can't have this conversation with my constituents because I'll yell at them and they'll yell at me. So you tell me."

The freshman's reply bewildered Emerson. "We've spent way too much money," he told her. "If this is the price we pay, so be it."

Emerson wanted to reply: *You asshole! Do you really not understand what could happen here?*

When she got home that evening, Jo Ann Emerson's greeting to her husband was "Just pour me a big glass of wine. I cannot believe that I had this conversation with somebody who was elected to Congress."

Jeff Duncan refused to accept it. He refused to believe that Harry Reid and the Senate were so immovable, so heedless to common sense and the urgency of the moment, that they would turn a blind eye to a serious fiscal remedy just as they had batted away H.R.1 and the Ryan budget plan. He refused to accept that this was just some therapeutic, box-checking exercise on the part of House leadership to cool the hot blood of the Tea Party freshmen.

On the afternoon of Thursday, July 21, the South Carolina freshman was standing on the floor next to fellow conservative freshman Tim Huelskamp of Kansas. "You know," Duncan said, "we ought to walk over there to the Senate tomorrow and look them in the eye while they're voting."

"That's a great idea," said Huelskamp. "We ought to get at least thirty of us and just be there, watching."

Viewing the occasion as an historic one, Duncan added, "I'd just kind of like to see the vote anyway."

Duncan's scheduler began sending out emails while the congressman notified Senator Jim DeMint. "That's great," the South Carolina delegation's political godfather said. He agreed to meet the gathering at Statuary Hall, the geographical midpoint between the two chambers.

Later that evening, during a marathon Foreign Affairs Committee meeting, Duncan passed a note to Renee Ellmers. *A bunch of us are going to go over to the Senate floor tomorrow and look them in the eye when they're taking the vote,* it read. Ellmers nodded that she was in.

Boehner convened another conference the next morning, Friday, July 22. Amid the hand-wringing over the impending Senate vote, Ellmers stood before the microphone and said, "Look, we're winning this argument! Let's stay on message! Cut, Cap, and Balance is what we passed! We've done our job—it's on the Senate and president now. And look, this is a huge deal. The president can go down in history as the one who signed a balanced budget amendment to the Constitution. I mean, Mr. Speaker, you should appeal to Obama's ego, because it's bigger than the deficit!"

The room erupted in laughter and applause. "Who gave you that line?" McCarthy asked her after the conference.

"That's *my* line, thank you very much," Ellmers sniffed.

"Well," laughed the whip, "it's your quotable quote!"

Immediately following the conference, Jeff Duncan stood in Statuary Hall with the three other South Carolina freshmen, DeMint, Senator Rand Paul, and a half-dozen other congressmen. They formed a tight huddle as DeMint did most of the talking.

"You've gotta tell Boehner to cut the bullshit," the senator said in a low voice. His face pursed in disgust, he continued, "When we go over to the White House like children . . ."

He then addressed the matter immediately at hand: the impending Senate vote on Cut, Cap, and Balance. "You shouldn't go down in the well while they're voting. But you've got floor privileges. You can just stand in the back, mill around, whatever. And if you see a senator and want to convince him, by all means do so. Okay?"

Jeff Duncan then said, "Senator, do you mind if we pray real quick?"

"Yeah, Jeff, let's do that," DeMint replied.

They bowed their heads. "Heavenly Father," Duncan said quietly, "we ask that you lift up the Senate on this historic vote. We know you were present when the nation was created. And we ask that you be present and give these guys strength this morning in the Senate. We ask this in Christ's name, Amen."

Then the group of a dozen or so, joined along the way by Ellmers and Ann Marie Buerkle, marched northward down the marble corridor toward the Senate.

They stepped inside the chamber.

A low murmur, almost melodic, was general throughout the surprisingly small and elegantly lit room. Along the floor stood several small groups of senators, talking pleasantly among themselves and completely unaware of the new visitors who had ambled in and now stood in the back, eyeing the inhabitants with the unease of shabbily attired plebians who had barged into a country club. As each senator entered the chamber, he or she simply made a gesture with a thumb, followed by the almost soothing feminine voice of the clerk: *Mr. Franken votes "no" . . . Mrs. Murray votes "no" . . .*

Harry Reid saw the visitors. The majority leader made his way to the back, welcomed them to the Senate, introduced himself, and then began to shake hands.

"Senator," said Duncan, "I sure would love to see some debate. I think the American people deserve that—not just a motion to table the bill . . ."

But Reid, standing not more than three feet away, did not acknowledge the freshman's words and continued to shake hands.

Ellmers looked for her fellow North Carolinian, Senator Kay Hagen. She and the Democrat had sat together during the State of the Union address. But this morning Hagen was nowhere in sight. Ellmers checked her watch. There were votes on Appropriations bills taking place down the hall. She left.

Duncan found West Virginia Senator Joe Manchin, a noteworthy moderate among Democrats. The South Carolinian made his pitch.

Looking around, Manchin said quietly, "If you could find three other votes, I'd go along."

Duncan could not find three other votes. Cut, Cap, and Balance was tabled on a 51–46 vote. He and the other House conservatives walked out of the Senate chamber. The senators remained huddled, as in a priesthood, and paid their departure as little mind as they had their arrival.

At 5:30 that same afternoon, Speaker John Boehner informed President Obama by phone that he was pulling out of the White House negotiations. "A deal was never reached, and was never really close," he said in a letter to his Republican colleagues. The letter cited two insurmountable stumbling blocks: "The president is emphatic that taxes have to be raised . . . The president is adamant that we cannot make fundamental changes to our entitlement programs." Boehner went on to say that he would now "begin conversations with the leaders of the Senate in an effort to find a path forward."

Curiously, Boehner did not mention in his letter the reason he and his staff would later cite for his having pulled out of the discussions—

which was that the president had "moved the goal posts" by insisting three days earlier that Boehner's initial offer of $800 billion in revenue hikes be increased to $1.2 trillion, in keeping with a proposal that had been unveiled that same day by a bipartisan group of senators known as the Gang of Six. Less than an hour after Boehner notified Obama that he was ending their negotiations, the president convened a press conference. He did not bother to conceal his anger. While acknowledging that he had made a counterproposal on revenues, Obama added that "when you've got a ratio of four dollars in cuts for every dollar in revenue, that's pretty hard to stomach."

Said the president, "It is hard to understand why Speaker Boehner would walk away from this kind of deal." He concluded tartly by saying, "And at some point, I think if you want to be a leader, you got to lead."

Eleven days remained until the D-day of August 2, 2011.

Allen West was surprised when he received an invitation to have dinner with the whip team on Monday, July 25. Not only had Kevin McCarthy never before asked him to join the group for dinner, but the Florida freshman wasn't exactly being looked upon favorably in recent days.

The previous Tuesday, West had been on the floor to defend Cut, Cap, and Balance—though first to correct yet another Democrat, this time Peter Welch of Vermont, who had confused him with the other black Republican, Tim Scott. "I'm not from South Carolina—I'm from Florida, but that's okay, I'm the guy with hair," West had ribbed Welch, before reiterating his support for the Republican bill and concluding, "I stand in support of H.R.2560 because this is insanity, and we cannot continue to do the same thing expecting different results."

He then left the floor. Upon arriving at his office on the seventh floor of the Longworth Building, West was told by a staffer, "Wasserman Schultz went after you!"

Immediately after West's speech, the Florida Democrat had spoken against Cut, Cap, and Balance. "And incredulously [sic]," she had said, "the gentleman from Florida, who represents thousands of Medicare beneficiaries, as do I, is supportive of this plan that would increase costs for Medicare beneficiaries—unbelievable from a member from south Florida . . ."

Well, that's not appropriate—going after me when I'm not there, he thought, and immediately he fired off an email to his Florida counterpart, copied to several Republican leaders:

> Look, Debbie, I understand that after I departed the House floor you directed your floor speech comments directly towards me. Let me make myself perfectly clear, you want a personal fight, I am happy to oblige. You are the most vile, unprofessional and despicable member of the US House of Representatives. If you have something to say to me, stop being a coward and say it to my face, otherwise, shut the heck up.

The two Floridians had a history. Wasserman Schultz had been close to West's Democrat predecessor, Ron Klein. When it emerged during the 2010 election cycle that West had penned op-eds for a biker magazine that also published outlandishly sexist commentary, the congresswoman had staged a protest outside the candidate's Deerfield Beach campaign headquarters. "He thinks it's okay to objectify and denigrate women," she told a TV reporter.

Though she had been joined by no more than fifty other protesters, the incident got under West's skin—and not just because his wife and two daughters did not consider him to be sexist. Instead, West seemed to view her action as a threat of sorts. When asked by a reporter in the wake of the Giffords shooting if he had ever felt in danger during his political life, West replied by saying that Wasserman Schultz had "incited a riot in front of my campaign headquarters."

Not many Republican congressmen—outside of the women's softball team, anyway—had nice things to say about the DNC chairwoman, who had been known to engage in hyperbole herself. Even so, West's comments were viewed within the GOP conference as excessive and not helpful to a party that was trying to win over suburban housewives and trying to recruit more female candidates. Some of the women from the class of 2010 were offended by West's hair-trigger reaction to a simple floor rebuttal. If he couldn't deal with rudimentary criticism from the opposing party, then how long did Allen West expect to last in the political arena?

McCarthy had approached West on the House floor. The whip told the freshman, "Look, I've got your back." But he also said, "You know, when I get upset about something, I write a letter and just send it to my wife or my friends. Just to let the steam out."

McCarthy viewed West as a serious man. And as someone who occasionally suffered rueful pangs for not serving in the military, McCarthy respected both West's courage and his strategic mentality. He noticed how the freshman was always among the very first to show up at conferences and always stayed until the end, almost never speaking but instead taking meticulous notes. So when Boehner unveiled his new debt ceiling plan on the morning of Monday, July 25, the whip thought it might not be a bad idea to bring Allen West along to the whip team dinner and take the freshman's temperature.

The dinner was at Art and Soul, a relatively new Capitol Hill establishment favored by Michelle Obama. As usual, McCarthy had gathered a mix of freshmen (Trey Gowdy, Tim Griffin) and more senior members (Charlie Dent, Marsha Blackburn)—and as usual, the whip threw out a couple of icebreaking questions. West divulged that his first concert was Earth, Wind & Fire, while his most embarrassing moment was at a University of Tennessee football game when a friend vomited all over him.

Talk eventually turned to the Boehner plan, which came in two stages. In the first stage, Congress would cut the deficit by $1.2 trillion and raise the debt ceiling by $1 trillion, thus funding government operations through the end of 2011. It would impose spending caps that, if exceeded, would trigger across-the-board cuts. Then a bipartisan "supercommittee" composed of twelve congressmen would identify an additional $1.8 trillion in savings that both chambers would have to pass without amendments, and the president would have to sign, before the debt ceiling could be raised an additional $1.6 trillion. At the same time, both the House and the Senate would have to vote on (though not necessarily pass) a balanced budget amendment to the Constitution by the end of 2011.

Tellingly, the Speaker had called radio talk show host Rush Limbaugh that morning to sell the überconservative on the plan. Nonetheless, many archconservatives felt that the cuts and caps were not sufficiently severe. In the meantime, Democrats insisted that the plan was a legislative nonstarter and thus an irresponsible waste of precious time before the August 2 deadline.

At the dinner, McCarthy asked West what he thought. Like every other Republican, the freshman had been hearing from Tea Party groups back home about how the debt ceiling should not be raised under any circumstances. West had advised some of his weaker-kneed colleagues, "Look, you've gotta stand. You've got to be able to come up here and evaluate legislation from the experiences you're having here. If they know they can pull your strings, then guess what—they will."

Or, as West had told one of his staffers, "If you allow the Tea Party to become a Roman mob, they'll dog you the rest of the time you're here."

Replying to the whip, West said, "The bill's not perfect. It's not everything I want. But you know, when you go to the National Training Center to hone your skills before going off to battle, I've been on the side of guys who won battles and also of the guys who lost battles. The guys who lost were the ones who sat around and tried to come up with a one hundred percent plan and cover every single thing. And we never got to rehearse it, because we ran up the time doing all this planning, and the other side would attack us and we weren't ready.

"Then," he went on, "I'd go out with the commanders who said, 'We're just going to get a seventy percent plan. And we're going to rehearse this. But the thing is, you'll be able to adapt quickly—this is a framework that we can flex off of.' So I think that's what we have here. It's seventy percent of what we want, but you can execute it one hundred percent."

"You've gotta say that in conference!" McCarthy exclaimed.

The conference was the next morning, Tuesday, July 26, and held at National Republican Congressional Committee headquarters, since the NRCC chairman Pete Sessions would be giving House members an update on recruiting and fund-raising efforts. After the NRCC presentation, Speaker Boehner went to the microphone. He was aware that his plan was getting little traction among his colleagues.

Almost forlornly, the Republican leader said, "Look, I've stuck my neck out here. I can't do this without you guys."

A few members stood and clapped when he was done. Feeling pressure, the other members stood as well. But the show of support was less than fervent.

When it came McCarthy's turn, the whip said to his colleagues, "This is a different fight now. This is a much bigger fight. This defines who wins or loses. The whole nation is watching. The president is afraid of this bill. That's because, in the end, this will *be* the bill."

Grinning, the whip then said, "You all know that I'm not only a student of politics, but also a big movie fan." The lights then dimmed. On the screen behind him rolled a clip from the Ben Affleck movie *The Town*, which McCarthy's chief of staff, Tim Berry, had brought up the evening before:

> Affleck: I need your help. I can't tell you what it is. You can never ask me about it later. And we're going to hurt some people.
> Jeremy Renner (after a brief pause): Whose car are we gonna take?

The Republican audience roared with approval. "And now I'd like to yield to Allen West, who gave a great talk last night at dinner," McCarthy said.

West then strode to the microphone. He repeated his story about the 70 percent plan beating the 100 percent plan. Then, riffing off the movie clip, the freshman declared: "Mr. Speaker, I'll drive that car."

West received a round of applause as well. The soft-spoken former football player Jon Runyan also said his piece. "I've been in a lot of situations like this where you can cut the tension with a knife," he told his colleagues. "But Mr. Speaker, I'm behind you. We made a lot of progress with Cut, Cap, and Balance. We got a first and ten with 'cut.' We got to second down with 'cap.' Yes, we ended up punting in the end. But there's also something in football called field position. We gained a lot of field position in the last week. Now it's time to win this."

Boehner wanted to bring his plan to the House floor that day. McCarthy told him that they didn't have the votes. At that point, they didn't even have half of the 217 needed for passage. The Speaker acquiesced. Voting was rescheduled for the afternoon of Thursday, July 28.

The day before the vote, the Dow Jones Industrial Average fell 199 points as the market nervously appraised the debt impasse. Meanwhile, Boehner's impatience with his colleagues began to show. "Get your ass in line," he growled during a conference. One of the Speaker's new favorite members, Greg Walden of Oregon, lit into RSC senior staffer Paul Teller for sending out emails to gin up opposition to the Boehner plan. The Speaker also tasked Pete Sessions to lean on members by re-minding them, "Remember, the NRCC gave you lots of support . . ."

The following afternoon at 1:30, Boehner, Cantor, McCarthy, and Hensarling participated in a press stakeout to declare the House Re-publicans' determination to pass Boehner's Budget Control Act a few hours later. Joining them was a freshman whom the Speaker's office wanted onstage as an assurance to Tea Party groups: North Carolinian Renee Ellmers. The Boehner plan, she acknowledged to the TV cam-eras, "is not one hundred percent of what our very conservative col-leagues want. But it is about seventy to seventy-five percent . . . This is not about who is most conservative. This is about common sense."

Leaving no doubt as to her intended audience, Ellmers concluded by saying, "And again, I call on my colleagues who may not be there yet . . . We're gonna get the vote, at the end of the day."

But, as it developed, not at the end of *that* day.

Just before the vote was scheduled, Raul Labrador was summoned to the Speaker's office.

Boehner knew that the Tea Party freshman was never one to mince words. So the Speaker cut to the chase: "Are you with me?" he asked.

"I'm sorry, I'm not," Labrador replied. "This is not a bill I can support. I actually think this is a terrible bill."

"Well, I need you here with me on this," Boehner pressed.

"I understand. But I can't vote for it."

Labrador saw the Speaker's strength as his weakness: he was fair and believed others would be, too. Boehner had actually told Labrador one time, "I trust Harry Reid."

Labrador had nearly come unglued. *Are you out of your mind?* Labra-dor was a lawyer. By training he had learned that it was wise to assume the worst in people. He didn't trust Reid. He thought Obama was lying to the American people about the government running out of money on August 2.

Then Labrador added, "But I've talked to several folks and I know how we can get out of this mess. If you can amend the bill to make it closer to Cut, Cap, and Balance, I think I can get you some votes. I've been talking to people all day—I think I can convince maybe ten people."

Despite Labrador's tough stances and his occasional obnoxious outbursts in conferences, the Republican leadership and the whip team admired his willingness to work toward a positive outcome. They saw Labrador as an eventual legislative heavyweight—assuming he could be persuaded to stick around long enough. The Idaho freshman hated being away from his young family, hated sleeping in his office; and for that matter, he was not altogether impressed with what he had seen from the House of Representatives. He had arrived in Washington thinking that term limits was a bad idea. Now, having seen how cynical and entrenched the senior members were, Raul Labrador had concluded that no one should be allowed to serve in Congress longer than six years.

Boehner brought in a legislative staffer. "Allen West would tell you, this bill *is* basically Cut, Cap, and Balance," the aide said.

"It's not even close," Labrador scoffed. He acknowledged that there were political considerations. West's district "is like sixty percent Medicare recipients." By contrast, Labrador's constituents were hard-core right wingers, the freshman told the Speaker. They made Labrador seem ideologically tame by comparison. The only way he and his conservative colleagues would vote for the Boehner plan was if it were amended to stipulate that the debt ceiling would be raised after a balanced budget amendment were to *pass* both the House and the Senate.

Boehner thanked Labrador, and the meeting broke up.

The entire Republican leadership team and whip staff had fanned out and were buttonholing on-the-fence members. The arm-twisters were finding that in this new era of banned earmarks and media hyperscrutiny, the tools of persuasion were limited. Louie Gohmert had emerged from Boehner's office telling reporters that even after his session with the Speaker, he remained "a bloodied, beaten-down 'no'"—which struck the whip team as laughable, since it was universally understood that the jut-jawed Texan did not respond well to threats.

Nor was it McCarthy's way to browbeat. Instead, the whip persisted, wheedled, enlisted friends, appealed to a member's sense of loyalty, evoked history, deployed cheesy *Braveheart* analogies . . .

Blake Farenthold bent and finally broke. After sending Boehner the letter in April with its fretful line, "My fear is that the debt ceiling is very possibly a hostage that we're unwilling to shoot"—to which the Speaker had never responded, leading the freshman to wonder if Boehner could even pick him out of a photo lineup—the friends he had from the financial markets convinced him that the debt ceiling matter was nothing to trifle with.

"I'm gonna vote for this," he told chief deputy whip Peter Roskam. Then Farenthold found himself shouting: *But you guys are killing me! You guys have got to give us some bones to throw to the Tea Party! We were brought up here to change Washington and everything you're asking us to do is easily portrayed as going completely Washington, DC!"*

Roskam assured him, "We will get you something."

Farenthold shared the same rant with Cantor. The majority leader smiled and said, "It is our goal to make the next five months of Congress a lot more pleasant than this one."

When Jeff Duncan learned that the six o'clock vote had been postponed, he decided to go the members-only chapel in the Capitol and pray on the matter.

Several reporters were staked out by the Speaker's office when Duncan walked past. "Congressman, are you going to a meeting with the Speaker?" he was asked.

"No, I'm not," Duncan replied. When they persisted, he said, "I'm going right here to the chapel to pray about this."

"Are you thinking about changing your vote?" one of them asked.

"I'm not praying for *my* vote," he said. "I'm going to lift *them* up, to pray for Speaker Boehner and President Obama and Harry Reid. And for America. So if you'd excuse me . . ."

His phone buzzed. It was Mick Mulvaney. "Duncan, where are you?"

"I'm in the members' chapel."

"Hold on. I'll be right there."

Duncan was already in the chapel when Mulvaney arrived, accompanied by Tim Scott and a reporter who had been following Scott. It was completely dark inside, except for the sunlight pouring through the dazzling stained-glass depiction of George Washington on his knees, praying in the snow at Valley Forge.

The reporter lowered her tape recorder and stared at the window. "Wow," she said.

After she had left, the three South Carolinians prayed and talked quietly for a few minutes. Mulvaney reached for the Bible, searching for a particular verse. Instead, he stumbled upon Proverbs 22:7: *The rich rules over the poor, and the borrower is the slave to the lender.*

It was as if Solomon himself were holding forth on the debt ceiling. "I'm done," said Duncan.

They went to the whip's office. There were about twenty members there—including McCarthy, Boehner, Cantor, Hensarling, Paul Ryan, and about ten "no" freshmen, among them Raul Labrador.

Boehner was three votes shy of passage. "This is what we're going to do," the Speaker told the group. "Raul had something to do with this. We're going to amend the bill." The new version would stipulate that either the House or the Senate would have to pass a balanced budget amendment before the debt ceiling could be raised.

"No," several of them said. They insisted on passage of the bill in both "the House *and* the Senate," not "or."

Mulvaney spoke for the South Carolinians. At least in the collective ear of the whip team, he indicated strongly that if the language could be changed to "the House and the Senate," the four of them would be on board.

Boehner and McCarthy left the office and went to speak with Senate Minority Leader Mitch McConnell. While the South Carolinians waited in a side conference room, a number of the freshmen invited themselves in. They implored the South Carolinians: *You're losing credibility when it looks like you have to get permission from your senator.*

A member of the leadership team shook his head and said of the South Carolinians, "They're making themselves irrelevant." But most of the Republican leaders were slightly more sympathetic. The problem wasn't just Senator DeMint. It was also the far more moderate other South Carolina senator, Lindsey Graham, who had announced his opposition to the Boehner plan. More than one of the South Carolina freshmen had told McCarthy and his whip staff, *There's no way I survive politically if I end up to the left of Lindsey Graham on this.*

McCarthy returned about an hour later, looking ecstatic. "We got it in!" he exclaimed—referring to the stipulation that the balanced budget amendment be approved by both the House and the Senate before the debt ceiling could be raised. "How many of you guys are gonna support this?"

A few members raised their hands—but not Mulvaney and the other South Carolinians.

"Why?" McCarthy exploded. "You just said you wanted this, I go over there and fight for it, I come back, and you're not for it? Screw it! No deal! We're done!"

Most of the people in the room had never seen the whip go ballistic before. "Whoa, whoa—don't leave, Kevin!" someone called.

McCarthy cooled down. It looked like they had the votes, even without the help of the South Carolinians. It was now after ten in the evening. "Let's bring it to the floor," he urged Boehner.

A brief discussion ensued, but Boehner was firm. "We are not doing a vote after midnight," he said.

This was his House. He was the keeper of the institution. There was no way he was going to pull a dark-of-night gambit like the notorious Medicare prescription drug vote of 2003.

"We're going to wait till tomorrow," Boehner said flatly.

McCarthy was deflated. He knew they could win the vote *now*. How things might be tomorrow, he couldn't say. But he also knew that Boehner was usually asleep at this hour. They would have to take it up on Thursday.

The following afternoon, the amended Boehner plan passed, 217–210. As Harry Reid had warned, the Senate promptly voted to table it.

The next day, Friday, July 29, the House preemptively rejected Reid's $1.2 trillion deficit reduction plan.

The table was now bare. There was no White House plan, no Boehner plan, no Reid plan—and almost no time left before August 2.

On Sunday afternoon, July 31, McCarthy was sitting in the twelfth-floor apartment of Nebraska Congressman Adrian Smith, which he had once shared with Smith until he became whip and decided he needed to be close to the Capitol at all times. McCarthy's cell phone rang. It was Arizona Senator Jon Kyl.

"Hey buddy," the whip said in greeting. The two men then fell into discussion about the debt ceiling deal that Mitch McConnell had just now consummated with his former senatorial colleague Joe Biden.

"It's gonna be tough," McCarthy told Kyl. "But I think I can get 150 to 170 votes."

The first of a dozen or so Republican congressmen began trickling through the apartment doorway, beginning with Sean Duffy. While Adrian Smith grilled steaks, they sat inside and drank wine and beer and caught the hour-long NBC special *Taking the Hill: Inside Congress*. They snickered when camera-craving Democratic Senator Chuck Schumer criticized the Republicans' usage of *The Town* in their conference. And they nodded appreciatively when Kevin McCarthy declared to host Brian Williams, "The world of buying votes are [*sic*] gone."

They clambered up to the rooftop for their steaks. A dazzling sunset blazed over them as they listened on their cell phones to Speaker Boehner explaining to the entire conference the details of the McConnell-Biden deal. The key elements were:

The debt ceiling would be raised immediately by $400 billion. The president could request an additional $500 billion, which could only be blocked by a congressional resolution of disapproval.

A trillion dollars in spending cuts would take place over the next decade by means of spending caps. If the caps were exceeded, across-the-board cuts in both nondefense and defense spending would be automatically triggered.

A Senate-House "supercommittee" would be empowered to identify another $1.5 trillion in cuts, which would enable the president to further raise the debt ceiling by the corresponding amount.

A balanced budget amendment to the Constitution would have to be voted on by the end of 2011 in both the House and Senate, though passage would not be a requirement.

Everyone on the rooftop that night was a "yes." But though the evening was convivial, an exhausted wariness gripped one of the attendees, Blake Farenthold. He didn't know what this vote would mean back home, but he could guess. Already his Tea Party supporters were disgruntled with him. Obama's approval rating was bad, but it was stratospheric compared to Congress's. Within the next week, it would dip to a record low of 13 percent.

Farenthold figured the low estimation was due to the perception that the House wasn't even trying. And he happened to agree. He himself had given too many programs the benefit of the doubt. No more. He now intended to vote for almost every cut. Washington needed to start behaving like it was broke. "No more, 'Instead of getting lobster

I'm getting steak,'" he would scoff. "No. You should be getting ramen noodles."

They didn't even cut the $2 million that the Department of the Interior had appropriated for summer concerts and fireworks! Come on! A private company would have picked up the slack! "Don't tell me that 'National Fireworks, brought to you by Lockheed Martin' wouldn't have happened! If we can't cut freakin' fireworks, we are in serious trouble."

But more than just program-slashing, he thought, why not be bolder? Why not defund the EPA and start from scratch? Why not eliminate the Department of Energy? To Farenthold, it would be a marvelous thing to replace the entire Appropriations Committee with freshmen. How about that?

Farenthold had recently lost his chief of staff and fired his communications director. His wife, who was present on the rooftop that night, had become the bad cop at the office, which apparently hadn't sat well with some of the staffers. But as Blake Farenthold thought about his restaffing, he was also contemplating what role he would like to have in the House of Representatives, going forward.

And what he had decided was this, as he would say later: "I want to be the communicator." Farenthold's belief: "Our conference sucks at it. We're so dead set on telling the truth—what the Democrats can say in two emotion-packed sentences takes us ten PowerPoint slides."

Farenthold was a "yes"—just this once more. But in the near future, the former talk radio host expected to be a voice. They could use him. How much worse could he be?

It was not like the Reverend Emanuel Cleaver to emote.

Both in his capacity as chairman of the Congressional Black Caucus and in the Democratic caucus as a whole, Cleaver tended to be a quiet, steadying presence. He gave the invocations at whip meetings, counseled Democratic members on personal matters, and otherwise picked his moments to speak up. While meeting with the whip team on one occasion, he reminded his associates that Moses had parted the Red Sea with the cane he held in his hand. "Use what you have," was the spiritual message. And during a caucus, when the discussion focused on the Democrats' alternative to the Ryan budget, the reverend went to the microphone and said that someone had asked him one time which of Cleaver's children did he love the most.

"My answer was, 'The one who *needs* it most,'" he told the caucus. "So on the budget, let's be balanced. But most of all, let's exert our efforts on behalf of those who need it most."

It had been a trying year for Cleaver after beating Sheila Jackson Lee for the CBC chairmanship. He had done what he could to broker peace between the sole Republican member, Allen West, and his progressive colleagues. After West had offended Keith Ellison with his anti-Muslim remarks, Cleaver had discussed a possible lunch between the three but could tell from Ellison's lingering anger that no good could come of it. It was equally evident to him that the 112th Congress had dedicated itself to eviscerating programs most beneficial to minorities. The appetite for such back-of-the-hand treatment was alarming but unsurprising to Cleaver, given how Steve King and Michele Bachmann had reacted during the previous session after the conclusion of the *Pigford v. Glickman* discrimination case, brought by African-American farmers. King and Bachmann had labeled the settlement "reparations"—leading Cleaver to think: *If you guys think this is reparations, believe me, we could do reparations a lot better than this.*

But the greatest emotional challenge for Emanuel Cleaver—greater, in a sense, than the notorious incident in March 2010 when a white man protesting the impending health care vote spat on him on the steps of the Capitol, prompting Maxine Waters to holler, "Have him arrested!," which Cleaver declined to do—involved his disappointment in the Obama administration. The CBC chairman and his colleagues had met with the president and his chief of staff, Bill Daley, more than once to protest the White House's supine response to the Republican agenda. During the H.R.1 program-slashing debate, Cleaver told the president, "Look, I was mayor of Kansas City. The community development block grant program? Huge for me. That's how I got infrastructure projects funded—how I did all sorts of things. If you cut that, Mr. President, the effects will be real." And yet Obama's own budget had proposed a $300 million reduction in the block grant program.

Of late, Cleaver, who grew up in the small Texas town of Waxahachie, had been conferring with his good friend and fellow Texan Jeb

Hensarling, along with Paul Ryan and Appropriations subcommittee chairwoman Jo Ann Emerson, about a project that would redirect federal funds in grant-making agencies to the districts that had been the most persistently impoverished. Many of these were white districts, like Emerson's. The three Republicans were enthusiastic about working with Cleaver. Boehner seemed open to it as well. Cleaver dared to envision a historic press conference—a Republican Speaker alongside the chairman of the Congressional Black Caucus, announcing a bipartisan initiative to attack persistent poverty in America.

But when Cleaver brought the matter up to Barack Obama, the former CBC member was less than encouraging. Not only did Obama believe such a bill was unlikely to pass during the 112th Congress; he also preferred that Cleaver not try to do so, for fear that it would complicate his ongoing negotiations with the Republicans.

And now this eleventh-hour debt ceiling compromise. When Cleaver scanned the outline of it on Sunday evening, he could see that it was of a piece with previous Obama White House capitulations. As he would later say, "It's hard to condemn the president for hope." But this plan—with the dubious setup of a supercommittee that was destined to disagree just as the larger body had, and with the trigger of across-the-board cuts that would almost certainly be undone later by the Congress—was sure to fail: "Stevie Wonder could see it coming."

The following morning, August 1, after opening his Twitter account, the reverend wrote: "This deal is a sugar-coated Satan sandwich. If you lift the bun, you will not like what you see."

The Democrats did not like what they saw. But Vice President Joe Biden, the co-chef of the sugarcoated Satan sandwich, came to the caucus that morning to explain it to them anyway.

"Look, I'm not gonna tell you how to vote," Biden stated from the outset. "And I accept the fact that you might see the politics or the substance different from how I do. But I want to tell you what we're doing here."

For the next two hours he and White House budget director Jack Lew answered questions about the McConnell-Biden plan. Many expressed doubts about the enforceability of automatic defense spending cuts. "This is Van Hollen's hobbyhorse," Biden replied, explaining that the Maryland Democrat had successfully pressed for inclusion of fire-walls that would protect nondefense discretionary spending from being cut unless defense funds were being cut as well.

Van Hollen stood and predicted to his colleagues, "I think the Republicans are going to pay a very heavy price for this, because of the extreme lengths they were prepared to go. The American people saw that they were literally willing to jeopardize the creditworthiness of the United States in order to try and force upon the country their budget agenda."

But, he acknowledged, "They won the framing. They changed the debate from investment in America to cutting."

Disappointment was palpable throughout the room, and at one point Biden became angry over suggestions that the White House had done a feeble job negotiating on behalf of Democrats. It was at that point that John Dingell went to the microphone.

"Treat him decently," the dean of the House told the others. "He's right on this. It's the best we can get." Dingell did not volunteer that he, too, was disappointed—most of all in the president's detached attitude, as if he were back in the classroom teaching constitutional law rather than striving to save a country from economic ruin.

The most compelling argument came from Dingell's recent protégé, Rob Andrews of New Jersey. "These people have been going after the president, if you haven't noticed," Andrews said. "They've compared him in pictures to a monkey. There's been a concerted effort to try to diminish his ability to lead by suggesting that he's not *capable* of leading.

"I don't want to be part of something like that," Andrews told his colleagues. "I want people to understand that he is, in fact, a functioning leader who can solve problems."

Further, Andrews observed, "It's the Republicans that are the party of antigovernment, while Democrats are the party of government. And if we fail here, if this bill goes down, it will reinforce the public's impression that the government doesn't work. And I don't care what the polls say. 'The government doesn't work' is an attack on the Democratic Party."

Immediately after the caucus, chief deputy whip Diana DeGette did an informal whip check—meaning a simple count without any attempts to persuade the members. About a third were "aye," another third were "no" or "lean no," with the remainder undecided. DeGette, who had concluded from studying the bill that it would gut virtually every federal program on which her Denver constituents depended, put herself down as a "lean no."

Meanwhile, Majority Whip McCarthy called Minority Whip Hoyer. The Republican told the Democrat that he would need one hundred of their votes.

Coming out of the dispiriting caucus, Hoyer was stupefied to hear McCarthy's request. "We got nothing out of this bill!" he snapped angrily. The minority whip said that the Democrats could provide at most twenty-five votes.

McCarthy replied that Hoyer could then call the president and be the one to inform him that the bill was going down in defeat. "The president agreed to this deal," he reminded Hoyer.

McCarthy knew, of course, that Obama's complicity in the "Satan sandwich" accounted for some of Hoyer's surly reaction. What he also knew but did not volunteer to Hoyer was that the Republicans' own conference that morning had been far from celebratory. Boehner had assured his fellow Republicans that "we got ninety-eight percent of what I wanted from my original deal," while Ryan had given an optimistic presentation of the details. But the cuts were far lower than what the conservatives had wanted, the caps were not permanent, and there was no mandatory balanced budget amendment.

McCarthy still thought he could get upwards of 150 Republican votes, though he had requested a cushion from Hoyer just in case. He wasn't sweating this one quite like he had the previous week's vote on the Boehner deal. On the other hand, there wasn't any time for orchestrated persuasions of individual members. Today was their last shot.

Rob Andrews approached McCarthy on the floor. "We can get to one hundred," he assured the whip. "We just have to work at it."

"Madam Speaker," Dennis Cardoza of California fumed when he saw Nancy Pelosi on the House floor, "the president of the United States is the worst negotiator who has ever owned that title! I mean, I didn't know Millard Fillmore, but . . . he's the worst. He doesn't know how to do this."

"Yeah," said Pelosi, "but he doesn't think so."

Pelosi shared Cardoza's disappointment. She thought the deal was a lousy one. Though she, Hoyer, and Biden had made a few calls to wavering members throughout the afternoon to tell them, "We might need you," Pelosi had not only not told anyone how to vote, she had not told any of her colleagues how *she* would vote. Pelosi had been a team player throughout the whole saga. Recognizing that the negotiations might ultimately require including entitlement reform as a component, she had carefully modulated her language in caucuses from "no cuts to Medicare" to "no cuts to Medicare beneficiaries." And she had resisted the temptation to say "I told you so" to Obama—who, back in December, had disagreed with the Speaker's belief that they should raise the debt ceiling during that lame-duck session. The president's belief had been that the Republicans would and should be equal partners in the debt ceiling discussion—implying, she thought, that he believed the Republicans would treat the matter in a reasonable fashion.

When the minority leader learned that day that McCarthy was requesting a hundred Democrats, Pelosi was beside herself. "These people come to the table, they want it all their way—then they can't provide two hundred and eighteen?" she fumed to a colleague. "You can only play that game so long. Do it one time, and it's the last time you do it."

Except, as Nancy Pelosi well knew, they had done this in fact twice—the first being the Continuing Resolution vote back in April. Once again, they had gotten their way with Obama. And once again, they were demanding that the Democrats show their solidarity with the President by voting for a sugarcoated Satan sandwich.

And Pelosi knew that she would have to do so, once again.

All but holding her nose, Nancy Pelosi stood in the well of the House chamber on the late afternoon of Monday, August 1, 2011, and asked her colleagues on both sides of the aisle, "Why are we here?"

The minority leader asserted that it was because "all of us in this body care about our country, have decided that public service is a noble pursuit, and that we have come here to make the future better for future generations." Pointing out that the Founding Fathers had created the Great Seal of the United States with the inscription *Novus Ordo Seclorum,* or "a new order for the centuries," Pelosi went on, "So confident were our Founders in their idea about generational responsibility, one to the next, that they were confident that our country, that what they were putting forth, would exist for the ages. For the ages. That was the challenge they gave us. That is the responsibility that we have."

But then she asked, "Why are we here today? Why are we here today, within twenty-four hours of our nation going into default, after months of conversation about how we would address the debt ceiling? . . . [T]his has never happened before. We have never, never tied the hands of a president of the United States. We have never placed any doubt in the public markets as to whether this would happen."

Pelosi cited a few virtues to the bill—namely, that it fulfilled America's obligations to its creditors, protected entitlement benefits, and placed equal weight on defense and nondefense spending. And though she criticized the legislation for requiring "not one red cent from America's wealthiest families," the Democratic minority leader said that "I feel a responsibility" to vote for it.

She stared out to her fellow Democrats and said, with landmark equivocation: "I urge you to consider voting 'yes,' but I completely respect the hesitation that members have about this." Then, in a bitter final shot at the opposition: "I hear that our Republican colleagues have said they got ninety-eight percent of what they wanted in the bill. I hope that their votes will reflect that."

A few minutes later, at 6:27 P.M., Paul Ryan stood. "Mr. Speaker," he said, "I move for a call of the House."

The rest of the House members began to file in. Ryan walked toward the Democrats, looking for the opposing floor manager, Chris Van Hollen.

He shook Van Hollen's hand and asked, "Are you voting for the bill?"

Van Hollen said, without enthusiasm, that he was.

A quorum was declared, and a recorded vote was demanded on the Budget Control Act of 2011. Almost immediately, Minority Leader Pelosi stuck her card in the voting slot and voted "aye"—a last dutiful waving of the pom-poms.

Kevin McCarthy stood beside the Republican whip table. He turned in one direction and then the next, intermittently looking up at the electronic voting board. As he had expected, the Democrats were holding back their votes. The Republicans were voting in trickles, with slightly more "ayes" than "nos."

Cantor grabbed him. "Barton's a 'no,'" the majority leader pointed out.

As the second-ranking Republican on the Energy and Commerce Committee, Joe Barton was particularly influential. The whip moved briskly to the back of the chamber, where the Texans habitually congregated. He found Barton standing behind the last aisle.

"Why are you voting against it?" McCarthy asked, clearly vexed.

Barton said that the negotiators had taken out a passage that he had wanted. The whip protested that they hadn't. They had already been through this in conference. Someone had shown Barton the passage that was still there. The Texan had ruefully acknowledged, "Dang it, now I gotta vote for it!"

But he hadn't. McCarthy saw that he was wasting his time. He headed back to the whip table. The "ayes" were approaching 160 with 118 dissenters.

"It's done," McCarthy's chief of staff, Tim Berry, said confidently. "We shouldn't go around and break people."

But McCarthy did not look particularly confident. His eyes darted around—to a member and then back to the board, member and board, a flicker of anxiety across that Californian composure . . . 180 to 131 . . .

From all the way across the chamber beside the eastern door there came a sudden uproar. Then a surge of applause that moved like an electromagnetic wave across the House of Representatives. McCarthy squinted. *If it's the president,* he thought, *I doubt they'd be standing and clapping . . .*

It was Congresswoman Gabrielle Giffords of Arizona. She had come to cast her vote.

Escorted by Pelosi, the sergeant at arms, and the House chaplain, Giffords stepped into the chamber. The congresswoman was sticklike and her long auburn hair had been cut short. But she waved vigorously and responded to the cheers with a broad smile.

McCarthy was agape. He clapped along with the rest. And with that wave of applause came a wave of "ayes" from both Democrats and Republicans.

Seemingly half of the congregation moved toward the frail figure as she held out her voting card, the one she had not used since January 7, and became the 251st House member to vote to raise the debt ceiling.

Jo Ann Emerson rushed toward the other side of the aisle to see her softball teammate. But the crowd was too dense—she worried that Gabby would be hurt. Emerson saw Diana DeGette, and the two women hugged.

She backed away, and found an empty seat next to John Dingell. Emerson kissed her old friend on the cheek.

"Isn't it wonderful Gabby's back?" she exclaimed, almost out of breath—while off to her left, John Boehner made his way to Giffords and with wet eyes threw his arms around her.

Dingell had celebrated his eighty-fifth birthday just three weeks earlier. As a matter of habit and prudence, he did not get too worked up about things (though he had certainly appreciated the birthday gifts from his staff: CDs of Chopin, the Red Army Chorus, the Detroit Symphony, the University of Michigan marching band, and Gilbert & Sullivan, along with Subway sandwiches and cake).

But yes, he acknowledged to his friend. He was glad to see the young lady back.

The Republican and Democrat sat together for several minutes—the one beaming unabashedly, the other gazing out into wherever it is that John Dingell gazes out into: some seam of history, perhaps, into which crises slip like dead leaves into an ever-churning river.

Jeff Duncan walked down the front steps of the Capitol and headed on foot toward the Cannon Building. With him were fellow South Carolinians Mick Mulvaney and Trey Gowdy, along with Steve Southerland. It was getting close to eight in the evening, and the heat of the August sun had eased as the men walked languidly alongside each other toward their offices, where, all of a sudden, there was no more work to be done.

All of them had been "nos." Duncan had not wished to be an obstructionist. He had gone over the numbers while Ryan went through the seven slides on the screen that morning in conference. Even using charitable estimations, Duncan calculated that under the new plan, America would still be running a $1.3 trillion deficit—while at the same time ratcheting up the debt ceiling to $16.7 trillion. And in the meantime, no one could say exactly where all of these proposed spending cuts would be coming from.

Duncan had written down, underneath his calculations: *Have I reduced the size and scope of government?*

He could not vote for it.

During the vote, after he had cast his "no," Duncan approached Boehner. "Mr. Speaker," he said, "thank you for the effort. For fighting the good fight."

They shook hands. "Duncan," Boehner said simply as their eyes met. He did not call the South Carolinian "hard head" this time. That fact had already been established. Within weeks, the Heritage Action for America group would rank freshman Jeff Duncan as the most conservative of all 435 House members.

As he and his fellow "nos" walked to their offices, Mick Mulvaney muttered, "I wish we could have done more."

Duncan responded that for freshmen, he thought they had done pretty well.

Now Jeff Duncan sat at his desk in Cannon 116. After tonight, Congress was in recess until September 7. Duncan's ten-year-old son, Parker, was in town for a weeklong tourist camp for kids called the National Treasures Experience. The father figured that he might spend some of the rest of the week doing some touring himself—particularly of the Capitol, so as to gain a broader understanding of the architecture and the paintings, little facts he could pass on to visiting constituents when he showed them around the building. Just the other day he had discovered a stairway leading out of a closet door beside Steny Hoyer's minority whip office. At such times, Duncan reminded himself that, impossible as it now seemed, he had only been in Washington for eight months.

Parker was staying at Duncan's apartment, and the two were living like bachelor slobs off a diet of pizza and fried baloney sandwiches. They'd gone to a Washington Nationals baseball game in which the Nats beat the Mets in extra innings. They'd been to the Air and Space Museum twice. They'd gone to the National Mall and tossed the football.

But now, on this first night of August, they had one more thing to do. While sitting in his office with Parker that evening, the congressman received an email informing him that Trent Franks of Arizona was on the floor for an hour-long special order to talk up the desirability of a balanced budget amendment. Because so many Republican members had already headed to the airport, Franks needed speakers. Would Duncan consider heading over to the Capitol?

Duncan grabbed his coat and his son and headed out the door.

He spoke for the first time on the House floor without benefit of notes. "What a great evening to talk about America living within its means," Duncan began. He pointed out that legislation with language for a balanced budget amendment had now been sent over to the Senate. He talked about his days as a small business owner—how he set a budget every year based on projected revenue inflows, and "I couldn't just hope that there was a money tree out in the backyard and continue spending money that I didn't have."

Duncan's oratory was plain and not apt to be confused with that of Fisher Ames, or even Nancy Pelosi. The people who had elected him to represent the 3rd District of South Carolina expected no more of him than to say as he believed, that it was time "to require Washington to live within its means the way families and small businesses and large businesses have to do all across this great land."

He closed, however, with something of a flourish, for Jeff Duncan anyway. First, he indulged in a bit of a boast—albeit a boast with cause. Referring to the balanced budget amendment to the Constitution, he said, "I am proud that I stand with eighty-seven members of our freshman class that really helped, I think, leadership see that this was a vital component to this piece of legislation." He added, "So I want to urge the American people to get behind this—to contact your senators, contact your House members."

Then he added a personal note. "I brought my little boy, who is ten years old," Duncan said. "He is sitting on the House floor with me today because I teach my children the value of not spending more than you can bring in. And they say: Dad, can we have that baseball? Can we have that item? I say: Son, we don't have the money in our budget this week or this month to purchase that. But let me make plans so that we can purchase that in the future.

"We live within our means," said the freshman. "Am I perfect? No. I have debt, but we have a plan to pay back that debt. The future of our children and our grandchildren is at stake. America knows. America got engaged in this, they got engaged in the last election cycle, and they know that Washington cannot keep spending more than it has."

Said Jeff Duncan, "Let's get our house in order, and let's create a way to start paying back that enormous debt. We can do that with a balanced budget amendment."

He walked down the aisle to where his son sat grinning. Parker kissed him on the cheek.

On the way out the door, a House clerk hustled up to them. "Excuse me," the clerk said to the congressman. "I don't think you mentioned your son's name. Why don't you give it to me? I'll make sure it goes in the *Congressional Record*."

Jeff and Parker Duncan walked out into the evening. The son would have his name enshrined in the American historical record alongside that of his father, who himself doubted he would ever forget that his boy had been there with him, during such a time as this.

CHAPTER TWENTY-THREE

Lower, Ever Lower

The next day, August 2, 2011, the Dow Jones responded to Congress and the White House's performance on the debt ceiling by dropping 266 points. All of the gains made that entire year on Wall Street were wiped out in a single day.

Three days later, Standard & Poor's downgraded America's credit rating from AAA to AA+ for the first time in history.

Later that month, Republican pollster Bill McInturff spelled out the link between America's political leaders and its economic woes in the starkest of terms. "The perception of how Washington handled the debt ceiling negotiation," McInturff wrote in a widely circulated report, "led to an immediate collapse of confidence in government and all the major players, including President Obama and Republicans in Congress. The collapse of confidence in government has substantially eroded already weak consumer confidence. Today's consumer confidence rating is the fourth lowest since 1952. Make no mistake: this collapse of economic confidence . . . is the direct consequence of the lack of confidence in our political system and its leaders."

The pollster's stern warnings were validated by the latest public opinion surveys that greeted federal officeholders when they returned in September to Washington from summer recess. President Obama's approval rating had dropped to 44 percent; Congress's, to 11 percent—and then, a month later, to 9 percent, a historic low. Seven out of ten who were surveyed believed that the House Republicans favored the rich and had no clear jobs plan.

Beneath the screeching, the posturing, and the stalemates, there had in fact been scores of congressmen quietly working with the other side in an effort to achieve results. Archconservatives Jason Chaffetz and Raul Labrador were huddling with archprogressive Luis Gutierrez over a comprehensive immigration reform package. Fellow Missourians Jo Ann Emerson and Emanuel Cleaver would, by December, succeed in directing funds to aid communities bedeviled by persistent poverty. Democrat Rosa DeLauro and Republican Don Manzullo had coauthored legislation that would incentivize manufacturers to dedicate monies to a community bank. Blue Dog Jim Matheson and GOP deputy whip Kevin Brady had teamed on a bill that would lower tax barriers to encourage American businesses to reinvest overseas earnings back home. Against the raging currents, Democrats and Republicans continued to paddle together, now and again. But these were renegade efforts, ones that the House leaders from both parties did not openly advertise and did nothing to encourage.

To no surprise, then, the "people's House" had become a leper colony.

Renee Ellmers volunteered to stay behind in Washington for a few days after the debt ceiling vote and face the media. The Republican leadership needed somebody to explain to the many skeptical Fox and talk radio hosts that the deal was a good one for conservatives—that a trillion dollars in spending had been cut, no taxes had been increased, and a pathway to a balanced budget constitutional amendment had been forged—and the telegenic Tea Party favorite was an obvious choice. It was when Ellmers finally returned home to Dunn, North Carolina, that she came to realize that she was stuck in the middle between two equally intense strains of discontent.

On the one hand, many of the conservative activists in her district were outraged that the debt ceiling had been raised at all. They didn't seem to understand that it was about paying America's outstanding bills, not about allowing future spending. Several of these hard-liners were of the belief that the best way for America to save money would be to simply shut the government down. Ellmers struggled to convince them that even if one could turn off all federal spigots, the cost of doing so would far outweigh the gains.

"Just stay away from Boehner," they would tell Ellmers, as if the Speaker's willingness to find practical solutions was symptomatic of an infectious disease.

Yet at least as many of her constituents were disgusted by what they perceived as the House Republicans' intransigence. "You guys need to be working together," they would lecture Ellmers. Here, too, the freshman detected strains of ignorance. Many of these folks literally did not understand that Congress consisted of two legislative bodies, both of which had to agree on each piece of legislation for it to pass—and that the upper body, the Senate, was controlled by a different party, one whose leader, Harry Reid, had decided on the strategy of doing little other than voting down everything that came out of the House.

But Ellmers was also caught between opposing forces in her own Republican conference. The other freshmen knew that she was close to Kevin McCarthy and the GOP leadership. Whenever she defended their decisions, a colleague was bound to pipe up, "Oh, you're just saying that because you're their favorite."

Boehner's doing a good job—they're all working hard, she would insist. It irked her that so many of her fellow freshmen behaved as if "every vote we've taken is the be-all-end-all, that history's going to judge us each time." As a former intensive care nurse, Ellmers was comfortable working as a team and trusting the surgeon to make the right decisions. Many of her freshman colleagues didn't share that tendency. Ellmers had stopped going to the weekly freshmen meetings with the Speaker because it distressed her to listen to her classmates criticize Boehner so harshly to his face.

"You've created a monster," she told McCarthy, adding that the leadership should end the freshmen meetings altogether. (McCarthy, for his part, imagined that the weekly get-togethers probably would be discontinued, though for a different reason: attendance had dwindled greatly, perhaps because the attendees saw little good coming out of them.)

Raul Labrador frequently voiced his disagreement at the meetings with Boehner. "I didn't come to Washington to be part of a team," the Idaho freshman would say. Like Renee Ellmers, Labrador had spent the month of August explaining his votes to angry constituents, the majority of whom were of the far right, shut-'er-down persuasion. They seemed to admire his independent streak even if Ellmers didn't. He returned to Washington confident that some of the other congressmen might have a 9 percent approval rating, but not Raul Labrador.

At a meeting with other Republicans one autumn morning in 2011, someone brought up a new messaging gambit conceived by the leadership to prove to the angry public that the House majority was doing everything in its power to put Americans back to work. It was a laminated card given to each House Republican, listing fifteen pieces of legislation that had passed the House, only to die in the Senate—"the Forgotten 15." Labrador stood up and criticized the list. It was a stretch, he said, to be claiming that legislating regulatory restraint over Internet providers, pesticide use, water quality, and the cement sector were tantamount to jobs bills.

"You're going to be against whatever leadership does," Renee Ellmers said dismissively.

"And you're just going to support *everything* they do!" Labrador replied.

In truth, Labrador didn't blame Boehner, Cantor, and McCarthy per se. It was more that he saw them as protectors of an institution that the Idaho freshman believed needed a thorough delousing. The friction between the entrenched Republican members and the upstarts had intensified. Labrador was hearing whispered threats that the dissenters on major votes would be punished. If that happened, Labrador could easily foresee a coup against Boehner. He could easily imagine a new Speaker being voted in, charged with tossing out all the committee chairmen and replacing them with Raul Labrador–style revolutionaries.

It only took about a dozen members to nearly unseat Newt Gingrich in the mid-1990s, Labrador thought. *You could find thirty members, easily.*

Yet Labrador was a practical enough legislator to believe that not every hill he climbed was worth dying on. In mid-September, the Republican House leadership brought to the floor yet another short-term Continuing Resolution to fund the government's activities, since the Senate had squashed the Ryan budget plan back in April. Labrador voted for the CR. Nancy Pelosi's Democrats promised to do the same. Then they reneged.

The House Democrats had spent the summer stewing over Obama's giveaway to the Republicans in the debt ceiling negotiations. Their spirits were improved considerably on September 8, when the president delivered a fiery speech before a joint session of Congress. Offering up a $447 billion initiative called the American Jobs Bill, Obama exclaimed numerous times throughout the course of his speech, "Pass this jobs bill!" The fact that it would be paid for by eliminating the Bush tax cuts for wealthy Americans ensured that House Republicans would not pass it (despite the fact that even a majority of Republican voters believed the same tax cuts should expire).

But to Democrats, that was the point. There was no pleasing these Republicans anyway. So why compromise when the opposition had no intention of doing so? Especially galling to the minority party was the recognition that McCarthy, the majority whip, had consistently required a sizable bloc of Democratic votes to pass the toughest bills— and yet the Democrats had nothing to show for their complicity.

Let's educate them that they need us, became the Democrats' abiding sentiment.

The CR included $1 billion in emergency relief in response to the year's many wildfires, hurricanes, floods, and other natural disasters. But a rare stipulation was added by the Republicans to entice its conservative members: the emergency funds would be offset by cutting a Department of Energy program that encouraged the development of high-mileage vehicles. Though the ranking Democratic member of the Appropriations Committee, Norm Dicks, recommended to Pelosi that they go along with the measure, the rank and file loudly refused to do so. Just as Boehner had done so many times that year, Pelosi for once deferred to her caucus.

Sure enough, forty-eight Republicans voted against the CR, even with the enticement of tying disaster relief to spending cuts. McCarthy needed Democrat votes. He didn't get them. Boehner's first big bill after the summer recess was defeated, 195–230.

Minority Whip Steny Hoyer found Kevin McCarthy on the floor right after the vote. "You're going to call us *now*, aren't you," the Democrat gloated.

"Oh, we'll be okay, don't worry," McCarthy shot back.

The whip had warned Boehner that they didn't have enough Republican votes to pass the CR. The Speaker, however, was emphatic. "I want to go to the floor," he had said. "Let the body work its will."

That didn't mean that Boehner was happy about the defeat. At the next Republican conference, he stood before the members, folded his arms across his chest, and with a flat stare said gruffly, "Now what?"

Boehner, Cantor, and McCarthy had endeavored to find an upside to

Congress's deepening unpopularity. Perhaps, they hoped, the freshmen would get an earful back home and return to Washington in September with a newfound eagerness to compromise. But it wasn't quite shaping up that way. The district maps that had been redrawn this year by predominantly GOP-controlled state legislatures as a result of the 2010 census meant that many Republicans now represented much more conservative territory—or, in some cases, much more Democratic, forcing them to migrate to a new district and run against a fellow Republican and in the process compelling them to prove their superior conservative bona fides. Right-wing advocates such as Heritage Action and Erick Erickson of RedState.com continued to rate members on their votes and agitated for primary challenges against less conservative members like freshman Martha Roby and the Missouri moderate Jo Ann Emerson. ("Wow, what did you do to piss off Erick Erickson?" Texas freshman Bill Flores asked Emerson one afternoon on the House floor. She had never heard of the conservative blogger whose October 21 post began with the headline, "Paging the Missouri Tea Party: Here's One to Primary.")

In short, whatever pressures to govern the freshmen faced were drowned out by pressures from the right. On top of that, their reelection fortunes depended on money from conservative donors. Blake Farenthold had raised a meager $102,000 during the third quarter of 2011. Farenthold couldn't stand asking people for money and was troubled by a system that dictated raising and spending a million dollars every two years so as to keep one's seat. The big checks seemed to go to Tea Party stars like Allen West. "Part of it is, you've got to be willing to set your hair on fire in front of the TV camera, and I'm not a set-your-hair-on-fire kind of guy," he would say.

For the moment, he had no primary opponent—but that was only because he had no district: the Texas legislature's redistricting map had been thrown out and replaced by a panel of federal judges with a far less GOP-friendly map . . . which in turn had been thrown out by the Supreme Court. Until new maps were drawn, Blake Farenthold did not know where he would be campaigning, or against whom. It seemed that the accidental congressman whose 2010 race concluded twenty days late was destined to remain behind the curve.

Jeff Duncan, on the other hand, had the same 3rd District of South

Carolina, anticipated no serious opposition, and had been proclaimed by Heritage Action to be the House of Representatives' most conservative member. Even in his blood-red district, Duncan had heard a few appeals for more compromise. He had his own ideas, of course, about what compromise looked like.

"What's it going to take for you to vote for this?" Kevin McCarthy had asked his freshman whip on the floor during the CR vote.

"Look, Hurricane Hugo hit South Carolina—we get the importance of disaster relief," Duncan told the whip. "I can sell my constituents on $8 billion in disaster relief. Just tack it on to the $1.019 trillion spending ceiling we have in the Ryan budget."

"The Senate's not going to vote for that," said McCarthy.

"To hell with the Senate. Let's vote some conservative bills out of the House. Bills that have our identity stamped on them."

Jeff Duncan was thinking precisely as the House Democrats now were. Since the opposition couldn't be pleased anyway, why not stick to one's principles?

Such was the state of governance in the House of Representatives in the fall of 2011.

Allen West happened to be sitting on the House floor next to eighty-eight-year-old Republican Ralph Hall of Texas during a tough vote when Boehner sidled up to the institution's oldest member. West listened as the two House veterans lamented the conservative defections now taking place.

"It's not like the old days, Ralph," the Speaker noted wistfully. "Without earmarks to offer, it's hard to herd the cats."

West was struck by that admission. He thought, *So you don't have anything to dangle anymore. But that's what true leadership is about. It's about how you take a diverse entity and get everyone focused on accomplishing a singular goal. Heck, I was commanding a company of 131 when I was twenty-eight years old. You have to provide a vision.*

The Florida freshman wasn't quite sure what vision was being articulated on November 1, when the Republican leadership brought to the floor House Concurrent Resolution 13, which reaffirmed "In God We Trust" as the official motto of the United States. "There are few things

Congress could do that would be more important than passing this resolution," cosponsor Lamar Smith intoned.

West found himself scratching his head. Nearly 14 million Americans were out of work. Congress's approval rating had hit rock bottom. *If West was making that call, that resolution would never have made it to the floor,* he thought.

But of course Allen West wasn't being asked to help make the calls. Far from it. In early November, Eric Cantor approached him on the House floor. "The new calendar for 2012 is coming out tomorrow," Cantor told him. The majority leader asked West to please refrain from publicly criticizing it as he had done when the previous calendar was released shortly after the 2010 midterm elections.

"Look, my point was proven," West said—meaning: *Our constituents want us staying here and taking care of business, not hanging out in our districts.* "And," he added, "if this calendar's the same as the last one, my point will be proven again."

The calendar would in fact be the same as before: a mere six Washington workdays in January, fourteen in February, fifteen in March, eight in April . . . It was in part because of this low-intensity legislating schedule that Allen West took to the House floor on December 8, stared into the C-SPAN camera, and said, "I must take the time to offer an apology to the citizens of the Twenty-Second Congressional District of Florida and to all my fellow citizens across this great nation . . . I would have hoped our exertions would have been, as a collective body, a bit greater."

Not for nothing had West's flattop gone grayer. In a way, life in the House was more stressful than being at war. "If I go into a combat zone," he said, "I know I'm coming with a plan to kill the enemy. Here, you see things develop, you say, 'Guys, come on, we can get there.' And it just doesn't happen."

Not everyone was ignoring West's advice. The chairman of the House Armed Services Committee, Buck McKeon, would recognize the Army veteran's expertise in December by appointing him to a select bicameral committee that would create guidelines and funding for the Department of Defense. For the most part, however, Allen West would remain his own sovereign entity amid a constellation of 435. The question was whether he would continue to burn bright and hold his place in the political solar system, or suffer a meteoric fate. The Tea Party star with no previous office-holding experience had grown into the role of legislator. He had authored the only spending cut bill to pass unanimously in the House. The whip team had used him to urge colleagues to accept compromise bills. West had come to realize, in his words, "As the military teaches, there are five forms of maneuver—you don't always have to do the frontal assault." His "yes" vote on the debt ceiling bill had even compelled a supporter back in Fort Lauderdale to say to him, "You dropped your bayonet."

Nonetheless, two formidable Democratic opponents were vying to take back his seat. The Republican redistricting cartographers in Tallahassee had done him no favors, reconfiguring the 22nd District in a way that replaced a few Republican strongholds with neighborhoods from the district of DNC chairwoman Debbie Wasserman Schultz. If the new map withstood court challenges, the former D+1 district would be more like D+5. Democratic Congressional Campaign Committee officials were crowing that Allen West would be forced to flee the 22nd District and instead challenge fellow GOP freshman Tom Rooney in the 16th.

"Soldiers don't abandon their posts," West would say. They also didn't commit suicide. West moved into the redrawn 18th district—living to fight another day.

It was Senate Majority Leader Harry Reid's novel proposition that if 535 congressmen and senators couldn't agree on how to solve America's deficit problem over a period of seven months, perhaps a dozen of them could within ten weeks. The wily majority leader knew better, of course. As Reid would later confide, he came up with the idea of the Joint Select Committee on Deficit Reduction, or Super Committee, fully expecting that it would fail.

The Super Committee held its first meeting on September 8. Signs of dysfunction were apparent from the start. Though several members at the table urged each other to "go big" by striving to find more than the $1.5 trillion in spending cuts required of the Super Committee, Republican Senator Jon Kyl warned the others that he would quit the proceedings if any of those additional reductions came from defense spending. Kyl also suggested that they begin by identifying areas that each side would be willing to cut—but the Democrats, recalling that this was how the Biden debt ceiling talks began, refused to play ball. Instead, said Chris Van Hollen, "We need to first agree on a framework, on the ratio of spending cuts to revenue increases." But no such ratio was ever agreed to—not on that day, and not at any other point.

The Democrat participants believed—naïvely, some of them would later admit—that the six Republican members would agree to forgo the Bush tax cuts for wealthy Americans. Not a shred of evidence anywhere suggested that any among the six had ever entertained such a proposition. Still, the Democrats hoped. They hoped that Kyl, who had decided not to run for reelection, would play the statesman. They hoped that Jeb Hensarling—the Republican House's conference chairman but largely unknown—might want to make a name for himself by producing the grand bargain that had eluded Boehner and Cantor. They hoped that House Ways and Means chairman Dave Camp, who had internally resisted the Ryan budget (though more on political and jurisdictional than policy grounds), would prove to be a voice of moderation.

Halfway into the Super Committee's ten-week tenure, no one had even offered a proposal—though in sidebar discussions, Kyl and Van Hollen mulled over a lesser revenue scheme involving a gas tax or user fee hikes on items like Medicare premiums, flood insurance, and Fannie Mae and Freddie Mac loans. (Neither man could convince his colleagues to adopt this approach.) On October 26, both sides finally exchanged competing plans. The Republicans offered a package of $2.2 trillion in deficit reduction over the next decade. The Democrats proposed $3 trillion in reductions, including $1.2 trillion in tax increases. Each side summarily rejected the other's plan. The Republicans then floated a proposal by Senator Pat Toomey that would raise revenues by about $250 billion—but largely through closing tax loopholes, and in the process locking in the $800 billion Bush tax cuts *and* lowering the top tax rate from 35 to 28 percent. The net effect of the plan would be a disproportionate burden on middle-income taxpayers. Though even antitax guru Grover Norquist proclaimed that it was a plan the Democrats could not possibly agree to, committee member Senator John Kerry spent days toying with a way to make it more palatable, and the Republicans appeared to have gained an edge in the negotiations.

Behind the scenes, the staffs of Dave Camp and Democratic Senator Max Baucus had been working on a completely separate package—one that would include roughly $600 billion in revenues from upper-income taxpayers, plus a $50 billion adjustment in the Consumer Price Index. The $650 billion figure had in fact come from Speaker Boehner, and his policy people had participated in formulating the specifics.

On Sunday, November 13, Camp and Baucus agreed on an outline for the package: a $100 billion down payment from closing corporate tax loopholes, another $500 billion generated from tax reform, and $50 billion from adjusting the CPI and lowering the top tax rate from 35 to 34 percent. Baucus presented it to Kerry, Van Hollen, and Senator Patty Murray in Murray's office that evening. All four Democrats were intrigued. (The other two Democrat members, Congressmen Jim Clyburn and Xavier Becerra, had been largely disengaged from all the negotiations.)

The problem lay with Camp's Republican colleagues. Hensarling and Kyl reacted coldly to the $650 billion revenue plan. Toomey, who at one time had been president of the antitax Club for Growth, had already been taking heat for his $250 billion revenue hikes and could go no further. On Monday the fourteenth, the committee met and went back and forth on the details of the Camp-Baucus option. But nothing was agreed to. By Tuesday—eight days before the committee's legislative deadline to submit a deficit reduction plan—the $650 billion bipartisan plan had fallen through the floorboards. The Republicans embraced the Toomey proposal. The Democrats, while proffering a $2.3 trillion reduction plan by Baucus, as a caucus began rooting for the Super Committee to fail—calculating that the better deal would be the $1.5 trillion automatic "sequestration" cuts in both defense and nonsecurity programs that would be triggered by the failure.

The Democrats got their wish, since failure is what the Super Committee ultimately produced . . . except that Republicans vowed that they would undo the sequestration trigger to protect defense programs.

At one point during the ten-week process, one committee member sighed to the others, "Failure to get an agreement—sort of sounds like a do-nothing Congress, doesn't it, guys?"

On this, if nothing else, there was agreement.

• • •

While the Super Committee talks were running their ignominious course, the House and the Senate easily passed a package of three Appropriations conference bills on November 17. The "minibus" legislation passed in the House, however, only because 165 Democrats voted for it. Fully 101 Republicans did not, including two members of the leadership team: conference chairman Hensarling and policy chairman Tom Price.

Livid, the Appropriations Cardinals demanded an audience with Boehner, Cantor, and McCarthy.

The twelve subcommittee chairmen and Chairman Hal Rogers met with the leadership trio in the Speaker's office on the morning of November 30. Rogers had particular reason to be irritated. The seventy-three-year-old, amply jowled, white-haired, cigar-smoking, silky voiced Southern gentleman had been representing Kentucky's 5th District since Reagan was first elected president in 1980 and had been an Appropriator since his second term. To receive Speaker Boehner's vote as chairman had required considerable pride-swallowing on Rogers's part. When Boehner decreed that two-thirds of the Appropriations Committee's sumptuous Capitol suite would become part of the Speaker's ceremonial quarters, Rogers did not squawk. When it became clear, after the results of the November 2 midterm election were in, that the committee would have to be stocked with hard-line conservatives, Rogers was acquiescent. And since it was abundantly clear that the days of earmarking were over—at least for now—the Appropriator once known as the Prince of Pork vowed not only to renounce the practice but also to enforce the ban with extreme prejudice. But Hal Rogers had grown tired of being a good sport.

"We got our legs cut out from under us," Rogers snapped. "There was no whipping of that vote. No discipline at all. Look, the electorate is going to judge all of us not by how many bills we can pass, but whether we can govern. They'll say, 'We've given you the majority to govern. Now: can you do that?' And we've just told them we can't."

Said Rogers, "You let us down, big-time."

McCarthy offered a halfhearted defense. Referring to a provision in the bill that increased the limit on Federal Housing Administration loans, the whip said, "We told you that if you put the FHA in there, it would collapse the vote."

The Cardinals were astounded. The FHA provision was a compromise with the Senate that Boehner himself had agreed to!

Sounding defensive, McCarthy nonetheless agreed that they had little control over how their members voted. Two other chairmen—Ryan of the Budget Committee and David Dreier of the Rules Committee—had recently voted against the balanced budget amendment to the Constitution. He added, "The fact is, we've got a bunch of younger members who don't understand that they're operating in the long term. It's a process, and I know it's frustrating. But they're beginning to see the bigger picture."

"But it's wrong to let them off the hook," said Rogers. "No punishment, no ramifications at all for doing the wrong thing . . ."

"We'd prefer to reward members for doing the right thing than punish members for doing the wrong thing," Boehner said.

The Cardinals objected. *They* were the ones who had been doing the right thing—cutting spending two years in a row for the first time since World War II, working their butts off to accommodate everyone—and all they were getting was grief. To add insult to injury, the Cardinals were required to raise more money for the National Republican Congressional Committee than other members were. As Interior subcommittee chairman Mike Simpson put it to the leaders, "We're having to raise extra money to reelect people who vote against our bills!"

"You need to strip them of their committee assignments," one of them said.

"Or take them off the CODEL [congressional delegation overseas trip] list," said another.

"That's not going to make this crowd more accountable," McCarthy warned.

"It'll just make martyrs out of them," Boehner agreed. The Speaker was mindful of the reality they lived in—one of unprecedented transparency, in which the slightest retribution would instantly be tweeted or become a banner headline on the *Drudge Report*. Every morning after waking up, Boehner would look at Facebook on his iPad to see if the fact that he'd had a margarita in a Mexican restaurant in Rosslyn, Virginia, had been announced to the public at large. It was a good thing, he reminded the Cardinals. It kept everyone honest.

"But then you're destroying our capability of coming up with anything significant on our big bill," said Rogers, referring to the "megabus" package of the remaining nine Appropriations bills that would be brought to the House floor in mid-December. The chairman recounted a warning he had been given by Steny Hoyer and ranking Democrat Norm Dicks on the House floor after the 101 Republicans had voted against the "minibus." The two Democrats told Rogers that the "megabus" had better be devoid of any sops to conservatives, such as riders that cut EPA funds. "Get the riders out," they instructed him.

"You've taken away our bargaining power," Rogers said. "So don't expect a hell of a lot."

Boehner had nothing to say to this. Cantor, the Cardinals noted, had been mute throughout the meeting. The majority leader's risk-averse nature had been exacerbated by the public outrage over the debt ceiling fiasco. His attack-dog press operation was now churning out fawning statements assuring voters that "we can't wait" to find areas of agreement with President Obama. When Cantor learned that protesters would be attending his speech at the University of Pennsylvania in late October, he canceled on the day of the appearance. Having now become the left's designated whipping boy, Cantor was now seeking to soften his image by accentuating his Jewish family history in speeches and offering to let a *60 Minutes* crew film him at home over Thanksgiving weekend. In the meantime, he was not looking to make any enemies among the Appropriators.

One of the more vocal Cardinals at the meeting, Agriculture chairman Jack Kingston of Georgia, had served in the House since 1993. He could not help thinking that his old friend Tom "the Hammer" DeLay would never have been so supine as today's Republican leaders. Nor would Nancy Pelosi. Nor would any Speaker in any of the state legislatures. *They'd say, "You're damn right I punished him for not voting my way." That's the rules of the game in any legislative body.*

Another veteran Appropriator left the room recalling conversations he'd had with some of the freshmen. "You're not in the minority," he had explained to them. "You're in charge! You don't throw hand grenades at your own people! You help them govern!"

Small wonder that the Appropriator's words had fallen on deaf ears.

The freshmen were allowed to carry on with impunity. "They're throwing hand grenades at the very place they own," he would later reflect. "It's a strange thing. They seem to revel in their rascality."

Rascality happened to be a John Dingell word—one that he had come to use with increasing frequency to describe the connivances of the Republican majority.

On the afternoon of December 13, 2011, Dingell sat in his Capitol hideaway—the sunny office space accorded the dean of the House—and reflected on the words he had used at the freshman orientation reception thirteen months ago to describe the House: *the most humanly perfect institution.* "The institution is still humanly perfect," he maintained. "The problem is, the inmates in it are not. There's all manner of rascality and bad behavior going on here. I'm more frustrated than I've ever been in my career."

Dingell shook his head as he considered that the House was supposed to be adjourning for the Christmas break in three days. But the Republican leadership had yet to bring to the floor its nine Appropriations bills, yet another Continuing Resolution to avert a government shutdown, and a measure backed by Obama (and thus viewed with disfavor by most Republicans) to extend a payroll tax cut to millions of Americans. Dingell personally viewed the payroll tax holiday as bad policy (for robbing revenues from Social Security) but clever politics, and he marveled at how obligingly the Republicans were allowing themselves to be portrayed by Obama as the party willing to raise taxes on the middle class. It would be another ten days before Speaker Boehner at last ignored the conservatives in his conference, capitulated to the White House, and brought the payroll tax cut bill to the floor under unanimous consent after all the House members had gone home for the Christmas holidays, so as to avoid one last rebellion among his ranks. Yet another thoroughly unnecessary eleventh-hour melodrama. Never in Dingell's career—never, he believed, in the history of the House—had it been so slow to tend to the nation's urgent business.

At least the institution still worked for him. During the summer recess, Dingell convinced EPA administrator Lisa Jackson to visit his beloved Detroit River International Wildlife Refuge. Jackson was sufficiently sold on the refuge that she agreed to procure a million dollars in EPA funds to help clean up a portion of the site that Dingell had recently convinced Chrysler to sell to the federal government—which, through Dingell's persuasions, then gave the land to the county. After the tract got cleaned up, he would then figure out how to transfer it over to Fish & Wildlife so as to officially make the land a part of the refuge. Dingell had the experience and the relationships—and, God willing, the time—to make it happen.

And just the night before, during a week choked with partisan rancor over the payroll tax issue, yet another piece of Dingell legislation had made it through the House. It was an oil pipeline safety bill that he had been laboring to pass for more than thirty years. After the devastating spill of crude oil into the Kalamazoo River in 2010, Energy and Commerce Committee chairman and fellow Michigander Fred Upton agreed with Dingell that the bill was needed and became its cosponsor. As always, the legislation was imperfect, as environmentalists were quick to point out. Still, that any bill adding new regulations to the oil and gas industry could prevail in a Republican-controlled House was a small miracle. Then again, the legislation was labeled the Pipeline Safety, Regulatory Certainty, and Job Creation Act, when of course the bill's purpose had nothing whatsoever to do with creating jobs. And for that matter, it was hurried to passage through a voice vote, for fear that a roll call would give conservatives time to organize against it.

Nonetheless, on January 3, 2012, President Obama signed the Dingell-Upton collaboration into law. It would be only the ninetieth piece of legislation from the 112th Congress to reach the president's desk for signature—a woeful output of historic proportions, especially considering that sixteen of those ninety bills pertained to renaming post offices and courthouses.

Perhaps, Dingell thought, the tea-baggers would be thrown out in 2012. Pelosi, for all her faults, was a peerless fund-raiser. A poll of swing-district voters conducted the previous week by Rosa DeLauro's husband Stan Greenberg found support for Republican incumbents fast eroding—leading Greenberg to conclude that "the House is surely in play in 2012." Certainly Nancy Pelosi was gung-ho about the prospects. She had hired Roy Spence, the Texas consultant, to interview the House Democrats and discern from their musings a common theme that could become their twenty-first-century answer to Reagan's

"Morning in America." Pelosi was already dropping the resulting slogan, "Reigniting the American Dream," into her speeches, though the average listener might be forgiven for wondering exactly what the buzz phrase meant and how it applied uniquely to Democrats.

Dingell had no particular reason to believe that the climate would improve if his party returned to power. He believed the "most humanly perfect institution" was imperiled by super-PACS that the Supreme Court had permitted to spend unlimited dollars in total anonymity; by redistricting, which threatened to wipe out moderate dealmakers and replace them with crowd-pleasers from the left or the right; by talk show screamers and lie-dispensing bloggers; and most of all, by its near-total lack of credibility in the eyes of the public. He tried to think if there was anyone living or dead who had polled as low as 9 percent.

"I think pedophiles would do better," he concluded.

In three hours Dingell would be back on the House floor to consider the payroll tax cut bill—albeit one that had been spiked with enough conservative catnip (spending cuts, the fast-tracking of an oil pipeline, curtailment of unemployment insurance) to guarantee that Harry Reid would pronounce it dead on arrival in the Senate the moment it passed the House. Impasse again.

"I'll bet you a new hat we're going to be here next week," John Dingell said. In truth, he did not seem to mind all that much. If tonight was like most nights, he would linger on the floor after all the votes—just sitting in his chair, his gaze pleasantly befogged while luxuriating in a half century's worth of triumphs and rascalities, more at home in the House than anyone had ever been. Then he would call his wife, the Lovely Deborah, and once home he might crack open a Stouffer's frozen dinner accompanied by a cranberry and mango smoothie, and then set the TV on to the Military Channel, until the marching soldiers and the cannon blasts would send him off to sleep.

And then, God willing, another day spent in that most humanly perfect institution, where he could still manage to get things done.

Evening, January 24, 2012

There were six of them, all Republican freshmen, seated around a dining room table two hours before Barack Obama's State of the Union address.

The venue was the Italian restaurant Landini Brothers, in Alexandria, Virginia. Ordinarily the group gathered at the Capitol Hill row house rented by Steve Southerland and ate the gumbo of Louisianan Jeff Landry—which was why they often referred to themselves as the Cajun Caucus. As the president's speech that evening left no time for Landry to cook, the Cajun Caucus instead drove to Old Town, pushing their way through the crowded Tuscan restaurant and upstairs to their secluded table, where they sat over pasta and iced tea and contemplated aloud what had transpired in the past year since they'd arrived as reinforcements for the beleaguered Republican leaders who had gathered in a different restaurant on the other side of the Potomac River three years earlier almost to the day.

All six men—Southerland, Landry, Jeff Duncan, Raul Labrador, Tim Huelskamp, and Tom Graves—were Tea Party conservatives. The brand of "reinforcement" they had brought to Washington had dealt their Republican leadership no end of aggravation. Public approval of the dysfunctional House Republicans now languished at 19 percent. Yet these six men were doing just fine with the voters back home in their blood-red districts. The only one among them with a primary challenge was Landry, and only because Louisiana's dwindling population in the aftermath of Hurricane Katrina had caused a fellow Republican, Charles Boustany Jr., to lose his 7th District and therefore to take a run at Landry's seat.

"Anything you need from us, Jeff," the others told their fellow freshman that night. "We'll come to your district. We'll raise money. Anything."

Landry and Graves had missed the annual House Republican conference the previous weekend, and so the other four men filled them in on the highlights. The affair had been pronouncedly less buoyant than the new majority's cocksure we-want-the-world-and-we-want-it-now conference in January 2011. Fresh off of the humiliating payroll tax cut debate, in which Speaker Boehner had finally turned a deaf ear to his Republican colleagues and meekly capitulated to the White House's demand for a two-month extension, Boehner's new mantra was, "Let's put the last year behind us. I want to push the reset button."

What did that mean? The men of the Cajun Caucus hoped it meant, "Start behaving like Republicans." But in the wake of the House majority's dismal approval ratings, perhaps John Boehner was saying, "Start finding ways to work together with the Democrats." In truth, they had no idea what was going on in their leader's head.

The best part of the conference, they told Landry and Graves, had been the PowerPoint presentation by Republican pollster Frank Luntz—the man who had organized the dinner at the Caucus Room three years ago. Luntz had told them, "You've been talking like conservatives, but acting like moderates. You've got to stop that. The American people would rather you talk like moderates and act like conservatives." Meaning: sound reasonable, but stick to your principles. That was music to the Cajun Caucus's ears.

While they ate, the White House released a few excerpts of Obama's upcoming address. Duncan was the first to reach for his buzzing Black-Berry. "You've got to be kidding me," he scoffed. Then he read aloud the offending excerpt: *Think about the America within our reach: A country that leads the world in educating its people. An America that attracts a new generation of high-tech manufacturing and high-paying jobs. A future where we're in control of our own energy, and our security and prosperity aren't so tied to unstable parts of the world.*

The others groaned.

Labrador then read aloud from another passage: *Let's never forget: Millions of Americans who work hard and play by the rules every day deserve a government and a financial system that does the same. It's time to apply the same rules from top to bottom: no bailouts, no handouts, and no cop-outs. An America built to last insists on responsibility from everybody.*

"As if!" the Idaho tea partier snickered.

"So do we wear the button?" someone asked.

"I intend to," said Duncan.

"Not if everyone else does—I don't like going with the pack," grinned Labrador.

They were referring to the large red button Duncan was wearing on the right lapel of his suit. 1000 DAYS, it read—signifying the amount of time that had elapsed since the Senate had last passed a budget. Duncan's office had printed 250 of the buttons and distributed them to his Republican colleagues. Perhaps half of them showed up to that morning's conference wearing the button—prompting Majority Leader Eric Cantor to exclaim into the microphone, "Great idea, whoever thought of that!" To which several loudly replied, "Jeff Duncan!"

But conference chairman Jeb Hensarling had also cautioned the members that morning, "The press is going to be watching you tonight. If you're texting or emailing during the president's speech, that's going to wind up on YouTube." And Boehner had been even more direct: "We're going to maintain decorum. No shouting. No wearing anything. No signs"—the latter admonishment due to Jeff Landry, who during President Obama's "pass this jobs bill" joint session speech last September had held up a placard that read DRILLING = JOBS. Landry was now proudly employing that slogan in his primary battle. That Boehner viewed such displays as unseemly was yet another reminder of the philosophical gulf between the Speaker and his unruly young charges.

Immediately following that morning's conference, as Duncan headed toward the House chamber so as to deliver a speech during morning hour debate, he had run into House Administration Committee chairman Dan Lungren, who told the freshman, "You can't wear that on the floor." Duncan reluctantly complied. He took his place in the line of morning-hour stalwarts: Walter Jones, who once again exhorted Congress and the president to "pull out our troops now" from Afghanistan; Minority Leader Nancy Pelosi, who paid tribute to the recent death of former Georgia Congressman Ed Jenkins, a proto–Blue Dog who served from 1977 to 1993, at a time when moderates who worked across the aisle were a flourishing breed; and Sheila Jackson Lee, who upon arrival in the chamber promptly deposited a pile of belongings on a third-row middle-aisle seat—thereby reserving it so that she could once again be seen that evening by a national audience, lit up in her bright green dress with her arms around the president of the United States as he fought his way to the podium.

When it came Jeff Duncan's turn to speak that morning, he began by saying, "All around the Hill today, you'll see members of Congress wearing a red button," and held it up for the benefit of C-SPAN viewers. "One thousand days, acting irresponsibly."

That night at dinner, Jeff Duncan declared to the others, "I'm gonna wear the button until someone tells me to take it off."

The other five nodded their approval, though none of them vowed to do the same. The Cajun Caucus paid up, piled into two cars, and made their way across the 14th Street Bridge, bound for the Capitol.

Once inside the impossibly crowded chamber, Duncan got separated from the others. Pressed up against him was a senior House Republican who peered down at Duncan's red button and quietly suggested that maybe this was not the time or place for such a display. The freshman slid the button off his lapel and put it in his pocket. He plopped down in the first empty seat he could find. Surrounding him were U.S. senators. Following a rogue impulse, Duncan pulled out the 1000 DAYS button and showed it to those around him. Archconservative Senator Mike Lee of Utah bobbed his head in approval. Democrat Tom Udall glanced at it with what Duncan interpreted as welling regret at his party's dereliction. Satisfied that he had made his point, the South Carolinian put his button away.

From his seat in the third row, Duncan could see a thin woman in a red jacket and glasses. It was Gabrielle Giffords. Last week the Arizona congresswoman had announced, in a heart-wrenching video marked by her clear eyes but halting speech as a result of her gunshot wound, that she would be resigning from Congress. Duncan joined his colleagues in giving Giffords a standing ovation. Though he'd never had an actual conversation with her, Jeff Duncan felt an ineffable kinship with the brave young woman who had come to symbolize the House—its earnestness and resilience, but also its mortal frailty.

He would stand and applaud a couple of other times that evening as the president spoke, a game showing of comity. But of course, the address was not intended for Jeff Duncan's ears—though in a sense, it was aimed squarely at him, campaign verbiage hurled by a wounded incumbent against what Obama hoped to frame as a Do-Nothing Congress: *I intend to fight obstruction with action. . . . Send me these tax reforms, and I'll sign them right away. . . . The opponents of action are out of excuses. . . . Both parties agree on these ideas. So put them in a bill, and get it on my desk this year. . . . So far, you haven't acted. Well, tonight I will . . .*

The Republicans poured out of the chamber the moment the address ended, as if repelled by force. Many of them as well as Democrats headed to Statuary Hall, garishly lit by dozens of camera crews— tonight a rotunda of comment seekers and comment givers, all haloed by marble scowls of statesmen from another time. Duncan was among them. He was scheduled to be interviewed by a Hearst TV channel— and for the occasion, the freshman had refastened his 1000 DAYS button to his lapel. But the crush of bodies was even more oppressive than in the House chamber. Standing all the way at the front of the line, already miked up, was Majority Whip Kevin McCarthy. Duncan counted fifteen interviewees waiting between McCarthy and himself.

"Forget it," he finally muttered. Duncan pushed his way back in the opposite direction from the media scrum, toward the House chamber, then out into the Capitol's main hallway, and finally out the eastern door, where the president's limousine awaited . . . where, aside from the Capitol police and Secret Service, there was nobody at all. He drew a fatigued breath and trudged along through the starless winter evening, looking no different from any other overworked Washingtonian in a suit except, of course, for that red button on his lapel. Duncan was proud of his little invention. As for the other 249 buttons? Likely they were already in desk drawers, mixed up among paper clips and rubber bands and scraps of other once-great ideas. Perhaps a button or two would survive the year, the decade, and even beyond, a rusty artifact for another generation to puzzle over: what were those thousand days, and who felt such a need to mark them—are they the stuff of statues or only of fighting words, and is it fair to ask what good they did . . .

NOTES

PROLOGUE: EVENING, JANUARY 20, 2009

xv   The venue was the Caucus Room: Interviews with ten of the fifteen participants. Also Matt Bai, "Newt. Again," *New York Times Magazine,* February 25, 2009.

xix   The U.S. unemployment rate: Bureau of Labor Statistics, February 10, 2009.

xx   First Federal Congress: Robert V. Remini, *The House: The History of the House of Representatives* (Washington, DC: Library of Congress, 2007); Rufus Wilmot Griswold, *The Republican Court; or, American Society in the Days of Washington,* 1867.

xx   "There are few shining geniuses": John Thornton Kirkland, *Works of Fisher Ames: With a Selection from His Speeches and Correspondence,* 1854, p. 33.

xx   "crazed with the chase": ibid., p. 74.

xxii   approval rating of 9 percent: CBS News/*New York Times* poll, October 25, 2011.

CHAPTER ONE: TEA PARTY FRESHMAN

3   "Mr. Duncan from South Carolina": Author personally observed.

3   Congressman-elect Jeff Duncan: Interviews with Duncan, November 18–19, 2010.

4   "I Believe": http://www.jeffduncan.com, campaign website.

5   the three House office buildings: Architect of the Capitol website.

5   Duncan surveyed: Author personally observed.

8   Glenn Nye: Interview with Nye, May 2, 2011.

8   "votes with Nancy Pelosi 83 percent": Scott Rigell campaign ad "Her Congressman," October 2010.

9   met in HC-5: Interviews with five members present at the meeting.

CHAPTER TWO: THE DEAN

11   At a weeknight party: Author personally observed.

12   "but then again": Interview with Dingell, April 21, 2011.

13   a town hall in Romulus: Video of town hall, August 6, 2009.

13 Dingell had faced: *National Journal Almanac* website, last updated July 1, 2011.
14 Michigan congressional delegation: Interviews with two of the attendees.

CHAPTER THREE: BAYONETS

16 a swearing-in ceremony: Author personally observed. Also interviews with West, January 12 and 25, 2011.
16 John Lewis: Interview with West, January 12, 2011.
16 James Clyburn: Interview with West, December 9, 2010.
16 Allen Bernard West: Interview with West, December 9, 2010. Also for Hamoodi interrogation, interview with Neal Puckett, June 28, 2011. Also for 2008 and 2010 elections, interview with Ron Klein, June 4, 2011.
20 plotting his campaign: Interview with West, January 3, 2011.
23 Boehner flew in: Interview with West, December 9, 2010.
23 Buck McKeon: Author personally observed. Also interview with West, January 25, 2011.
23 new working calendar: West letter to Cantor, December 16, 2010. Cantor staff response: Michael O'Brien, "GOP freshman charges Cantor with crafting lax work schedule," *Hill,* December 16, 2010. Cantor nonresponse: Interview with West, January 25, 2011.

CHAPTER FOUR: CITIZENS IN THE DEVIL'S CITY

27 Duncan held a prayer breakfast: Assistant Emily Umhoefer personally observed.
27 "May this Territory": Fourth Annual Message of John Adams, November 22, 1800.
28 Washington in its first few years: Remini, *The House;* Griswold, *The Republican Court;* Benjamin Perley Poore, *Perley's Reminiscences of Sixty Years in the National Metropolis,* vol. 1, 1885. Daniel Carroll: John Michael Vlach, "The Quest for a Capital," Ruth Ann Overbeck Capitol Hill History Project lecture series; also Duddington Place website. "Spider lobbyists": Perley Poore, *Perley's Reminiscences,* p. 33.
30 Ellmers was a registered: Interview with Ellmers, December 21, 2010. McCarthy trip: Interview with McCarthy, December 10, 2010. "Please let go of my arm": YouTube video of the incident, uploaded June 14, 2010. Two NRCC sources verify that the two who accosted Etheridge were NRCC interns. Victory mosque: Interview with Ellmers, December 21, 2010; also "No Mosque at Ground Zero" TV ad, September 22, 2010.
31 Farenthold was a shy: Interview with Farenthold, January 18, 2011. "Fluke winner": David Wasserman, *Cook Political Report,* December 17, 2010. Reception buffet: Author personally observed.
33 At 2:03 P.M. on January 5: Author personally observed. Boehner and Dingell: YouTube video, January 5, 2011. Cantor and Democrat remarks: *Congressional Record,* January 5, 2011.
34 read sections of the U.S. Constitution: Author personally observed. Goodlatte:

Goodlatte press release, January 5, 2011. Duncan: Interview with Duncan, January 18, 2011. Ames and First Amendment: 109 1 *Annals of Congress* 766, August 20, 1789; also see Marc M. Arkin, "Regionalism and the Religion Clauses: The Contribution of Fisher Ames," *Buffalo Law Review,* Spring 1999. (Curiously, none of Ames's surviving writings mentions his authorship of the First Amendment's final language—perhaps because the great orator had little use for any amendments to the Constitution, viewing them as a sop to anti-Federalists that would "stimulate the stomach as little as hasty-pudding." Kirkland, *Works,* p. 54.)

CHAPTER FIVE: GABBY

35   Blue Dogs hosted: Interviews with five of the attendees.

35   After raising: Carolyn Classen, "How did Giffords win?" *Tucson Citizen,* November 14, 2010.

35   Her boomerang trajectory: Vera Fedchenko, "27-year-old charts Ariz. firm's course," *Tire Business,* February 16, 1998; Lorrie Cohen, "Goodyear buys out El Campo," *Tucson Citizen,* July 3, 1999; Emily Heil and Anna Palmer, "Motorcycle Mama," *Roll Call,* May 5, 2008; Gabrielle Birkner, "Giffords' Jewish journey: From Israel to service and study," *Forward,* January 24, 2011.

36   "Whatever you say": Conservatives for Congress Committee in Tucson ad, posted May 21, 2010. Anonymous assailant: Dan Nowicki, "Vandal hits office after Giffords' vote," *Arizona Republic,* March 24, 2010. Crosshairs: SARAHPAC map posted on Palin's Facebook page, March 23, 2010. Giffords response: Chuck Todd and Savannah Guthrie interview with Giffords on MSNBC, March 25, 2010. Kelly ad: posted on Jesse Kelly campaign website.

37   "Listen, young lady": Interviews with two of the attendees.

37   "absolutely the Tea Party": Chris Cillizza, "Raising Arizona," *Washington Post,* March 15, 2010. "Gabrielle is not like other": Giffords for Congress ad videos and speech transcripts. Debate with Kelly: YouTube of Sierra Vista debate, October 20, 2010.

39   she discussed the matter with Pelosi: Interviews with Pelosi and Giffords aides.

39   "there's a big difference": YouTube video of Giffords on election night, November 2, 2010.

CHAPTER SIX: THE INSTITUTIONALIST

40   Boehner had been at his home: Interview with two Boehner staffers. Pelosi and Christmas tree: Annie Groer, "Rep. Giffords voted against Pelosi for House Speaker [*sic*]—but that was SO last week," *Politics Daily,* January 13, 2011. "I am horrified": Boehner statement, January 8, 2011. "And frankly": Transcript of phone call, January 9, 2011.

41   In 1808: Benson John Lossing, *Harpers' Popular Cyclopaedia of United States History from the Aboriginal Period to 1876* (New York: Harper, 1881), p. 481. Sickles versus Key: *New York Times,* February 28, 1859, April 13, 15, 16, 27, 1859. Ryan assassination: Report of a Staff Investigative Group to the U.S. House Commit-

tee on Foreign Affairs, May 15, 1979. Capitol shooting: Martin Weil, "Gunman shoots his way into Capitol," *Washington Post*, July 25, 1998. Anthrax: Tom Daschle, "The unsolved case of anthrax," *Washington Post*, October 15, 2006. Shuler threat: Interview with Shuler, March 3, 2011. Markey: Interview with Markey, July 12, 2011. Udall: "Mark Udall receives death threat at Denver office," *Huffington Post*, May 25, 2010. "I know many": YouTube video of Boehner statement, March 25, 2010.

43 Chaffetz came to Boehner: Interview with Chaffetz, July 8, 2011.

45 "I stand opposed": Scott Lilly, "Republican earmarks: Fool me twice?" *Huffington Post*, March 11, 2010.

46 FOR A MAJORITY: Quoted from the thirty-seven-page document. Majority leader vote: Interviews with four attendees. 122–109: Ken Rudin, "The Boehner upset," NPR, February 3, 2006.

47 CANTOR RULE: Author personally observed. McCarthy and Boehner to Tea Party: Interview with McCarthy, May 5, 2011. Pledge: Pledge to America website. "out of touch": Dan Balz, "Boehner defends criticism of financial overhaul as excessive," *Washington Post*, June 30, 2010. Noem: *Argus Leader*, October 20, 2010.

49 "end earmarks": Jake Sherman, "Cantor calls for earmark moratorium," *Politico*, October 13, 2010; Cantor, "A step towards curing Washington's spending disease—eliminating earmarks," *Politico*, October 13, 2010.

50 "by being led": Interview with Lott, May 13, 2011.

CHAPTER SEVEN: STATE OF THE WEINER

52 "Am I to understand": *Congressional Record*, January 7, 2011. "And just a word": *Congressional Record*, January 17, 2011. "You know": *Congressional Record*, January 19, 2011. (Author personally observed all of these.) "House Mouse": YouTube video of Weiner floor statement, April 1, 2011.

53 had predicted on CNBC: Weiner on CNBC, August 17, 2009. "I don't think": Meredith Shiner and Maggie Haberman, "Left laments Barack Obama's move to center," *Politico*, January 24, 2011.

55 "a pyromaniac": YouTube video of Weiner-McCaughey debate, October 5, 2009.

57 January 25: Author personally observed.

CHAPTER EIGHT: MADAM MINORITY LEADER

58 "win the future": State of the Union address, January 25, 2011. Retreat: Felicia Sonmez, "Obama pays short visit to House Democratic retreat," *Washington Post*, January 21, 2011.

58 a self-styled messaging coach: Author personally observed.

59 Shuler had called her: Interview with Shuler, December 21, 2010.

60 $65 million: "Anti-Pelosi ads break records," CNN, November 8, 2010.

60 "we have to pass": YouTube video of Pelosi speech, March 9, 2010.

60 "I know how to win": Interview with Pelosi, July 19, 2011.

61   the whip race: Marc Sandalow, "House Democrats pick S.F.'s Pelosi for minority whip," *San Francisco Chronicle*, October 10, 2001.

61   "felt like a ten-pound anvil": Zachary Coile, "Pelosi sketches strategy on key issues," *San Francisco Chronicle*, January 22, 2009.

62   "brain dead": "Pete Stark: Dem moderates 'brain dead,'" *Politico*, August 27, 2009.

65   The unemployment figure: Peter S. Goodman, "Joblessness hits 9.5%, dampening recovery hopes," *New York Times*, July 2, 2009.

65   House Democrats caucused: Interviews with five attendees.

CHAPTER NINE: CONTINUING RESOLUTION

69   "Tantalus Club": *Oswego Daily Palladium*, March 18, 1902; *Washington Times*, December 18, 1902; *Washington Herald*, February 1, 1911; "The small talk of Washington," *New York Times*, April 7, 1904, February 29, 1904; "British Ambassador a hit," *New York Times*, December 19, 1902; "Tantalus Club forms a Cabinet," *Washington Times*, February 3, 1905; also copy of Tantalus Club menu at the Shoreham, 1907.

70   Duncan deposited it: Author personally observed.

71   Grover Norquist: Jonathan Strong, "Conservatives push 'anti-appropriations committee,'" *Daily Caller*, October 19, 2010. RSC letter: "Rep. Jeff Duncan invites cosponsors to bring back the Byrd Committee," January 24, 2011. Cantor: pen-and-pad transcript, February 8, 2011.

72   the Triangle: Author personally observed.

73   At the end of January: Interview with Duncan, February 16, 2011, and with two other attendees. $100 billion versus $32 billion: Andrew Stiles, "Cutting the full $100 billion," *National Review Online*, February 10, 2011.

76   "This new number": Interview with Labrador, September 23, 2011. "I will not lose me": Elise Viebeck, "Lifetime of grief management readied Southerland for Congress," *Hill*, October 17, 2011.

77   "Look": Interview with Duncan, February 16, 2011. "That's the coward's way out": Interview with West, February 15, 2011, verified by two other attendees.

77   Majority Whip Kevin McCarthy: Interviews with McCarthy, December 21, 2010, and March 23, 2011; see also Draper, "How Kevin McCarthy wrangles the Tea Party," *New York Times Magazine*, July 13, 2011. McCarthy backstory: Interviews with McCarthy, March 23, 2011, and mother Bert McCarthy, March 24, 2011. "Watch this guy": Interview with Lott, May 13, 2011. "You can't have": Interview with McCarthy, March 23, 2011.

81   a meeting with the Cardinals: Interviews with seven attendees.

83   "Do we just": House Appropriations agriculture subcommittee hearing, April 1, 2011.

84   "I am trying to support": House Appropriations financial services subcommittee hearing, February 11, 2011; also interview with Yoder, February 17, 2011.

85   "This is a rather literal": Flake press release, September 28, 2007.

87   "Transparency and openness": Hoyer pen and pad, February 15, 2011.

88   "What are we doing": *Congressional Record*, February 15, 2011.

89   Pelosi was watching the tally board: Author personally observed.
89   Jeff Duncan also wanted: Interviews with Duncan, February 16, 2011, and March 14, 2011.
92   Blake Farenthold had been: Interviews with Farenthold, March 3, 2011, and April 13, 2011.
95   "I go to bed": Boehner on C-SPAN video, June 12, 2007.
95   "this outlandish massacre": *Congressional Record,* February 17, 2011.
97   "looks and talks": *Washington Post,* January 9, 1956. "If I can be half the man": *Detroit News,* January 22, 1956. Civil Rights Act: *Detroit News,* March 28, 1956. Cabaret tax: *Detroit Labor News,* March 1, 1956. Taft-Hartley: *Machinist,* March 29, 1956. FDA: *Detroit News,* January 25, 1956.

CHAPTER TEN: MOMENT OF SILENCE

99   "Mr. Speaker": Author personally observed; also *Congressional Record,* March 1, 2011.
101 Walter Jones was: Interview with Jones, March 8, 2011. *Mother Jones:* Robert Dreyfuss, "The three conversions of Walter B. Jones," *Mother Jones,* January/February 2006.
103 Sam Johnson was escorted: Author personally observed; also *Congressional Record,* February 17, 2011.

CHAPTER ELEVEN: BLACK REPUBLICAN OUT OF FLORIDA

105 Josiah Walls: Samuel Denny Smith, *The Negro in Congress, 1870–1901* (Chapel Hill: University of North Carolina Press, 1940), pp. 75–78; Peter D. Klingman, *Josiah Walls: Florida's Black Congressman of Reconstruction* (Gainesville: University of Florida Presses, 1976). "Sir, the Negro": Smith, *The Negro in Congress,* p. 138. "I cannot live": "Southern Negro's plaint," *New York Times,* August 26, 1900. De Priest: Elliott M. Rudwick, "Oscar De Priest and the Jim Crow restaurant in the U.S. House of Representatives," *Journal of Negro Education* 35, no. 1 (Winter 1966), pp. 77–82.
106 desire to be a player in the CBC's: Interviews with West, February 15, 2011, March 2, 2011, April 8, 2011, April 26, 2011.
109 a town hall in Pompano Beach: Author personally observed, February 21, 2011.
109 CPAC convention: YouTube video, February 21, 2011; also interview with West, March 2, 2011. Sinise: Interview with West, March 29, 2011. Borgnine photo: Author personally observed. Beck: Glenn Beck radio show, April 11, 2011.
110 For a Tea Party icon: Interview with West, March 2, 2011. Heritage Action: Heritage Action website (West scored a 74). Frank: *Congressional Record,* February 17, 2011. "I have never seen": West press release, February 18, 2011. "Barney Frank at midnight": Interview with West, March 2, 2011. West legislation: *Congressional Record,* April 4, 2011. State of the Union notes: Author obtained a copy. White House reception: Interview with West, February 15, 2011.
111 flew to Atlanta: Interview with West, April 8, 2011; also Kyle Wingfield, "Allen

West on growing up in Atlanta, and ladders versus hammocks," *Atlanta Journal-Constitution,* March 25, 2011.

CHAPTER TWELVE: RADICALIZATION

112 Duncan was now sitting through: Interview with Duncan, March 14, 2011.
113 There was a single mosque: Interview with Duncan, March 14, 2011; interview with Oglesby, April 19, 2011. New Jersey case: "Cain claims Muslims tried to influence sharia law in OK and NJ," Politifact Georgia, July 27, 2011.
113 In early March: Transcript of Committee on Homeland Security hearing, The Extent of Radicalization in the American Muslim Community and That Community's Response, March 10, 2011.
116 Sheila Jackson Lee: Interview with Duncan, March 14, 2011.

CHAPTER THIRTEEN: WOMAN OF A CERTAIN RAGE

117 The legendary Houston: *Jet,* November 30, 1972. "epitome of the new politics": *New York Times,* October 23, 1971. "militancy is expressed": *Sepia,* October 1972. LBJ and Mills: *Washington Star-News,* January 14, 1973. Rodino currying favor: Lawrence E. Taylor, "Sketches of members on Judiciary panel," *St. Louis Post-Dispatch,* April 21, 1974; also interview with Jordan's AA Bud Myers, May 1, 2011. "brightest member": Taylor, April 21, 1974. Jordan and National Archives: Mary Beth Rogers, *Barbara Jordan: American Hero* (New York: Bantam, 2000). Jordan's speech: YouTube video, July 25, 1974. Outside: Interview with Myers, May 1, 2011. Retirement: Jordan statement given to *Time,* January 6, 1978; Rogers, *Barbara Jordan.*
120 "I should not deny": Interview with Jackson Lee, June 22, 2011. Sixteen amendments: numbers 238, 239, 240, 398, 399, 400, 401, 472, 473, 474, 475, 476, 579, 580, 581, 582. Jared Polis had the second-most among Democrats with fifteen. Among Republicans, Steve Pearce had the most amendments, with twenty.
121 a staggering fifty-two different caucuses: Jackson Lee website.
122 The tradition of the jar: Interviews with five congressional staffers.
122 Michael Jackson's funeral: *Congressional Record,* June 25, 2009; Super Bowl ad: *Congressional Record,* February 8, 2011; soccer stadium: *Congressional Record,* February 9, 2011.
123 a job fair: Karen Masterson, "Catering to voters," *Houston Chronicle,* September 1, 2002. Swimming pools: Ken Fountain, "Rep. Lee, energy firms to the rescue to keep 8 Houston pools, 7 centers open," *Houston Examiner,* June 20, 2011. Riverside General Hospital: Lindsay Wise, *Houston Chronicle,* June 7, 2010. Houston Ship Channel: Port of Houston newsletter, February 22, 2010.
123 offered up an amendment: Author personally observed; also *Congressional Record,* May 4, 2011.
124 Jackson Lee's abusiveness: The first of these was Tim Fleck, "What's driving Miss Sheila?" *Houston Press,* February 20, 1997. *Washingtonian* poll: In the "meanest" category, Jackson Lee was number two in 2006 (behind Bill Thomas), number

one in 2008 (ahead of Obey) and again in 2010; *Washingtonian,* September 2006, September 2008, and September 2010.
125   failed in her bid: Interviews with two attendees.

CHAPTER FOURTEEN: "YOU HARD HEAD"

127   And so the five: Interview with Duncan, April 18, 2011.
127   The following day: Interview with Duncan, May 23, 2011; interview with McCarthy, March 23, 2011.
128   the whip's vault of metaphors and homilies: Interviews with McCarthy, March 23, 2011, April 5, 2011, and April 15, 2011; also interview with Rick Berg, April 7, 2011.
129   McCarthy loved the freshmen: Interview with McCarthy, March 23, 2011.
131   "Touching gloves": Interview with McCarthy, May 5, 2011.
131   "I love chaos!": Interview with Berg, April 7, 2011; interview with McCarthy, March 23, 2011.
132   organized another dinner: Interview with McCarthy, March 23, 2011; interview with Michael Grimm, April 14, 2011; interview with Adam Kinzinger, May 4, 2011.
132   Raul Labrador: Interview with Labrador, May 12, 2011, and with three other attendees.
133   On the House floor: Interview with Duncan, May 23, 2011.
133   Government Shutdown Prevention Act: Cantor press conference, March 30, 2011.
133   Kevin McCarthy approached: Interview with Farenthold, April 13, 2011.
133   "I am disgusted": West press statement, April 7, 2011.
133   "I thought I'd let you know": Interview with West, April 8, 2011. "the representative of South Carolina": *Congressional Record,* April 8, 2011.
134   Steny Hoyer received a call: Interview with McCarthy, April 15, 2011; interview with Hoyer, May 12, 2011.
135   "You hard head": Interview with Duncan, April 19, 2011.
135   "was a miserable experience": Interview with Roskam, May 4, 2011.
136   Paul Ryan: Katherine Mangu-Ward, "Young, wonky and proud of it," *Weekly Standard,* March 17, 2003; Christian Schneider, "Rebel without a pause," *Wisconsin Interest,* July 2010; Erik Gunn, "That hair, those eyes, that plan," *Milwaukee Magazine,* July 1, 2005.
138   "There are parts": Monica Davey, "A young Republican with a sweeping agenda," *New York Times,* August 2, 2010. Cantor and Ingraham: Fox News interview, August 26, 2010. Obama: Transcript of conference, January 29, 2010. "full of gimmicks": Transcript of health-care summit, February 25, 2010.
139   Denny Hastert had told Ryan: Interview with Ryan, May 5, 2011.
139   listening sessions: Draper, "How Kevin McCarthy wrangles the Tea Party."
140   The result was: ATF blog, April 5, 2011. Cato Institute: April 5, 2011, Cato blog reprint of op-ed by Michael F. Cannon, *Kaiser Health News,* April 4, 2011. Heritage Foundation: Quoted in *The Path to Prosperity,* p. 59. Krauthammer dissent: Charles Krauthammer, "Paul Ryan's brave budget blueprint," *Washington Post,*

April 8, 2011. "It's been great": Interview with Roskam, May 4, 2011. "You could write": Interview with LaTourette, May 11, 2011.

142 McCarthy and Ryan: Interview with McCarthy, April 15, 2011.

143 "It's a vision": Transcript of Obama speech, April 13, 2011. "Autism": Interview with Ryan, May 5, 2011.

143 "I think Ryan's": Interview with McCarthy, April 15, 2011.

143 "You're never going": Interview with McCarthy, April 15, 2011; confirmed by Van Hollen's office.

145 Friday afternoon: Author personally observed.

145 At that morning's conference: Interviews with five attendees.

147 The two budgets: Author personally observed. Hoyer whip strategy on RSC budget: Interviews with three participants, also interview with McCarthy, April 15, 2011. Ryan congratulating McCarthy: Interview with McCarthy, April 15, 2011, and with Ryan, May 5, 2011.

150 Later that afternoon, McCarthy: Author personally observed.

151 Kathy Hochul: Hochul and Corwin press statements, April 15, 2011.

CHAPTER FIFTEEN: DRAFT HORSE

155 Cherokees: Cherokees of South Carolina website. Huguenots: Bertrand van Ruymbeke, *From New Babylon to Eden: The Huguenots and their Migration to Colonial South Carolina* (Columbia: University of South Carolina Press, 2006). John Duncan: Interview with Duncan, September 6, 2011. Huger: http://bioguide .congress.gov. Keitt: Letter from Keitt published in *New York Times,* August 3, 1857; "Keitt and Burlingame," *New York Times,* June 23, 1856; "Brooks and Keitt," *New York Times,* July 16, 1856; "The debate in the House on the summer assault," *New York Times,* July 9, 1857; "Keitt knocked down by Grow," *New York Times,* February 6, 1858; "Another painful occurrence in the city of Washington," *New York Times,* May 28, 1856; "A Southern bobadil," *New York Times,* September 22, 1856. Mills: Interview with Derrick, April 17, 2011.

156 "disgraceful and un-American": Duncan open letter, June 18, 2009.

156 Three days after: Author personally observed, April 18, 2011.

157 He visited the Bosch: Author personally observed, April 18, 2011.

159 Keith Jennings: Author personally observed, April 18, 2011.

159 a Tea Party event: Author personally observed, April 18, 2011.

160 South Carolina delegation: Author personally observed, April 18, 2011.

161 "Rogers knew": Interview with Duncan, May 23, 2011.

162 *New York Times* had published a story: Jennifer Steinhauer, "Close-knit, new to the House and resistant to blending in," *New York Times,* April 10, 2011.

163 "the draft horse": Interview with Duncan, June 23, 2011.

CHAPTER SIXTEEN: THE WINNING MESSAGE

164 On the morning: Dan Rostenkowski archives, Loyola University. "Socialized medicine": Congress of Industrial Organizations radio interview, September 16,

1945. AMA campaign: Democratic Study Group letter from staff director Bill Phillips to members, February 23, 1965, Rostenkowski archives. "Cruel hoax": Undated clip, Rostenkowski archives. "No longer will": Johnson remarks at signing ceremony, July 30, 1965.

165 $500 billion: Glenn Kessler, "Fact checking the GOP debate: $500 billion in cuts to Medicare?" *Washington Post,* June 15, 2011. 2006 versus 2010: Aaron Astor, "The age gap tells all," *Moderate Voice,* November 3, 2010.

166 Franks switch his vote: Interview with two GOP officials, confirmed by Franks's office. "We won it": Pelosi press statement, November 22, 2003.

167 "supports a budget": DCCC video ad, May 12, 2011. "Medicare, Medicare and Medicare": Chris Cillizza, "Of grand bargains, Medicare and silver bullets," *Washington Post,* July 7, 2011.

167 "I hope you get cancer!": Interview with Ellmers, June 3, 2011. "You want to kill": Interview with Grimm, May 4, 2011.

168 At Cavalry Chapel: Author personally observed, Fort Lauderdale, FL, April 26, 2011.

169 Pelosi called Roy Spence: Interview with Spence, June 18, 2011, with Pelosi, July 19, 2011, and with three other participants.

CHAPTER SEVENTEEN: SIDE POCKETS ON A COW

171 "We're celebrating": Author personally observed, April 21, 2011.

173 That changed when Dingell: Interviews with three committee members.

175 "as useful as feathers": Edmund L. Andrews, "Veteran House Democrat guards turf on energy," *New York Times,* July 21, 2007.

177 a recent op-ed: Thomas Friedman, "How to fix a flat," *New York Times,* November 11, 2008.

179 Dingellisms: The author has heard Dingell recite many of these, and also has a full list of same in his possession.

180 "nannyism": Robin Bravender, "Conservatives burn over Fred Upton's light bulb law," *Politico,* November 12, 2010. "The voters have spoken": Upton undated memo to "Interested Parties" re: "Energy and Commerce Chairmanship."

181 the port at Charleston harbor: Interview with Duncan, August 2, 2011; Gowdy at South Carolina delegation event, April 19, 2011; also interviews with two other members and three staffers involved in efforts to procure the funding.

183 international wildlife refuge: Interviews with three individuals involved in the funding procurement. Salazar meeting: Author personally observed, July 6, 2011.

CHAPTER EIGHTEEN: "HERE IS YOUR SHIELD"

186 Ben's Chili Bowl: Author personally observed and interviewed, July 7, 2011.

CHAPTER NINETEEN:
"DROPPING OUT OF THINGS IS WHAT I DO"

193 On the afternoon: Author personally observed, June 1, 2011.

195 "A to Z Spending Cut Plan": David E. Rosenbaum, "Washington Memo: In jargon-filled talk about budgets, a debate of politics over substance," *New York Times,* July 19, 1994.

196 dining room with John Dingell: Interviews with Andrews, July 19, 2011, and with Dingell, June 23, 2011.

197 "Friday dump": From Weiner's Twitter account, May 27, 2011. "These Friday night visits": YouTube of Weiner on Maddow's show, May 27, 2011. "Certitude": YouTube video of Russert interview with Weiner, June 1, 2011. "OK howz about": From Weiner's Twitter account, June 1, 2011.

199 ballroom of the Sheraton hotel: YouTube video of press conference, June 6, 2011.

CHAPTER TWENTY: "YOU ARE *WRONG!*"

203 On June 1, 2011: Interviews with four of the participants.

203 "an extreme anti-woman agenda": *Congressional Record,* February 15, 2011. "The Senate": C-SPAN video, April 8, 2011.

206 One freshman: Interview with Ellmers, July 22, 2011; also see Draper, "How Kevin McCarthy wrangles the Tea Party."

208 "Uncertainty, burdensome": YouTube video, June 25, 2011.

209 At the hearing: YouTube video, June 21, 2011.

210 "I love it!": The author was the reporter in question.

211 "go storming the White House": Interview with Ellmers, July 22, 2011. Feminist: Marin Cogan, "GOP freshmen women go on offense," *Politico,* June 20, 2011.

CHAPTER TWENTY-ONE: COFFEE WITH YOUR CONGRESSMAN

215 At seven-thirty on a spring morning: Author personally observed, and interviewed Farenthold, April 28, 2011. Farenthold's wealth: *Roll Call,* December 15, 2011.

CHAPTER TWENTY-TWO: THE HOSTAGE

222 the spring 1790 session: Winfred E. A. Bernhard, *Fisher Ames: Federalist and Statesman, 1758–1808* (Chapel Hill: University of North Carolina Press, 1965); Richard Labunski, *James Madison and the Struggle for the Bill of Rights* (New York: Oxford University Press, 2006). "settle upon our posterity": Jacques S. Jaikaran, *Debt Virus: A Compelling Solution to the World's Debt Problems* (Macomb, IL: Glenbridge, 1992), p. 98. "I despise politics": Kirkland, *Works of Fisher Ames,* p. 88.

224 Bureau of the Public Debt: Author personally observed; interviews with McCarthy, May 5, 13, and 24, 2011, and June 5, 2011.

225 His office had in fact sent out a letter: Interview with Farenthold, April 28, 2011.

226 listening sessions: Interviews with three attendees.

227 At 10 A.M. on June 1: Interviews with six attendees.

229 led by Vice President Joe Biden: Interviews with three attendees.

233 "I want to let you know": Interviews with four attendees.

234 Jay Powell: Interviews with three attendees.

234 a conference on Friday: Interviews with four attendees.

237 "I have to tell you": Interview with Labrador, July 30, 2011.

238 Boehner's four friends: Interviews with two of the participants.

239 "I can't think": Boehner press conference, July 14, 2011.

240 "You know": Interview with Duncan, August 2, 2011.

240 "Look, we're winning": Interview with Ellmers, July 22, 2011.

241 "You've gotta tell Boehner": Author personally observed.

241 inside the chamber: Author personally observed; interviews with Ellmers, July 22, 2011, and with Duncan, August 2, 2011.

242 "A deal was never": Boehner letter, July 22, 2011; "when you've got": Obama press conference, July 22, 2011.

243 Allen West was surprised: Interview with West, July 28, 2011.

243 "I'm not from": *Congressional Record,* July 19, 2011. "Wasserman Schultz went after": Interview with West, July 28, 2011. "Look, Debbie": West email, July 19, 2011. "He thinks it's okay": YouTube video of Wasserman Schultz at protest, October 22, 2010. "incited a riot": Interview with West, January 12, 2011.

245 whip team dinner: Interview with West, July 28, 2011.

246 The conference was the next: Interview with West, July 28, 2011, and with four attendees.

248 "is not one hundred percent": Author personally observed.

249 "a bloodied": Lisa Mascaro and Michael A. Memoli, "Republicans search for votes with Boehner plan in jeopardy," *Los Angeles Times,* July 28, 2011.

250 "I'm gonna vote": Interview with Farenthold, August 2, 2011.

250 chapel in the Capitol: Interview with Duncan, August 2, 2011.

251 They went to the whip's office: Interviews with four attendees.

253 "No more": Interview with Farenthold, August 2, 2011.

256 "It's hard": Interview with Cleaver, December 15, 2011.

256 But Vice President Joe Biden: Interviews with six attendees.

260 a recorded vote: Author personally observed; also *Congressional Record,* August 1, 2011.

262 Jeff Duncan: Interview with Duncan, August 2, 2011; also *Congressional Record,* August 1, 2011.

CHAPTER TWENTY-THREE: LOWER, EVER LOWER

266 the Dow Jones: Christine Hauser, "World markets staggered by weak consumer data," *New York Times,* August 2, 2011. S&P downgrade: Charles Riley, "S&P downgrades U.S. credit rating," CNN, August 5, 2011. McInturff: "A Pivot Point in American Opinion: The Debt Ceiling Negotiation and its Consequences,"

Public Opinion Strategies, August 2011. Poll: CBS News/*New York Times* poll, October 25, 2011.

266   Beneath the screeching: Interviews with Chaffetz, February 25, 2011, Labrador, June 2, 2011, and Gutierrez, March 2, 2011. Emerson/Cleaver: Interview with Cleaver, June 24, 2011; also see language in Appropriations Subcommittee on Financial Services omni report, released December 16, 2011. DeLauro/Manzullo: H.R. 110, Manufacturing Reinvestment Account Act of 2011. Matheson/Brady: H.R. 1834, Freedom to Invest Act of 2011.

267   Renee Ellmers: Interview with Ellmers, October 27, 2011.

268   "I didn't come": Interview with Labrador, December 1, 2011.

269   "Pass this jobs bill!": Obama speech, September 8, 2011.

271   "Paging the Missouri Tea Party": RedState.com post, October 21, 2011.

271   "Part of it is": Interview with Farenthold, October 25, 2011.

272   "What's it going": Interview with Duncan, December 6, 2011.

272   "It's not like": Interview with West, December 12, 2011. 2012 calendar: Posted on majorityleader.gov. "I must take the time": *Congressional Record,* December 8, 2011.

274   Super Committee: Interviews with six individuals connected with the negotiations.

277   Livid, the Appropriations Cardinals: Interviews with four Cardinals and three others connected with the discussion.

280   "The institution is still": Interview with Dingell, December 13, 2011. Poll: Democracy Corps poll, December 9, 2011.

EPILOGUE: EVENING, JANUARY 24, 2012

283   seated around a dining room table: Interviews with two of the participants.

284   *Think about the America within our reach:* State of the Union address, January 24, 2012.

286   "All around the Hill today": Author personally observed.

286   Once inside the impossibly crowded chamber, Duncan got separated: Interview with Duncan, January 25, 2012.

287   Duncan was among them: Author personally observed.

ACKNOWLEDGMENTS

I undertook this project immediately after the 2010 midterm elections, when the Republican Party regained control over the House of Representatives. Observing that this GOP takeover had been made possible by the election of eighty-seven newcomers—about one-third of whom had never before held any kind of political office—I suspected that both the tenor and substance of the House were about to undergo dramatic change. My intuition was that as the Republicans' point of the spear against the administration of President Barack Obama, the House was sure to be relevant and, at the risk of sounding crass, highly entertaining. So the day after the midterms, I notified both my agent and my publisher that I wanted to put aside the altogether different book project I had been working on for the past two years. Instead, I informed them, I aimed to produce a narrative of the 112th Congress as seen through the eyes and activities of its members, particularly its newest arrivals. After picking themselves up off the floor, my publishing team agreed that this was a good idea.

The conceit for the book was to immerse myself in the House—to spend every day that it was in session on the Hill, doing interviews and observing the activities of this world-renowned yet (at least in book form) little-explored democratic institution. Though it would have been a fool's pursuit to attempt to speak to all 435 congressional members, I did what I could to visit with a sizable cross section and was gratified by the openness of nearly all whom I approached. Between November 2010 and December 2011, I interviewed over fifty House members, some of them as many as fifteen times. I also benefited greatly from the insights of about two dozen former members, in addition to numerous current and former senior House staffers. In all, I conducted more than three hundred interviews for this book. A number of my sources requested that our interviews be "on background" in order for them to speak candidly. Where a quote or fact is not accompanied by an endnote, the reader should assume that the information in question came from one or more on-background interviewees. For that matter, many facts obtained by on-the-record sources were verified by others on background.

I knew at the outset that this would be a character-driven narrative; I just didn't know who the characters would end up being. Several months of interviewing went by before I concluded that among the protagonists, three would receive the lion's share of space: Allen West, a Tea Party sensation with no political experience; Jeff Duncan, another Republican freshman, but one who lacked West's celebrity and thus would encounter the familiar challenges of earning distinction among a body of 435; and the freshman class's institutional counterweight, Democrat John Dingell, the longest-serving House member in history. I'm particularly indebted to them and to their excellent staffs for enduring my many impositions. At the same time, I'm deeply thankful to all the other House members and staffers with whom I spoke for the book. Though any honest rendering of a Congress that achieved record lows in public standing could not be a particularly glowing one, I emerged from my experience with great admiration for the intellect and dedication of virtually every representative and staffer whom I encountered.

I could not have accomplished this book without my assistant Emily Umhoefer, whose job description came to include not only research and transcribing but also sitting in on House committee meetings and minding my dog Bill while I was away. Emily's dependability and hilarious take on House-related vagaries kept me sane throughout an otherwise frantic timeframe; I'll never be able to thank her enough. I also appreciate the archival research that Dan Kaufman contributed. Morgan Wimberley, Sarah Wheaton, and Ian McCue deserve thanks as well for the research they contributed to the book I put aside for this one.

Accomplishing this book required taking a year off from my magazine work. For their patience and support, I'm very grateful to Jim Nelson and Mike Benoist at *GQ;* to Barbara Paulsen, Victoria Pope, and Chris Johns at *National Geographic;* and to Ilena Silverman and Hugo

Lindgren at *The New York Times Magazine*, where the lengthy feature I published on House Majority Whip Kevin McCarthy in June 2011 formed a kind of template for how I would write this book-length story.

Most of this book was written in blissful seclusion at the Glade, a lovely farmhouse in Wytheville, Virginia. For that memorable and very productive experience (which I highly recommend to writers and non-writers alike), I want to thank the Glade's owner, Jack Stuart, and its very able caretaker, Bill Mello.

Throughout my career, I've benefited from the perspective and encouragement of literary friends, and that was certainly the case as I slogged my way through this project. Special thanks, then, to writer pals Sara Corbett, Mike Paterniti, Frances and Ed Mayes, Lisa Depaulo, Mark Leibovich, Peter Baker, Mark Salter, Kathleen Parker, Elise Hu, Jonathan Martin, Matt Bai, Manuel Roig-Franzia, Ceci Connolly, Maureen Dowd, Ashley Parker, Lee Smith, Hal Crowther, Allan Gurganus, Ann Hornaday, Jim Shahin, Mark Halperin, Jacob Weisberg, Greg Curtis, Jan Reid, Skip Hollandsworth, and Marty Beiser. In the non-ink-stained category of Washington, D.C., friends, I'm grateful for the diversion supplied by Todd Harris, Doug Heye, John Scofield, Jessica Shahin, Susan McCue, Danielle Landau, Susan Raines, Jim Duffy, Louis and Dena Andre, Brad Garrett, Elisa Poteat, Gary Greco, and certain others who cannot be named here lest the merest association with me wreak havoc in their professional lives.

The best ally a writer—or maybe anyone—could have is Sloan Harris at ICM, my agent and friend for the past fifteen years. Sloan's judgment, literary and otherwise, has been crucial to me. I'm lucky to have him and his assistant Kristyn Keene in my corner.

I'm equally fortunate to be an author for Free Press. In allowing me to put my other book project to the side and wade into this one, editor in chief Dominick Anfuso and publisher/president Martha Levin demonstrated a level of faith that I'll always appreciate. Martha's support has extended far beyond what any author has a right to expect from someone so high up on the publishing food chain. Meanwhile, Dominick's excellent editing of the first draft improved the story in numerous ways. Thanks as well to Dominick's ferociously hard-working assistant, Sydney Tanigawa, and to all the rest at Free Press, including vice president and director of publicity Carisa Hays, publicist Jill Siegel, director of social media marketing Claire Kelley, production editor Edith Lewis, copyeditor Tom Pitoniak, and attorney Elisa Rivlin.

It's almost absurdly reductive to say that my parents and my brother John (to whom this book is dedicated) have always been there for me. But I feel absurdly lucky to say it anyway. Finally, I won't embarrass Lara Andre by listing here the countless ways in which she has made a difference in my life. I'll just say (with apologies to Fisher Ames) that in these days of faction, our togetherness means everything to me.

INDEX

ABOUT THE AUTHOR

Robert Draper is a contributing writer to the *New York Times Magazine* and *National Geographic* and a correspondent to *GQ*. He is the author of several books, most recently the *New York Times* bestseller *Dead Certain: The Presidency of George W. Bush*. He lives in Washington, D.C.